THE BAUSELL
HOME LEARNING GUIDE

Teach Your Child to Read

THE BAUSELL HOME LEARNING GUIDE

Teach Your Child to Read

R. Barker Bausell, Ph.D.,
Carole R. Bausell, M.Ed.,
and Nellie B. Bausell, M.S.

Illustrations by Kelly Glancy

THE SAUNDERS PRESS
W.B. Saunders Company
Philadelphia • London • Toronto

THE SAUNDERS PRESS/SAUNDERS PAPERBACKS
W. B. Saunders Company
West Washington Square
Philadelphia, Pennsylvania 19105

IN THE UNITED STATES
DISTRIBUTED TO THE TRADE BY
HOLT, RINEHART AND WINSTON
383 Madison Avenue
New York, New York 10017

IN CANADA
DISTRIBUTED BY
HOLT, RINEHART AND WINSTON, Limited
55 Horner Avenue
Toronto, Ontario
M8Z 4X6 Canada

© 1980 by W. B. Saunders Company

Copyright under the International Copyright Union

All rights reserved. No part of this book may be duplicated or reproduced in any manner without written permission from the publisher.

Print Number 9 8 7 6 5 4 3 2

First Edition

Library of Congress Cataloging in Publication Data

Bausell, R. Barker,
The Bausell home learning guide.

1. Reading (Primary)—Handbooks, manuals, etc.
2. Domestic education—Handbooks, manuals, etc.
   I. Bausell, Carole R., joint author.
II. Bausell, Nellie B., joint author. III. Title.
    LB1525.B38   372.4'1   79-67117
           ISBN 0-7216-1593-7
ISBN 0-03-056737-8 (Holt, Rinehart and Winston)

Acknowledgments

A book such as this cannot help but owe a great deal to the multitude of scholars and researchers who have labored to improve the science and art of reading instruction. Although there is no way we can thank each of them individually we would like to acknowledge the contribution of a few of the Masters whose work we have found most helpful.

First and foremost we would like to acknowledge the work and teaching of Dr. Russell G. Stauffer. We have found his already classic text, *Teaching Reading as a Thinking Process* (Harper & Row, 1969), invaluable for both the language experience and the word recognition/study sections of the present book.

In addition no truly comprehensive reading program could avoid indebtedness to Dr. Emmett Albert Betts for his many contributions including *Foundations of Reading Instruction* (American Book Company, 1946). We similarly found Dr. William S. Gray's *On Their Own in Reading* (Scott, Foresman & Company, 1948) and Dr. Arthur W. Heilman's *Phonics in Proper Perspective* (Charles E. Merrill Publishing Company, 1968) especially useful for the sections dealing with phonics in this book.

On a more personal level we would like to thank Dr. Paul R. Daniels of The Johns Hopkins University for his very considerable expertise and helpfulness in suggesting authoritative sources and materials. A dept of gratitude is owed Ms. Carol Meyers for her aid in helping us prepare the manuscript.

Most of all, however, we would like to sincerely acknowledge support and guidance of our editor, Howard E. Sandum, without whose vision this work would not have been possible.

Contents

1	Teaching Your Child Yourself	1
2	Getting Your Child Ready to Read	14
3	Reading to Your Child	26
4	Teaching Letter Recognition	33
5	Teaching Letter Sounds, or Beginning Phonics	69
6	Reading the First "Book": Preprimer #1	118
7	Reading the Second "Book": Preprimer #2	184
8	Reading the Third "Book": Preprimer #3	257
9	Reading the Child's Own Experience Stories	284
10	Teaching More Advanced Phonics Skills	294
11	Continuing Reading Instruction	377
12	Where Do We Go From Here?	396

1
Teaching Your Child Yourself

The natural and most effective learning environment for human beings is one adult instructing one child. Since our species must learn so much more than any other in order to function, maybe this is why we are generally born one at a time rather than in litters, and why we take so long to mature.

Isn't it odd, then, that we expect our children to learn, in groups of thirty or more, instructed by a stranger, all they need to know to function in a complex technological society? It is natural for us to have high aspirations for our children. It is not realistic to expect an educational institution to accomplish this task unassisted.

If you want more for your child than what the public schools can give, then you must help achieve those aspirations yourself. For most parents this means that you have to help teach your children yourself.

This book is designed to show you how to do that. It will teach you everything you need to know to teach your child the single most important and complex skill he will ever be required to learn: *reading*. Between infancy and adulthood, we must master a multitude of skills, the key to most of which is reading.

Let's talk first about some practical questions: 1. *Will teaching my child to read work?*, and 2. *Is it necessary?*

Does Parental Teaching Work?

Few questions in education can be answered so emphatically in the affirmative. In studies comparing children taught reading by their parents with those whose parents did not teach them, the results are overwhelming:

Children taught to read by their parents significantly outperform children not so taught on reading tests. Furthermore, this advantage is maintained over time.

These findings were confirmed (1) in different locations (such as Los Angeles, Denver, and New York), (2) at different times (1958 to 1976), (3) by different investigators, (4) using different procedures, and (5) studying different populations of varying socioeconomic levels.

Some additional conclusions based upon this research follow.

1. Preschool children can learn basic reading skills from their parents.
2. Parents can learn to effectively use techniques for teaching these skills to both preschool and school-age children.
3. Reading *to* children is also associated with early reading success.
4. Active reading (for example, asking and answering questions) is superior to passive reading.
5. Parents with good reading habits themselves tend to have children with superior reading ability.
6. One method of parental teaching isn't superior to another.
7. *No harmful effects (including physiological, social, or psychological) of early reading instruction have ever been documented.*

We not only know that parental instruction works, we know that it works through the operation of two of the most basic principles in learning theory:

PRINCIPLE #1
Everything else being equal, the more a child is taught, the more will be learned

This principle is as simple and commonsensical as it sounds. Unfortunately, although it is probably the oldest and best known law in the psychology of learning, it is largely ignored. In the traditional school setting, one teacher must present a topic to thirty children for the same length of time regardless of individual needs.

Parental instruction, on the other hand, takes full advantage of the fact that the amount of learning is related to the amount of teaching. This applies whether the parent begins instruction *before* or *after* school age is reached.

PRINCIPLE #2
Tutoring and small group instruction is more effective than classroom instruction

Although this principle might also seem obvious, having been recognized by educators from Socrates to Rousseau, it was acknowledged and verified by educational researchers only recently. It was one of the authors of this book who first documented that children learn more when taught one-to-one than under any other conditions![1]

While interesting for its own sake, this line of research does not offer a great deal of applicability for the public schools. As a society we cannot afford one-to-one instruction and it is nearly impossible for a teacher to incorporate much individual teaching in a classroom of twenty or thirty students.

---

[1] R. Barker Bausell with W. B. Moody and R. N. Walzl, "A Factorial Study of Tutoring Versus Classroom Instruction," *American Educational Research Journal* 10 (1973): 591–97; R. Barker Bausell with W. B. Moody and J. R. Jenkins, "The Effect of Class Size on the Learning of Mathematics: A Parametric Study with Fourth-Grade Students," *Journal of Research in Mathematics Education* 4 (1973): 170–76.

The same is definitely not the case with home schooling, however. In teaching your child at home you can capitalize directly on both learning principles by providing as much instruction as needed within an individualized setting. So if parental instruction works, and it unquestionably can work successfully, then there is a further question that you as a parent must ask yourself:

Is Parental Teaching Necessary?

To answer this question you must examine your aspirations for your child in the light of the public schools' role in society. If you want your child to achieve at a level approaching his *maximum* capacity, then it is unrealistic to expect the schools by themselves to accomplish this for you. To expect otherwise is to fail to understand the basics of learning and the reasons behind the development of public school education.

Schools in this country were established originally to give a large number of children the best education possible under the circumstances. No one ever seriously believed that these one-room schools would give all enrolled children a chance in life equal to children of parents able to hire tutors and later enroll them at prestigious private academies and universities.

Our educational system is much more egalitarian today in the sense that many more children are given an opportunity to pursue advanced studies and, hence, professional careers than they once were. In many other important ways, however, our public schools have not changed that much. They are still structured for maximum efficiency; their objective is still to give the best available education to the greatest number of people. It is here that parental aspirations differ from the aims of the schools, since parents care most that their own child reach maximum personal potential. As we have explained, fixed-time intervals and large classes are incompatible with this goal.

By the same token, just as the schools are interested in group performance, the parent wants to see individual performance. Schools will compare an individual child to all the children of his age in the country, but the parent is primarily interested in comparing the child with no one but himself! The parent should be concerned with how much the child learns in relationship both to how much he *needs* to learn and how much he *can* learn.

Since neither of these quantities are measurable, the best a parent can do is to see that the child receives the most effective form of instruction. For most parents and children this will be individualized home instruction beginning as early as the third or fourth year of life.

Of course, all children will not display the same readiness or desire to learn to read at that young age. Nor has the opportunity been lost if the child has already started school. *This book is designed for parents of both preschool and school-age children, those showing precocious abilities as well as those developing more slowly.*

It is important, however, that you do everything in your power to prevent your child from receiving a slow start in school or from falling too far behind once there. Serious consequences can result, such as repeated failures which result in a loss of self-confidence and esteem; eventually, the child will expect less and less of himself.

Even when this serious stumbling block can be avoided, the step-after-step nature of most learning can pose a real problem to a child who receives a slow start or falls behind in school. The learning of simpler concepts is usually necessary before more complex ones can be mastered. In other words, what is not learned today may prevent something else from being learned tomorrow.

The sad reality in our time is that our schools are simply not set up to help children catch up once they fall behind. Such children require a great deal of individual attention for which, unfortunately, teachers do not have enough time when there are other children to be taught. All too often the result is that the faltering child keeps falling farther and farther behind. Eventually he may qualify for a special education or learning disabilities class. At this point he may be so far behind that catching up becomes very difficult.

You, the parent, can prevent this from happening, except in the rarest of circumstances. Even in those instances where a child has real, identifiable learning problems, he will be better off with your help than without it. By early intervention you are more likely to detect those problems yourself, thereby giving you the option of seeking professional help, when it is desirable, at a point at which the prognosis is brightest.

"Falling behind" or "receiving a slow start" are terms that do not tell the whole story, since they tend to compare the child's performance only to a group. As a parent, you are interested in your child's learning as much as he possibly can. For some children, performing only slightly behind their peers is a great feat, indicative of great effort on their part. For others, being among the "best" students in an entire school may indicate a shameful waste of talent and potential.

No one can tell you how much nor how soon your child can learn. Anyone who pretends to be able to do that, whether as educator, psychologist, pediatrician, or whatever, is a charlatan. The only way for you to find out how far your child can go is to provide him with all the support, help, and opportunity you can. For the vast majority of parents this consists of teaching their children long before they begin school and continuing long afterwards. This book is devoted to showing you how.

How to Use This Book

This volume is designed both for children who have had no formal reading instruction, and for those who have been taught reading but haven't progressed beyond the primary grade levels. In the latter group are those reading at or below the third-grade level, regardless of age (some children past the third grade still read considerably below that level).

The book offers a carefully sequenced program which, if conscientiously followed, can take your preschool or school-age child having little or no knowledge of letters or words to a point at which literally hundreds of words are known by sight; many more words never encountered in print can be recognized via word attack strategies; and a wide range of children's stories and books can be read fluently and with understanding.

This impressive achievement will be accomplished through five sequences of formal lessons, beginning with teaching recognition of the twenty-six letters of the alphabet and ending with the child's reading stories and books of your and his choosing. Throughout this entire sequence you will be *reading to your child* as well as teaching him to read. You will be expected to supplement both activities with other natural child-rearing behaviors involved in fostering a positive self-concept, physical well-being, language development, and a sense of discipline in the child.

These nurturing behaviors are discussed briefly in Chapter Two and are assumed to be known in the vast majority of homes where a book like this will be used. With the exception of physical readiness, best checked by a pediatrician, all of these achievements can be fostered by direct parental instruction. Therefore, they will probably require little specialized attention prior to your actual teaching.

Chapter Three deals with a topic crucial to the success of the entire enterprise. In it the importance of reading to the child is discussed, as well as the best way of doing so. Regardless of your child's age, the instructions in this chapter should be read and followed carefully. Being read to is a beneficial experience for which a child is never too young or too old.

Chapter Four begins the formal reading instruction. The names of the letters of the alphabet are taught, along with a few simple words. Competency tests and a teaching/recording device called a "Word Box" (both of which are discussed below) are introduced as ways of measuring how successful you were in your initial teaching venture, and which lessons need to be retaught. The instruction in this chapter is appropriate for most children aged three and older, although it will be too elementary for many school-age children.

Chapter Five introduces the *sounds* associated with many of the letters taught in the previous chapter. In addition, recognition of more words is taught, along with the assisted reading of actual sentences containing them. This instruction is designed to follow letter recognition and is also appropriate for all school-age children who do not "pass" the competency tests discussed below.

The teaching of Chapters Six, Seven, and Eight will be one of your most rewarding experiences. You will observe your child actually begin to read by means of little stories constructed from a tightly controlled vocabulary. They may be appropriate for the preschool or school-age child as indicated by the competency tests, which will again serve as a placement tool as well as a means of identifying lessons in need of review. It is also here that the Word Box assumes its most important role in the teaching, reviewing, and recording of words encountered in reading.

Chapters Nine and Ten form a single instructional unit and take up where Chapter Eight left off. You will be teaching your child to (1) read ever more complex stories, (2) recognize more words, and (3) learn more complex letter/sound relationships. Chapter Nine will be an especially interesting experience because the child will be reading stories which *he* dictates using any words he pleases. Chapter Ten introduces some of the more useful phonics concepts. They will prove helpful in sounding out and recognizing new words.

The Eleventh chapter is the most ambitious. It is designed to extend the process of reading ever more complex words and stories. At the same time, it will be teaching a word attack system that will allow the child to recognize new words without outside aid. In this chapter you will also be told how to choose books so that the skills learned in previous chapters can be used with any reading materials.

The Competency Tests

Chapters Four, Five, Six, Seven, Eight and Ten all contain tests designed to serve two basic purposes: 1. *evaluation,* in order to see how effective your instruction is, and to pinpoint specific problem areas for reteaching, and 2. *placement,* in order to determine which lessons need to be taught to the school-age child.

Each competency test should be given before instruction for children who have already received reading instruction. The parent of such a child will begin with the tests in Chapter Four and proceed step-by-step through the book. When the child's score indicates a problem area (as defined in the directions for each test), the specified lessons will be taught and the same test readministered to evaluate the effects of instruction.

Evaluation versus Placement

The only difference, therefore, between the use of the competency tests for preschool or school-age children lies in the situation that preschool children are assumed not to have acquired the skills taught in this book, and, hence, are given the tests following instruction only. This assumption could result in a great deal of wasted time for children who have already received some reading instruction, however; thus the tests are given them before (as well as after) teaching, to ensure that the skills in question have not already been acquired. The tests are readministered as many times as necessary to both groups until a given unit has been mastered.

Difficulty. The competency tests in this book are difficult, so don't expect glowing results each time you give them. They have been designed this way for a reason: You want to be sure that your child has *mastered* a skill before it is passed over, and you want to make sure that this skill can be applied in the reading process.

In this sense our tests are different from the ones your child will (or does) take in school. The purpose of our tests is not to compare your child to his peers nor to assign a grade. Their only purpose is to influence your teaching, to guide you in knowing exactly which lessons need to be retaught or reviewed. Thus they measure no skills other than the ones in the lessons with which they are concerned. We think that an occasional disappointment is a small price to pay for knowing exactly what your child has and has not learned, and thereby knowing exactly what to do about it.

The Word Box

The Word Box is a tool for recording words that your child has learned to recognize. It is nothing more than a container for 3″ by 5″ index cards on which known words are written.

The box itself has two sections. One simply contains the child's entire repertoire of known words in alphabetical order. (Alphabetical dividers can be purchased to go along with the index cards.) The other contains an envelope entitled "New Words" in which those words recently encountered are placed until they are mastered. (You are encouraged to keep an alphabetized list of the entire contents of the Word Box to guard against loss.)

The Time Chart

It is also very important for you to keep an accurate record of the amount of teaching time devoted to each topic. This information can have great diagnostic use. We suggest that you conscientiously maintain the following time chart:

Figure 1–1
Time Chart

Child's Age ____

Chapter	Section	Lesson	1st Session (Minutes)	2nd Session (Minutes)	3rd Session (Minutes)
4		1	___	___	___
		2	___	___	___
		3	___	___	___
		4	___	___	___
		5	___	___	___
		6	___	___	___
		7	___	___	___
		8	___	___	___
		9	___	___	___
		10	___	___	___
		11	___	___	___
		12	___	___	___
		13	___	___	___
		14	___	___	___

\# words in word box = ☐

Chapter	Section	Lesson	1st Session	2nd Session	3rd Session
5	1	1	___	___	___
		2	___	___	___
		3	___	___	___
		4	___	___	___
		5	___	___	___
		6	___	___	___
		7	___	___	___
		8	___	___	___
		9	___	___	___
		10	___	___	___
		11	___	___	___
		12	___	___	___
		13	___	___	___
		14	___	___	___
		15	___	___	___
		16	___	___	___
		17	___	___	___
		18	___	___	___
		19	___	___	___

\# words in word box = ☐

	2	1	___	___	___
		2	___	___	___
		3	___	___	___
		4	___	___	___
		5	___	___	___
		6	___	___	___
		7	___	___	___
		8	___	___	___
		9	___	___	___
		10	___	___	___
		11	___	___	___
		12	___	___	___

Figure 1–1 (continued)

Chapter	Section	Lesson	1st Session (Minutes)	2nd Session (Minutes)	3rd Session (Minutes)
			# words in word box = ☐		
6	1	1	_____	_____	_____
		2	_____	_____	_____
		3	_____	_____	_____
		4	_____	_____	_____
		5	_____	_____	_____
		6	_____	_____	_____
		7	_____	_____	_____
		8	_____	_____	_____
		9	_____	_____	_____
		10	_____	_____	_____
		11	_____	_____	_____
			# words in word box = ☐		
7	2–1	1	_____	_____	_____
		2	_____	_____	_____
		3	_____	_____	_____
		4	_____	_____	_____
		5	_____	_____	_____
		6	_____	_____	_____
		7	_____	_____	_____
			# words in word box = ☐		
	2–2	1	_____	_____	_____
		2	_____	_____	_____
		3	_____	_____	_____
		4	_____	_____	_____
		5	_____	_____	_____
		6	_____	_____	_____
			# words in word box = ☐		
	2–3	1	_____	_____	_____
		2	_____	_____	_____
		3	_____	_____	_____
		4	_____	_____	_____
		5	_____	_____	_____
		6	_____	_____	_____
		7	_____	_____	_____
		8	_____	_____	_____
			# words in word box = ☐		
8	3	1	_____	_____	_____
		2	_____	_____	_____
		3	_____	_____	_____
		4	_____	_____	_____
		5	_____	_____	_____
		6	_____	_____	_____
		7	_____	_____	_____
		8	_____	_____	_____
		9	_____	_____	_____
		10	_____	_____	_____

12 / Teach Your Child to Read

Figure 1–1 (continued)

Chapter	Section	Lesson	1st Session (Minutes)	2nd Session (Minutes)	3rd Session (Minutes)
			# words in word box = ☐		
9		Story 1	——	——	——
		Story 2	——	——	——
		Story 3	——	——	——
			# words in word box = ☐		
10		Preliminary Lesson	——	——	——
	1	1	——	——	——
		2	——	——	——
		3	——	——	——
		4	——	——	——
		5	——	——	——
			# words in word box = ☐		
	2	1	——	——	——
		2	——	——	——
		3	——	——	——
		4	——	——	——
		5	——	——	——
			# words in word box = ☐		
	3	1	——	——	——
		2	——	——	——
		3	——	——	——
		4	——	——	——
		5	——	——	——
		6	——	——	——
		7	——	——	——
		8	——	——	——
		9	——	——	——
		10	——	——	——
		11	——	——	——
		12	——	——	——
		13	——	——	——
		14	——	——	——
		15	——	——	——
			# words in word box = ☐		
	4	1	——	——	——
		2	——	——	——
		3	——	——	——
		4	——	——	——
			# words in word box = ☐		
	5	1	——	——	——
		2	——	——	——
		3	——	——	——
		4	——	——	——
			# words in word box = ☐		
11		Story 1	——	——	——
		Story 2	——	——	——
		Story 3	——	——	——
			# words in word box = ☐		

To use the chart, simply record the number of minutes you spend teaching each lesson each time you teach it. For example, suppose you spend twenty minutes teaching the **long *e*** lesson in Chapter Ten and the child learned the concepts involved as demonstrated by the fact that he later answered the **long *e*** items correctly on the competency test. Trouble was encountered with the next lesson, however, and you were forced to teach it twice with sessions lasting twenty-five minutes the first time and fifteen minutes the second. This information would be recorded on the time chart as follows:

Chapter	Section	Lesson	1st Session (minutes)	2nd Session (minutes)	3rd Session (minutes)
10	1	1	20	x	x
		2	25	15	x

You do not have to record the length of each session to the nearest second, but you should try to estimate the approximate number of minutes spent each time you sit down with your child. (For Chapters Nine and Ten you will also have to estimate how much of each session was spent with the language experience story and how much with phonics instruction.)

Evaluating Your Progress

As a way of helping you with the important and admirable enterprise upon which you are about to embark, the authors of this book would like to offer the following service. If at *any time* you would like to see how you are doing compared to other parents using this book, mail a copy (keep the original for your own records) of the time chart filled out as far as you have progressed, plus copies of each competency test worksheet you have completed, and we will send you a comparison report free of charge.

Send the copy of the time chart, competency test worksheets, and a legal size, self-addressed, stamped (30¢ postage) envelope to:

> Dr. R. Barker Bausell
> P.O. Box 19109
> Towson, MD 21204

2
Getting Your Child Ready to Read

Some children learn to read with great ease, others learn very slowly. Over the years, educators have advanced various explanations for these differences. Our position is that the pace of learning is largely determined by the child's early experiences and environmental stimuli. It arises generally from two sources.

Researchers have found that children who arrive at school with a wider range of intellectual experiences (such as having been taught the letter names, read to by their parents, and exposed to books and magazines within the home) also tend to learn more quickly to read. Most educational theorists also stress the importance of early experiences. Jean Piaget viewed the child as a naturally active organism whose intellect is shaped by his interaction with the environment; Jerome Bruner maintained twenty years ago that "any subject can be taught in some intellectually honest form to any child at any stage of development"; and B. F. Skinner conceives of a child as the sum of his behaviors, which are almost totally determined by environmental stimuli.

There is no question that a child's intellectual performance can be influenced *to some degree* by early experiences, of which none are as varied and stimulating, and ultimately beneficial, as the ones that lie between the covers of books. We are not interested in trying to develop something as vague as your child's intellect, however. We want to teach you, the parent, how to teach your child *specific, measurable, reading skills*, which are the primary key to almost all subsequent learning. If this influences his intelligence, fine. If not, he will at least be able to read!

How to Use This Chapter

Before you can actually teach your child to read he must first *learn how to learn*. Toward this end we will suggest some activities to foster those attributes that contribute to the development of this skill. The activities themselves are by no means the only way in which these talents can be developed, but they will serve as an excellent point of departure for the parent who wants to stimulate the child's early learning development.

Chances are that you already incorporate most of these strategies in your home. If so, just skim this chapter. But they are far too important to leave to chance and we know for a fact that many parents do not use them. There is reason to believe, in fact, that the use of these strategies encourages the development of the very characteristics that make the difference between homes producing good readers and those producing children who have a great deal of difficulty.

The specific areas on which we will concentrate in this chapter, therefore, are:

1. Physiological readiness.
2. Self-concept.
3. Discipline.
4. Listening.
5. Language development.
6. Developing an interest in books.

Physiological Readiness

Beginning with infancy, a child should have physical activity, language stimulation, a balanced diet, and adequate rest. Regardless of sex the child should have balls to throw and catch, be allowed to climb, swing, slide, and jump, use crayons and scissors, and manipulate puzzles and blocks. Through such activities children not only develop perceptual-motor skills, but also learn to play with other children and thereby develop important social skills. All these things contribute to the child's later success as a learner.

Many learning problems can be prevented or corrected easily, if promptly and accurately identified. There is no excuse for allowing children to have trouble in school because they don't see well or have an uncorrected hearing problem. It is your responsibility as a parent to have a specialist check your child's vision and hearing, especially if he experiences difficulty learning. By the same token, speech or language difficulties should be referred to a speech pathologist who has experience with children of the same age.

Some learning problems persist without our being able to correct or identify their cause. They are often grouped under such labels as learning disabilities, dyslexia, hyperactivity, minimal brain dysfunction, or mild intellectual handicaps. Labels like this aren't particularly helpful because each of them includes children who differ dramatically from each other.

Learning disabilities, for example, include difficulties in areas as diverse as visual, auditory, perceptual-motor, cognitive, and language processes. Dyslexia has been used very generally to describe reading problems and very specifically to refer to letter and word reversals. Whatever the label, a behavioral description of the problem is necessary. If this problem cannot be corrected through professional help, a modification of the educational process is called for and one-to-one instruction is the most effective educational modification known. Furthermore, because the lessons in this book contain numerous suggestions to further adapt one-to-one instruction for the child who does not learn the first time something is taught, the program is as applicable to children with learning problems as it is to those who learn easily.

Some of the characteristics of our program which allow the parent of a child with learning problems to tailor the teaching to special needs include:

1. The program enables you to find out immediately when something is not understood, thereby avoiding continual frustration on the part of the child.

2. The teaching of concepts can proceed as slowly as necessary.

3. As much repetition and review is provided as needed.

4. The child is involved as an active participant in the learning process through dialogue and through being able to manipulate materials.

5. The pressure found in most learning situations is reduced by de-emphasizing failure, not giving the child more to do than he can successfully complete, making him aware of his strengths rather than emphasizing his weaknesses, and keeping instruction as low-key as possible.

Self-concept

It will probably come as no surprise to you that the way a child feels *about* himself is important to his success as a learner. Since you have more influence on this factor than anyone else in his environment, the best way for your child to feel good about himself is for you to:

1. Provide opportunities for him to do things of which he will be proud and which will help him feel that he is learning and growing.

2. Let him know that you value, are proud of, and are interested in the things he does.

3. Take time to be with your child, listen to him, encourage him in his interests.

4. Be positive or offer positive suggestions, and *never, never reward your child's efforts with criticism and sarcasm.*

Those four precepts pretty much sum up the philosophy underlying this entire book. The teaching activities we describe are designed to incorporate them. If you are unable to apply them, then you should not attempt to teach your child yourself.

Discipline

To many people discipline means the same as punishment. We see discipline as something much broader, which might better be described as *standards of conduct*. Parents set standards initially for their children and then modify them over the years as their children grow more mature.

Ultimately these standards become self-imposed, rather than externally imposed, but for that to occur the child must be taught discipline by the parents in the first place. We won't presume to try to tell you how to accomplish this with your child, but we will say that a child constantly in conflict with his teacher, whether at home or in school, is not receptive to learning. The very nature of the teaching situation requires a disciplined interaction between a teacher—who presents the stimuli—and a student—who attends or reacts to it.

Listening

Before children become fluent and avid readers, they obtain new information primarily through their ears. A child who has not learned to listen attentively will be severely handicapped both in the amount of knowledge he brings to the learning setting and in the degree to which he can absorb information from that setting.

Many factors influence effective listening, some of them so obvious—such as hearing, vision, and anxiety—that they are often overlooked.

Hearing. Normal hearing is essential for effective listening. Children sometimes suffer a temporary mild hearing loss because of a buildup of wax in the outer ear canal, or an accumulation of fluid in the middle ear as a result of a cold or overgrown adenoids. When this happens a child may seem inattentive, slow to respond, or indifferent. A teacher, whether parent or classroom teacher, may think the child has a poor attitude toward learning; someone who doesn't know the child well may even think he is not very bright. In any case, the listening and learning capabilities will be hindered until the problem is corrected, so by all means see your pediatrician if you think there might be a difficulty. Identifying the problem is ninety percent of the solution because you can compensate for it in your instruction and teach him to compensate when someone else teaches him.

Vision. Strangely enough, the eyes are also important to listening. All of us engage in some unconscious lip-reading and face-watching when we listen, which helps us ascertain not only what is being said but also how the speaker feels about what he is saying. When we don't have this opportunity, we are forced to be much more explicit in what we say—for example, when we speak over the telephone. A child with poor vision, or one who has simply not learned to use visual clues in listening, may thus miss a good deal of what is said to him. Furthermore, looking at something also helps maintain interest in the subject and thereby indirectly influences listening. Young children, for example, like to look at pictures while they listen to a story and often lose interest when they cannot.

Anxiety. Children who are preoccupied with a problem have difficulty focusing their attention on anything for long, and this can definitely make for poor listening. It is to be hoped that your child will come to you for help when he has a problem; if he doesn't, you should seek him out. Remember that to maintain a close and warm relationship with your child, you too must be a good listener.

Strategies for enhancing listening skills. Listening can be developed and improved like any other skill. Here are a few suggestions you may find helpful:

1. *Assess the cause of the problem.* We can't overstate the importance of ensuring that your child's vision and hearing are normal. If they are and he is still a poor listener, consider the possibility of other factors, such as:

(a) Are you expecting him to listen for too long (that is, beyond his attention span)?

(b) Are you using an inappropriate vocabulary (for example, too many words he doesn't understand)?

(c) Is he interested in what is being said to him?

2. When addressing your child, speak clearly, using words he understands. To get his undivided attention, speak to him in a quiet area, ensuring eye contact between the two of you. See if he can repeat what you have told him in his own words.

3. There are several activities you can use to enhance a child's listening ability, the most effective of which undoubtedly is reading to him. As you will see in Chapter Three, your reading should be accompanied by questions based on what is happening in the story you are reading. When your child develops ease in handling those "who," "what," and "where" questions, you should make them slightly more difficult. "Why" questions require not only attentive listening but also some thinking on the child's part.

Other listening activities children often enjoy are:

(a) *Story completion.* Begin telling or reading a story, stop, and ask the child to complete it. By paying special attention you can determine whether or not he responded to all the elements you gave him. You might even throw in an unusual twist or two to see if he was listening.

(b) *Focusing on individual sounds (rhyming).* It is natural for children to enjoy playing with language. Babies, after all, learn to speak by experimenting with sounds. Rhyme is a form of language play of which children are especially fond, and games using them not only improve listening skills, but also lay the foundation for future instruction in phonics. One such game is the recitation of nursery rhymes, allowing your child to fill in the rhyming word when you pause. You can also make up your own verses. Have a good time and allow yourself to be silly! You can invent rhymes using objects in the room; for example:

He shut the door
And sat on the _____. (floor)

When the room was dark
The dog would _____. (bark)

Sit in this chair
And comb your _____. (hair)

Or you can use animals; if the child has trouble with this, you might use pictures of the words you are suggesting:

I saw a cat
Sitting in a _____. (hat)

Here is a duck
Riding in a _____. (truck)

We saw a snake
Swimming in the _____. (lake)

As you can see, there are endless possibilities for helping your child become a more effective listener. You can develop these skills with little or no extra effort on your part, in the normal course of talking, reading, giving directions, or playing with your child, and have fun at the same time. This much is certain: the child will have to be able to listen in order to be able to learn to read.

Language Development

When you consider that reading is a mental process requiring comprehension of both oral and written language, it is not particularly surprising that the same children who fail to learn to read in school are often the ones who arrived there with poor language development in the first place. It is truly a tragedy that this occurs, because every parent is an experienced language teacher. With just a little extra effort every child with normal capacity for learning language could be given an adequate language repertoire.

It is your function as a parent to teach language; it happens so naturally that many are never even aware of their teaching role. Learning language comes just as naturally to the child as teaching it does to his parents. Children are great imitators. They will learn their parents' native tongue simply by repeating the sounds they hear in their immediate environment, but for optimal learning this imitative process must be both stimulated and encouraged. Almost all parents do this to some degree, and today the job is made a great deal easier by the ever-present influence of television. Still, we doubt if all parents realize just how *crucial* verbal exchange is to their children's later learning experiences.

The most important fact to keep in mind is that the child basically learns through imitation. This means that the language he hears you using, the language he hears his playmates using, and the language he hears coming from the television set will be the language he develops. If your spoken language is sloppy and grammatically incorrect, your child's will be also. If you talk to your child in baby talk for the first three years of his life, he will communicate with you and the world in kind. Language is simply too important to be left to chance, and although the repetition of television jingles—which seem to have replaced the nursery rhymes of yesteryear in some homes—is excellent practice for a child, there is no substitute for the systematic, continual, and conscious stimulation of a child's language development by his parents.

The child learns language through a communication process involving an exchange of ideas. As with all forms of learning interaction between you and your child, the more gentle and natural the exchange, the more will be learned. If your child says to you that "daddy goed home," in response your tone of voice should not be scolding or even correcting. It should simply let him know you understand while also showing him the way to learn to construct the verb "to go": "Yes, daddy went home."

Should your voice communicate displeasure or impatience, chances are the child will be discouraged from talking to you. This is one of the worst mistakes parents can make. Besides hurting their ultimate rapport with their children, they are also actively retarding their children's language development. Consistently telling a child to be quiet or ignoring him will have an identical effect.

Besides reading to your child, which is discussed in detail in the next chapter, there are several strategies you can use to help your child's language development:

1. Looking at pictures together. One of the best opportunities for both increasing a child's vocabulary and teaching him to speak in grammatical sentences involves looking at pictures and picture books with him. At a very early age the child will be able to name only a few objects in each picture, but your sessions together can nevertheless be quite fruitful. A typical interaction might progress something like this:

After showing your child a picture containing a dog, for example, you might ask *What is this?* The child may simply answer "dog."

Yes, that is a dog, or *Yes, that is a big, black and white dog.* By answering in complete sentences, using appropriate pauses and emphases, you are encouraging the development both of new vocabulary and of more complex grammatical units. Never make an issue of the child's errors or failure to incorporate what you are "teaching." Language development is a long-term project and efforts to hurry it will only have the opposite of the intended result.

As the child's vocabulary expands he can be encouraged not only to name objects, animals, and people in pictures but also to say what those animals and people are doing. With only a little guidance, some children are capable of going beyond the immediate situation to guess what will happen next. The primary objective of these interactions is to give the child practice in verbal communication; additional benefits will be the stimulation of creative thinking and self-assurance. The more verbal your child becomes, the better his chances of becoming a good reader.

2. Story telling. You should also not overlook the importance of story telling in language development. Children often ask for the same story again and again whether it is told or read. Sometimes parts of a particular story will become so familiar that they will often be quickly supplied if omitted or skipped, which means that these favorite stories have become part of their language repertoire.

In addition to make-believe tales spun by an imaginative parent, children love hearing about incidents from their parents' childhood. Fortunate indeed is the child who has a grandparent with the time and interest to talk, read, and tell stories. Many grandparents can offer a wealth of folklore as well as the wisdom of a lifetime to share with their grandchildren.

3. Concept development. A child's concept development, which is an important part of language development, can be fostered in many ways. Looking through magazines together, for example, a parent and child can name or cut out pictures of foods, people, animals, vehicles, clothes, and so forth. Once a child becomes proficient at this level, more refined discriminations and classifications can be tried. The child who has identified things that can be eaten, for example, can be asked to sort out fruits, vegetables, meats, desserts, drinks, and other food.

In this way the child not only engages in language development but also learns to classify or order his thinking, and to see that an assortment of different things may be unified because of underlying similarities. Later on this ability will be essential for reading with full comprehension, writing with clarity, and even expressing ideas orally in a precise fashion.

Developing an Interest in Books

Researchers have known for some time that children who learn to read easily and early come from homes that contain a great deal of written material which they observe the adults in their families reading. These findings aren't accidental. Children learn that which they consider important and that for which they have developed an interest or taste.

There is no better way to instill such an attitude in a child than to show him how much fun and enjoyment lie within books. We have devoted the next chapter entirely to issues related to reading to your child. The activities given there will go a long way toward developing a lifetime interest in books and reading.

Where to Go from Here

If you follow the spirit of the activities suggested in this chapter in all your dealings with your child, and if you foster his physical, psychological, and language development, then your child will learn to read very soon in all but the rarest circumstances. Practically everything we have said in this chapter is commonsense. The chances are that you already deal this way with your child. Because we believe these ideas are crucial, and because they affect the way we suggest you teach your child in later chapters, we have felt it necessary to list them.

The most effective strategy for developing most of the skills discussed in this chapter is, as we have stressed, reading to your child. For that reason we suggest that you keep this chapter in mind while you read Chapter Three. Its purpose is the same: *Getting your child ready to read.*

3

Reading to Your Child

Systematically teaching a child to recognize simple words or even to name the letters is not the first step in teaching a child to read. *The first step is to read to him.*

This chapter discusses how that step is best taken through the consideration of five questions parents commonly ask:

1. *Why should I read to my child?*
2. *At what age should I read to him?*
3. *How often should I read to him?*
4. *How can I know the best books to select?*
5. *What's the best way to read to a child?*

Why?

Until recently, reading to children simply seemed like a pleasurable form of parent–child interaction without offering a great deal of significance aside from the enjoyment it brought the child. We know differently today in specific ways.

Study after study has demonstrated the link between reading *to* children and their success in acquiring early reading skills. In

Denver, for example, preschoolers were compared on a test of basic early reading skills with the following summary results:

> Those children who performed the best on the basic reading tests had been *both* taught reading *and* read to by their parents, but those who had only been read to by their parents performed *significantly* better than those who had not been read to.

This is by no means an isolated finding. In studies conducted in New York and Los Angeles, researchers found that almost all children who learned to read before going to school, some of whom had actually learned to read with no formal instruction at all, had been read to by a parent or older sibling.

Reading to children has many other far-ranging benefits. It lays the foundation for a more intimate personal relationship between parent and child; it helps language development; it helps the child learn to solve problems; it increases his general store of knowledge; and, on a more elemental level, it teaches him what print is and not to feel threatened by it.

The list could go on and on. The fact that no activity, when properly done, is more enjoyable nor ultimately more beneficial to the child will be reason enough for any reader of this book.

When?

You can't start reading to a child too soon. Babies may not understand what you say or read to them, but they enjoy and benefit from listening to your voice. The toddler loves to hear a parent recite simple nursery rhymes and to look at, and point to, objects in colorful picture books as they are read. As the preschool child gets older the range of stories and books that he can appreciate grows as rapidly as he does, and their importance for reading development grows also.

Even after the child has begun to read, you should continue reading to him. Throughout the elementary school years and even into the early teens children still enjoy listening to a good reader. It is an excellent means of exposing children to good literature which they will not, or cannot, read on their own, and when made into a regular family function, its benefits can be extended indefinitely.

How Much?

Just as you can't begin reading to a child too soon, you also can't read too often or too much if you take care not to exceed his attention span. Since young children have difficulty focusing on anything for very long you should become sensitive to your child's individual limits and tailor your reading sessions accordingly.

It is a good idea to set aside a fixed time period each day to enable you to budget your time properly and to give your child something to look forward to. We personally recommend 20- to 30-minute sessions, depending on the individual child, since the shortest time period ever demonstrated to be effective is ten minutes.

Which Books?

Although most of the books children enjoy (for example, alphabet, picture, and story books) are relatively modest in price, the cheapest source with the greatest variety to choose from is unquestionably the public library. Therefore most parents who read to their children on a regular basis use it for the bulk of their books, and buy only those that prove to be favorites. Exceptions, of course, are gifts for special occasions or treats picked up while shopping in grocery, variety, or drug stores.

Regardless of where books are obtained, a few general guidelines should be considered relating to the age of the child. Keep in mind that these are only general suggestions and that wide individual differences exist between children at all age levels.

1. Children under three years of age. Books should be selected primarily on the basis of their illustrations. Choose books with pictures to which your child can relate, things with which he is familiar. Illustrations should be clear, colorful, and show size in realistic proportions. The text should be limited and closely coordinated with the pictures. Books that ask the child to point to and identify objects in the pictures are enjoyed by this age group, as are nursery rhymes (probably nothing will ever replace *Mother Goose!*).

2. *Three- to seven/eight-year-olds.* Continue to select books with a lot of pictures but now pay special attention to the text as well. It should closely follow the pictures and be repetitious. The child's interests should again dictate the topics. Don't be surprised if a child at this stage (or even younger) has a favorite book which he wants to have read over and over to the point where he can recite certain phrases and sentences in unison with you. This is quite natural and serves an important function, so humor him while continuing to read new material as well. This age group still loves rhymes—keep a good book of rhymes at home and involve the child in repeating them.

3. *Age eight and beyond.* When the child has become less dependent on pictures and more interested in the story line itself you may turn to more involved, more interesting fiction. Continue to let his interests dictate what you read. Most children develop strong preferences for certain types of stories (such as books about horses, detectives, trains, sports) to the point where many parents wonder whether these are cause for concern. Don't worry. Be happy that your child enjoys your reading to him. You can always try occasionally to expand his horizons. Children around this age often begin to appreciate "the world of make-believe," for example, enjoying such things as fairy tales, fables, folk tales, and legends.

A children's librarian can be of invaluable help in directing you to books appropriate to the age and interests of your child. Lists of children's books which have received special awards are another excellent source for obtaining quality titles available in most libraries. The John Newbery Medal for text and the Randolph J. Caldecott Medal for illustrations are probably the best known awards; lists of past winners of both are usually available in public libraries. Many other groups, however, some of which specialize in topic areas (such as science, mystery stories, adventure), give awards for excellence in children's books as well. The Children's Book Council publishes a small paperback collection of lists called *Children's Books: Awards and Prizes*, which is updated every two years. In it each award is explained and followed by the winners in each category. If your library does not have a copy you may order this worthwhile guide by writing to:

The Children's Book Council, Inc.
67 Irving Place
New York, NY 10003

The American Library Association compiles its own "Notable Books List" and starting in 1978 made it much more useful to parents by including the age level for which each book is appropriate. This list can be ordered from:

The American Library Association
50 East Huron Street
Chicago, IL 60611

Other sources with age-level designations also exist, such as *The New York Times Book Review Supplement*, and lists compiled by some of the larger individual children's libraries based on committee reviews.

Although all of these sources can prove quite helpful, none can completely absolve you of the responsibility for screening the books you choose to read to your child to assure both their appropriateness to his interests and your family's values.

How?

Most parents' initial reaction to someone advising them how to read to their children is either to feel vaguely insulted or to answer: "What difference does it make how I do it as long as I do it?"

Interestingly enough, how children are read to is almost as important as whether they are read to. Researchers have documented the fact that certain styles of parental reading are more often related to early learning success than others. The child's role in the process is the determining factor.

Some reading styles are "active"; some are more "passive." The parent who encourages discussion about the reading is stimulating language development as well as interest in the reading process itself, with the most dramatic results showing up later when the child himself begins to read. Reading to a child as we see it, then, is an active, *interactive* process. The number and types of questions you ask, and how much your child talks and is encouraged to do so, is as important as the words being read.

This interaction begins before and continues well *after* the reading session. Before beginning the reading, therefore, you and your child should examine the picture on the cover of the book (or on the first page of a story), with the child discussing what the story might be about and what he knows about the topic. For the actual reading itself, make sure your child can look comfortably at both the pictures and the text. This usually requires that the two of you are seated close together, side by side or with the young child in your lap. Be sure to take advantage of the remarkable potential of the voice for creating mood and generating interest by using different speaking tones and volumes.

Never discourage the child from interrupting you with questions or comments, and be sure to give explanations related to his experiences in words he understands. By the same token, don't hesitate to stop and ask questions occasionally yourself while you read. You may begin by asking simple questions such as what has happened in the story so far, or what did such and such character say or do. Later, when the child gains ease and confidence with factual relationships, go to "why" questions, such as "Why did this or that character behave in this particular way?" When the child has gained some assurance in answering these questions, go on to more difficult kinds, such as "What else could they have done?"

After the story has been read, be sure to follow up relevant questions raised before and during the story to make sure that the child has both listened and understood.

Discuss what happened; why it happened; what could have happened; and so forth. It is also important to give the child a chance to evaluate the story, to tell you things he liked and disliked; in short, to develop his personal tastes and opinions.

Questions about words. In the course of reading and rereading your child's favorite stories from books that are always at hand, it is not uncommon for the child to begin asking questions about *words*. He may ask you *which* word says "elephant," for example, or point to a word and ask, "What does it say?"

This is a normal step in the development of a young human being. He asks more and more questions to learn about his environment and the people, actions, and things that are important in his life. Be sure to answer these questions about words just as you do all his other questions. Your answers will not only increase the child's motivation to learn to read, they will also increase his confidence that one day he *will* learn. Recognizing one word in a favorite book, in fact, may show him that he is already a little bit of a reader.

4
Teaching Letter Recognition

The Task

The chief purpose of the fourteen lessons in this chapter is to enable the child to recognize the twenty-six letters in the alphabet in both capital and lower-case formats. The key word here is *recognition*, which does not mean that your child will simply learn to recite his ABCs. It means, rather, that the child should learn to recognize the letters of the alphabet in the sense that an infant learns to recognize the parents' faces and to eventually attach the titles of Mother and Father to the appropriate combination of features.

Although as the child acquires language he learns to attach more and more labels to more and more objects that have meaning to him (such as a favorite toy, body parts, foods), the young child normally has no real experience in recognizing and labeling such abstract and stylistic shapes as the things we call letters. As adults it is difficult for us to realize just how similar to each other all those little "chicken scratchings" must appear the first time they are encountered.

Children, for example, are used to a chair being a chair no matter its position: a chair is still something to sit in whether it is facing us, facing away from us, or turned upside down. Imagine, therefore, the potential confusion when a child learns that a **b** turned around (**d**) or upside down (**p**) is no longer a **b** but two entirely different letters. Imagine also, if you will, the child who has just learned these differentiations and is presented with a **b** and a **B** and told that these things are both **b**'s.

As simple as the tasks you are going to be teaching your child in this chapter may appear to you, they probably won't seem all that simple to the child. You should also be aware that your child is going to learn some individual letters much easier than others. He may, for example, find letters in which the capital and lower-case counterparts differ only in size—like **Xx**, **Ss**, and **Cc**—easier to learn than letters in which the upper- and lower-case formats differ primarily with respect to position on the line—**Pp** and **Yy**. These in turn might be easier to learn than letters having very few similarities between formats—such as **Rr**, **Gg**, and **Aa**. Alternately, you might find that he also has difficulty in telling an **M** from a **W**, a **u** from an **n**, and a **b** from a **d**, or that he consistently forgets that the only difference between a **P** and an **R** is a single diagonal line. All these differences are problems for most children only at first. A small number of children continue to experience these difficulties into the primary grades. The lessons in this chapter are set up in such a way that they can be used to teach the letters to any child and when supplemented by generous doses of perseverance, common sense, and patience on your part almost any child should master them.

Format of the Lessons

The letters in this chapter are therefore taught by introducing them through words familiar to the child, words which have some meaning in his life. By adopting this strategy we are beginning the initial stages of reading instruction (1) by showing the child that reading is relevant to his experiences and life, (2) actually teaching him to recognize words, and (3) demonstrating to him, on an intuitive level, that reading is simply an extension of oral language processes which he has already mastered. To start with isolated letters is to miss capitalizing on all these opportunities, and to risk the possibility of giving the child the idea that reading is a mechanical process involving memorizing symbols and attaching meaningless names to them.

Teaching the letters meaningfully is more natural and enjoyable to the child since the lesson is first tied into the child's life-stream. It progresses from the introduction of a word to recognition of its letters and then to recognition of the word itself. The words we have chosen are from signs, from important people in the child's life, and from fun activities. Each lesson uses the same basic format: an oral preparation, followed by a series of activities designed to teach skills related to the lesson objective.

The first model lesson is designed to familiarize you with the basic lesson format and even includes a detailed plan which can be used word-by-word. In subsequent lessons you will be able to improvise within the same activities as you see fit. Supplementary activities are provided to vary the routine and help eliminate confusion in more difficult lessons.

There are fourteen lessons in all, and if your child successfully completes them, he will have mastered all the letters of the alphabet, both upper- and lower-cases, as well as acquired a sight vocabulary of fourteen words. The final lesson is followed by a series of three tests designed to help you determine which letters have been mastered and which are candidates for additional instruction.

General Guidelines

Some guiding principles will make teaching the lessons easier for you and more effective for your child. Let's go over them briefly.

1. Be prepared. Prepare for the lesson before sitting down with your child, by reading the lesson plan and preparing all materials. Most materials require lettering. This should be done as simply as possible, taking care to observe size differences between tall and short letters. Refer to the chart below for basic letter formations.

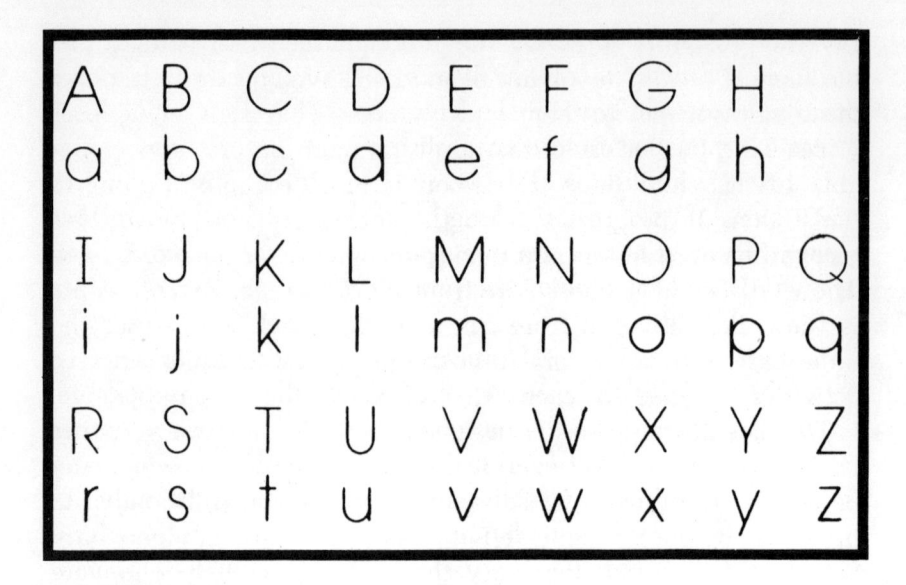

```
A  B  C  D  E  F  G  H
a  b  c  d  e  f  g  h
I  J  K  L  M  N  O  P  Q
i  j  k  l  m  n  o  p  q
R  S  T  U  V  W  X  Y  Z
r  s  t  u  v  w  x  y  z
```

You will find that not having to prepare or search for materials during the lesson will make it a lot easier to teach and will help to increase your child's attention span as well.

2. Don't work beyond your child's attention span. You can help lengthen your child's attention span by approaching each activity energetically, praising small accomplishments, and encouraging the child to be an active participant by having him talk and handle materials.

Your child's attention span will vary according to his age, personality, mood, the amount of sleep he got the night before, how active his day has been, when he last ate, and a host of other factors. Although not as variable, your attention span too will vary along similar lines, so there is really no way we can tell you exactly how many minutes each particular lesson should take. As little as fifteen to twenty minutes per day can still be extremely beneficial. Of course, additional instruction will result in additional learning, but no learning will occur if you try to force a child who has lost interest.

Don't feel that you have to complete a lesson every time you sit down. Each lesson has been divided into activities for the express purpose of providing natural stopping places. Each lesson provides plenty of opportunities to review previously taught material, so *use your judgment.* Whatever you do, however, never drag a lesson out beyond the point at which your child loses interest. When that time comes, stop.

Quitting five minutes early every now and then isn't going to make any difference in the long run as far as how much your child learns, but it can make a good deal of difference in how much the two of you enjoy the process.

3. Be flexible. The lesson format and activity sequences have been designed to fit the needs of as many children as possible, but in the final analysis your child is different from all other children. Use your knowledge of these differences to actually *improve* these already effective materials whenever possible. As we discussed in the first chapter, one reason parental teaching works so well is that no one knows your child as well as you. Teaching your own child at home is the ultimate in individualized instruction; capitalize on it every chance you get.

This means that if it is obvious to you that your child knows a lesson by the time you are half through the scheduled activities, then skip the rest and go on to the review exercises. If he doesn't seem to benefit from one type of activity, substitute another which teaches the same concept. If he has a great deal of trouble discriminating between upper- versus lower-case forms of letters, then teach the capital letters first and wait until he has mastered them before teaching the lower-case counterparts. If the script for an activity seems stilted, or doesn't reflect the way you and your child talk, then by all means rephrase it. If we use a word you don't think is in your child's vocabulary, then substitute one that is. In other words, improvise. Be creative.

4. Be goal-oriented. Always keep in mind what you are trying to get your child to learn and bend your best efforts toward that end. If this requires establishing a routine in which you work with your child every day between 2:00 and 2:30 p.m., fine; it will give him something to look forward to. If your child is easily distracted, find a spot in your house where you can shut off the outside world; turn off the TV, take the phone off the hook if necessary. In other words, do whatever is necessary to make the teaching of the lessons which follow in this and subsequent chapters as profitable and as enjoyable as possible.

Materials

(1) **Word Box.** This is a box into which will go all the words the child studies and learns beginning with those in this chapter. Its uses are explained below. A cigar or greeting card box or a 3" x 5" index card filing box will do.

(2) **Word cards.** These are 3" by 5" (or larger) index cards found in drugstores and office supply stores. You will be writing one word on each of these cards.

(3) **Letter cards.** These are index cards cut apart into small cards. One letter is written on each card.

(4) **Felt tip pen.** Any pen for writing the words will be fine.

(5) **Wide-lined primary paper.** These practice tablets are found in drugstores and variety stores.

(6) **Crayons, pencils, ruler or straight edge.**

(7) **Paper.** Any plain, inexpensive paper should be kept on hand for spontaneous demonstrating, practicing, or coloring.

The Word Box

This filing box is one of the most important aides for the teaching of reading, serving record keeping, teaching, and reviewing functions. Each of the child's words is printed in lower case letters (not capitals) on an index card and placed in it. It has two compartments: one consisting of words which have been mastered and one labelled "New Words" consisting of words which have been studied but not yet mastered. The compartments can be separated with some kind of divider or the "New Words" section can be kept in an envelope at the front end of the box.

You will use the Word Box throughout this book. When new words are introduced you will file them in the "New Words" section or envelope. In each lesson you will review the contents of this envelope by having the child read or study the words. When you are convinced a word has been learned you will file it in the "known words" section of the Word Box which will be referred to simply as the Word Box. Occasionally you will review the entire contents of the box to make sure that the child remembers all his mastered words. If he fails to read one he used to know, place it in the "New Words" section for review during the next session.

If you communicate the importance of placing a word in the Word Box and approach the entire process with excitement, most children take great satisfaction in this permanent record of their reading achievement. Some, in fact, enjoy periodically taking the cards from the box and playing with them. We suggest that you encourage this activity, although you would be wise to keep a separate list of the words contained in the event that some cards are inadvertently destroyed or lost.

Getting Started

You now know what you are going to teach in this chapter, you have an idea of the format the lessons will take, and you have received some general suggestions to make the experience rewarding. The only thing left for you to do is to read the remainder of the chapter to obtain (1) a feel for the task at hand, (2) ideas for activities and materials you may want to use earlier in the sequence in case they are needed, and (3) directions and specifications for constructing needed materials.

Once you have done this you will be ready to begin teaching your child letter recognition, a skill researchers have found to be highly related to early success in reading. This skill will also make the teaching of letter sounds (Chapter Five) and the words these sounds make far easier. You will be ready, in other words, to begin to teach your child to read. May it be rewarding to you both.

MODEL LESSON #1
Teaching the letters **Ss, Tt, Oo, Pp**

The four letters introduced in this lesson will be taught via the word "stop." Most children know this word and are familiar with stop signs. We will make the most of this familiarity to construct a meaningful and interesting context for the lesson.

Laying the Groundwork

You should start teaching this lesson several days before you and your child actually "sit down" for the first session. The next time the two of you go outside, point out the first stop sign you run across and ask your child if he knows what the sign means. Explain that it tells cars that they should stop at that corner and discuss the importance of traffic signs such as this. Point out the red background and white letters and note that the sign has four letters which spell the word "STOP." You can make a game of pointing out all the stop signs you see. If your child knows how to count, make a game of counting all the stop signs you see; if he doesn't, you can count out loud for him, thus laying the groundwork for eventually teaching him that skill as well.

Materials

1. A large stop sign drawn on a sheet of paper which the child can color red.

2. Word card for "STOP."

3. Word card for "stop" (lower case).
4. Letter cards for S-T-O-P and s-t-o-p.

ACTIVITY #1
Introducing the capital letters

Sit next to one another, preferably at a table or desk away from distractions. If your child is right-handed, sit to his right. If he is left-handed, sit to his left.

Take out the stop sign you have prepared.

Do you know what this sign says?

He will probably say, "Yes, that is a stop sign." If he answers correctly, encourage him by saying:

That's right. This sign says "STOP."

If he does not identify it correctly, simply say:

This is a "STOP" sign. See, this word says stop.

In either case, discuss the games you have been playing identifying stop signs. Review their function, importance, and other characteristics.

Next show your child the index card with "STOP" written in capital letters.

Today we're going to learn the names of the letters in the word "STOP." Listen to me say them.

Starting with **S** and proceeding through **P**, point to each letter as you say its name.

S-T-O-P spells "STOP."
The first letter of "STOP" is S.

Point to it.

We always start to spell words on this side of the card

—point to the left—

with the first letter and go this way.

Sweep your hand from left to right across the card. Point to the first letter again and say:

Can you remember what the first letter of "STOP" is?

If your child answers correctly, say:

That's right, the first letter is S.

If he does not remember, say:

The first letter is S.

Point to it.

Now what is the first letter?

Compliment him when he repeats the name correctly.

Do you remember what the next letter is called?

Point to the **T**. If he responds correctly, compliment him and proceed to the next two letters in the same fashion. If he does not remember, say (while pointing):

*The second letter in "STOP" is called **T**.*

Again, proceed to the next two letters using the same strategy. After you have completed this exercise say:

Can you point to each letter in "STOP" while I say it?

Pronounce the letter names in order (using the same index card) as your child points to them. If he has trouble, gently guide his finger to point to the correct letter.

Now let's point and say the letter names together.

Hold his hand so that the two of you can point and recite the names together. Go slowly, rhythmically, and gamelike. Do it as many times as you feel that it is productive or as your child wants.

Now, let's see how many letters you can say by yourself. Remember, always start over here with the first letter.

Point to the S.
However many letters your child remembers, say:

Very good, you remembered _, _, _, and _.

Say and point to the letter names correctly remembered.

Let's say them one more time together.

Be sure to go over the letters in order, setting a slow pace so that if the child forgets one he can join in, trailing your voice.

ACTIVITY #2
Using the capital letter cards

I'm going to give you the letters in "STOP" on little pieces of paper. I want you to place each letter on top of the same letter on our word card.

Point to the index card you have been using.
Spread out the individual letter cards in mixed-up order.

Can you find the S and put it over the first letter in "STOP"?

Help him place the S card over the S on the word card if need be and say:

Now we have the S in place. Can you find the second letter and place it over the T on the word card?

As your child places the **T** (again if help is needed, supply it), say:

*That's good. The first letter of "STOP" is **S** and the second letter is **T**. Do you remember what the next letter is called?*

If he knows it, compliment him. If he doesn't, say:

*The next letter in "STOP" is called **O**.*

Proceed to the final letter using the same matching game.

ACTIVITY #3
Practicing and reviewing

Can you point to each letter in "STOP" while I say it?

Pronounce the letter names in order, using the same index card as in Activity #1, as your child points to them. If he has trouble, gently guide his finger to the correct letter.

Now let's point and say the letter names together.

Hold his hand so that the two of you can point and recite the names together. Go slowly, rhythmically, and gamelike. Do it as many times as your child wants.

Good! Let's see how many letters you can say by yourself. Remember, always start over there with the first letter.

Point to the **S**.
However many your child remembers, say:

Very good, you remembered _, _, _, and _.

Say and point to the letter names correctly remembered.

Let's say them one more time together.

Be sure to go over the letters in order. Set a slow pace so that if the child forgets a letter he can join in, trailing your voice.

ACTIVITY #4
Tracing

Take out a sheet of paper, pen, and crayons.

Watch while I write the word "STOP," and then you can go over it with a crayon.

Write the letters as large as you did on the word card. Write slowly, saying each letter name as your child watches.

Why don't you pick a crayon and trace over each letter in "STOP" like this.

Illustrate with the nonwriting end of your pencil or pen, then give the child the paper you just wrote on. If he asks for help you can either demonstrate the tracing process or guide his hand while he traces. As he finishes each letter, say:

Good. You've traced the S (for example), *now see if you can trace the T.*

As he works, point out the differences in the way the letters are constructed. Show him how the **S** is made of two curves, for example; how the **T** is made of two straight lines, one on top of the other; how the **O** is round like a circle; how the **P** is a little bit like a circle on a stick, or any combination of descriptions you can think of. The point of the exercise is to begin focusing your child's attention on the way the letters look, not to be able to write them perfectly.

ACTIVITY #5
Introducing the lower-case letters

We've learned the letters in "STOP" just like they're written on stop signs. Did you know that there are two ways to write "STOP"? One is with big letters like the ones on the signs. The other way to write "STOP" is by using small letters. Every letter can be written both big and small. Let's learn how to write "STOP" using small letters now.

Show the child the word card with "stop" written in lower-case letters.

This is how "stop" is written with little letters. Let's say the letters as I point to them.

The child should have very little trouble with this activity; if he does it will probably lie with the **T**–**t** difference. Simply say something like:

This is the way a small t is written.

Point out each letter again, saying its name, and then ask your child to say the name while you point to them in order.

ACTIVITY #6
Using the capital and small letter cards

Here are the big and little letters written side by side.

Show the child the letter cards with both upper- and lower-case letters.

See, the big and small S's look the same.

Point to each as you mention the similarity. Help him trace both with his finger.

Look at the big and small T's (point). *The big T has one line on top of the other.*

Take the child's finger and trace the **T**, vertical line first, followed by the horizontal line.

Now, look at the little t. It's a little different. The little line isn't on top of the big one.

Help the child trace the lower-case **t** with his finger, vertical line first.

The big and little O's are the same, just like the S's.

Point to the two **O**'s. Help him trace them with his finger.

Let's look at the P's now. They're the same except the little one has a tail that hangs down.

Point out the difference by writing **P** and **p** on the wide-lined paper and showing how the little **p** hangs down below the line.

See how the little p is written?

Help him trace it, emphasizing the portion extending below the line.

Now, let's see if you can match the big letters with the little ones.

Take out the two sets of individual letter cards. Spread the capital letters out keeping them in order, but mix the lower-case letter cards up and say:

Put the little s with the big S.

Help him if he has trouble. If he does it correctly, say:

That's right. This is the big S and this is a little s.

Point to both.

Repeat the process for the three remaining letters. If your child has trouble with one, point out the similarities and differences between the two forms again. If you feel he needs more practice, repeat the process, matching the capitals with the lower-case letters. You may also wish to repeat the tracing exercise in Activity #4 using both capital *and* lower-case letters if you think it will help him learn the letter names.

Tell me once more what this word is.

Show him "stop" on the word card. He should have no trouble at all. If he does, show him the upper-case word card ("STOP"), and remind him that the two words are the same. When the child identifies it, be highly complimentary and remind him that he just learned to read his first word. Try to build some anticipation for the next lesson in which more letters and another word will be learned.

ACTIVITY #7
Word Box

Show the child the Word Box and explain that it is where he will collect all the words he learns to read. Then file the word card for "stop" (lower case only) in the "New Words" section.

A Note to the Parent

You have now taught your child over 15 percent of the letters in the alphabet; the rest will be *easier* to teach because:

1. You now have something to build on.
2. No other lesson in this chapter will require you to teach this many letters at one sitting.

3. Both you and your child have gained some ease in using the sequence of activities that goes into teaching the letters.

4. You have established a precedent for your new, formalized teacher-student relationship.

5. Your child has experienced real success in learning.

If, for one reason or another, your child had difficulty with this first lesson you may be asking yourself if he will ever learn to read at such a slow pace. The answer is a resounding "Yes" for two reasons. In the first place you shouldn't assume that if your child has trouble learning initially he will always have trouble. As long as you continue to display patience and understanding he will continue to improve. Secondly, your child will eventually learn more quickly because you will improve as a teacher with time and experience.

If your child did learn slowly during this first lesson, chances are that he may forget quickly. When this happens—and all children and adults do forget some of what they learn—don't despair. Above all *don't lose patience or degrade your child in any way*. Forgetting is as natural a process as sleeping or eating. It occurs when we don't use something or when it doesn't have particular relevance for us. Your job as teacher entails making sure that your child uses what you teach him through regular lessons and review sessions, and making sure that what is being taught is considered relevant. You should point out that letters and words are encountered everywhere in our environment.

Summary of the Lesson Format

The basic format just presented will be used for the remaining letters of the alphabet, so detailed instructions for teaching each lesson will not be given. Instead we suggest that you refer back to the preceding model format or the following summary to occasionally refresh your memory as you progress through the remaining lessons.

In addition to preparing materials and laying the groundwork for a lesson in advance, the actual teaching process will involve the following seven steps (plus supplementary activities as desired):

1. **Introducing the capital letters.** The letters to be taught in a lesson will be introduced through familiar words. Each word will contain both previously learned letters and new letters. The introduction of these letters is an *active* process, involving both parent and child.

2. **Using the capital letter cards.** The letter cards, prepared in advance of the lesson, are used to gain familiarity with each letter contained in the word card.

3. **Practicing and reviewing.** Practice is given recognizing the letters contained on the word card, always proceeding from left to right.

4. **Tracing.** The child is familiarized with the unique shape of each letter by tracing over the letters with crayon as you write them for him.

5. **Introducing the lower-case letters.** The familiar word is shown printed in lower case format. The child is introduced to each letter individually and told its name.

6. **Using the capital and lower case letter cards.** The capital and lower-case letter cards are compared with differences and similarities in shapes discussed. The child is taught to match the capital letter cards with their lower-case counterparts.

7. **The Word Box.** This is one of the most essential steps in teaching your child to read. It should be included in each lesson you teach because it is basically an ongoing record of words which have been learned and which need to be reviewed. The "New Words" section of the box is also a valuable teaching aid, reminding you of which words need additional practice. The Word Box will be used throughout this book, so it is important to keep it updated.

8. **Supplementary activities.** In addition to ABC books, alphabet strips, or a chalk board, activities are presented throughout the chapter which can be substituted for any of the above steps (with the exception of the Word Box) or used as additional instruction when needed.

Supplementary Activities

Future lessons will suggest at this point supplementary activities which may be substituted for a regular activity or serve as an additional teaching strategy for certain letters with which the child may have difficulty. The decision of whether or not to employ a particular supplementary activity is up to you, but bear in mind that their occasional use helps vary the routine and prevent boredom.

Below are three supplementary materials which can be used with any lesson, or which can serve to reinforce learning the letters *between* lessons.

Supplementary Materials

1. The alphabet strip. This is a long narrow sheet of paper which displays the alphabet in order (Aa Bb Cc . . . Yy Zz). It can be hung either on the wall of your study area or in the child's room to serve as a continual reminder of the letter shapes and alphabetical order. Alphabet strips can either be purchased or constructed by drawing the letters on wide-lined primary paper and taping the sheets together.

2. ABC books. Either coloring books or story books which match pictures with each letter of the alphabet can be used to introduce the particular letters being taught or to reinforce their learning following the lesson. These books are also excellent for helping the child learn to recite the alphabet.

3. The chalkboard. A small chalkboard can be purchased from most department or toy stores which can be used to help the child copy or trace the letters. When it is kept in his room the child may enjoy writing on it as a play activity.

LESSON #2
Teaching the letter **Gg**

The word we are going to use, "GO," combines a relatively difficult letter, **G**, with an easier one already learned, **O**. Lesson #2 should progress more quickly than Lesson #1 since it really has only one unfamiliar letter and because the two of you are more familiar with the sequence of activities.

Materials

1. A round sign drawn witth the word "GO" inside which the child may color green.

$$\bigcirc \text{GO}$$

2. Word cards for "GO" and "go."
3. Letter cards for **G-O** and **g-o**.

ACTIVITY #1
Introducing the capital letter

The letter **G** will be introduced by the word "GO."

Today we're going to learn a different word. This new word means the opposite of "STOP." Can you guess what it is?

Show him the "GO" sign. Since "GO" signs are not nearly as common as stop signs (although many green lights do contain the word), he may not recognize the word. Also remember that the word "opposite" may not yet be a part of your child's vocabulary. If he does not recognize "GO," say:

After a car stops at a stop sign, it can _____.

Continue to prompt him if he has trouble. For example, if he plays Monopoly ask what he must do if he lands on the jail sign. Once he either guesses the word or you have to break down and tell him, point to the sign and ask him if he recognizes either of the letters. **O** should be recognized. If it is, make a major production out of it. If it is not, remind the child that the **O** (point to it) was also in "STOP." If he simply does not remember, tell him that the round letter in both "STOP" and "GO" is indeed an **O**.

You may now repeat as many of the activities listed in the lesson format summary as it takes to teach the child to recognize capital and lower-case g's and the word "go." Be sure to include Activity #7 (Word Box), but feel free to substitute supplementary activities for any of the others.

SUPPLEMENTARY ACTIVITY
Playing with words

By following the list of activities in the model lesson as applied to the word "GO," the child should now be familiar with both the letters and the word written in both upper- and lower-case formats. This means that he has now studied two words ("stop" and "go"); it is now time to see whether or not he can tell them apart. If he can, and if the meaning of each is known, then your child has actually begun to learn to read.

One way to evaluate recognition and understanding of these words is to simply take out both cards for each of the two words (written in upper- and lower-case formats), mix them up, and have him tell you what word is written on each as you present them. You may vary the exercise occasionally by asking what a word *means*.

A second method—and you will be able to think of many more—is to play a game using the four word cards. You might, for example, have your child stand on the opposite side of the room (or you could play the game outside) and walk toward you each time he sees the word "GO" (or "go") and stop every time the word "STOP" ("stop") is read. You, of course, will flash the cards in whatever order you choose. Failure to respond to a word correctly will result in the child's having to return to the starting point. You should get an excellent idea whether or not the two forms of each word are known. If a word is not known, playing this game should help.

LESSON #3
Teaching L and W

Two new letters, **L** and **W**, will be introduced in this lesson using the same general sequence of activities employed for the first two lessons. By not varying the basic format too much we are helping you and your child to fall into a familiar routine of having a couple of new letters introduced at each lesson via a familiar word. The child receives practice in the recognition of these letters both in their upper- and lower-case formats, and receives some practice in recognizing the word itself.

Materials

You will again use the same basic materials as in Lesson #1, substituting the letters **S–L–O–W** in both upper and lower cases. Since you are still dealing with words appearing on signs, make a diamond-shaped caution sign with the word "SLOW" written on it.

ACTIVITY #1
Introducing the capital letters

SUGGESTED SEQUENCE

Introduce the word "SLOW" with a discussion of its meaning along with the meaning of the sign you have just constructed. The word contains two letters already familiar to your child, **S** and **O** (which have appeared in both words learned so far).

Start the lesson by asking if he recognizes the two letters already studied. Praise him lavishly if he does, supply him their names if he does not. You may then follow the same sequence as suggested in the model lesson.

It should be emphasized again that this is nothing more than a suggested sequence. As always you may alter, delete, or add steps depending upon your child's interest and how quickly he learns, just as long as you teach the upper- and lower-case forms of **L** and **W**, provide some kind of mechanism for review, attempt to teach recognition of the word "slow" itself, and use the Word Box as already described.

LESSON #4
Teaching the letters **Aa** and **Kk**

Prior to the lesson, a concentrated effort should be made to point out "WALK" and "DO NOT WALK" lights on street corners. Lay the groundwork for this and Lesson #5 several days in advance (by discussing the meaning of "WALK"—"DO NOT WALK" lights, playing counting games with them) so that the actual lessons can begin on familiar ground.

ACTIVITY #1
Introducing the capital letters

The new letters contained in the word "WALK" should not, in themselves, present any particular problem, although the differences between the upper- and lower-case **A**'s are a problem for some children. As always you should use the familiar letters (**W** and **L**) as sources of review and reinforcement. Follow the lesson format summary.

ACTIVITY #7
The Word Box

Try to plan the lesson itself so that you have at least five minutes to devote to review. When that time comes take the word cards contained in your child's Word Box and ask him (1) what word is written on each and (2) the names of the letters contained in each word. If the child can no longer recognize a word already filed in the box, transfer it to the "New Words" section. If, however, one of the words in the "New Words" section is now known, transfer it with great fanfare to the portion of the Box marked for mastered words. If the child doesn't recognize one of the letters contained in any of the words, make sure that letter is reviewed in subsequent lessons.

LESSON #5
Teaching the letters **Dd** and **Nn**

Hopefully, you have been pointing out "DO NOT WALK" lights to your child since before you started Lesson #4, so the groundwork for this session has already been laid. (In the event the pedestrian lights in your community incorrectly use the contraction "DONT WALK," you may construct your word cards accordingly, as long as you include the apostrophe.)

ACTIVITY #1
Introducing the capital letters

The two new letters introduced in this lesson are **D** and **N**, both of which have upper- and lower-case variations. Be sure to point out these differences at the appropriate point in the sequence and to ask the child to find both letters on his new alphabet wall chart.

SUPPLEMENTARY ACTIVITY
Pulling out letters from the word cards

As a variation in the review process you might take out all five word cards used to date and spread them out on the work surface. Ask the child to identify each word and then to:

Pick out a letter that you would like for me to write down.

When he does (and make sure he names it as well as points to it), you should write that letter on a sheet of paper in both upper- and lower-case formats.

Now pick out another letter for me to write.

Write the second letter (again after he says it and points it out) under the first.

Now, pick another letter besides these two.

Point to the two letters you have written on the sheet of paper. Continue the process until all eleven letters are written out. When your child picks a letter already chosen, say:

No, we have already written a _. Pick a different letter this time.

Point to the letter already chosen on the sheet of paper. Once you have completed the process you may work from the written sheet to the word cards if you see fit, perhaps by asking the child to find all the **O**'s, for example, on the word cards.

LESSON #6
Teaching the letters **Ee, Xx, Ii**

Continuing the theme of teaching letters and words contained in signs, point out to your child the EXIT signs found in public buildings, movie theaters, stores, and other places. The chances are good that though he has seen these signs many times he will not have paid attention to them and may not even know the word orally unless you have made a point of teaching it. If you have neglected to do so, now is a good time to start, since knowing the meaning of this particular sign is a potentially important piece of knowledge for any child (not to mention a convenient way to introduce the letter **X**).

ACTIVITY #1
Introducing the capital letters

This lesson is unique in the sense that all the capital letters involved contain only straight lines in their makeup. You might point out this fact and even see if the child can copy the word.

LESSON #7
Teaching the letters **Qq** and **Uu**

The two letters **Q** and **U** are the last to be taught through words contained in signs. "QUIET" signs, of course, are hardly commonplace outside libraries or hospitals, but the word itself is certainly very much a part of the child's oral vocabulary. What you can do, therefore, is make up a sign with the word "QUIET" written on it, attach a string to it, and agree on some ground rules that will allow the child to hang the sign wherever he chooses to "study." This will require the cooperation of family members.

LESSON #8
Teaching the letters **Mm, Hh,** and **Rr**

The theme of the words from which the letters are derived now switches from signs to people the child knows. Obviously one of the best known people in the child's experience is his mother, and although he may call her by a different name (such as Mom, Mommy, Ma), the title of "Mother" is at least familiar.

You may develop the lesson by telling the child that he is now going to learn the letters in the names of people he knows. You might want to produce a picture or some other identifier and ask the child if he knows who is represented. You could discuss different names for "MOTHER," finally deciding to choose the more formal name as the one to work with.

Teaching Letter Recognition / 59

The actual letters to be learned in this lesson are **M**, **H**, and **R**. All three have troublesome characteristics: the **M** because it is sometimes confused with **W**; the **H** because of the difference between upper- and lower-case forms; the **R** both because it possesses a truly difficult shape (straight, curved, and diagonal lines in the same letter) for children, and because of the radical differences between upper- and lower-case forms.

Take special pains to point out these problems during the lesson's sequence and supply ample practice time for mastering them, but aside from that you should simply continue to use those procedures you find work best for your child. Be sure not to neglect the review activities at the end of the lesson; the more new letters and words are introduced the more difficult discrimination between them can become. If you are not careful you may find your child reaching a point where he seems to be forgetting as much as he is learning.

LESSON #9
Teaching the letter **Ff**

Continuing the theme of learning the letters in names of people your child knows leads logically to the word "FATHER," which not only conveniently contains one of the seven letters not yet introduced, **F**, but also affords practice in using two of the relatively difficult letters introduced in the previous lesson, **H** and **R**.

SUPPLEMENTARY ACTIVITY
Matching upper- and lower-case letters

Before beginning this activity you should write the letters covered so far in two columns as illustrated: upper case in the first column in alphabetical order; lower case in the second column in mixed up order. If the wall chart containing all twenty-

A	d
D	w
F	q
G	n
K	g
L	v
N	p
O	a
P	l
Q	k
S	f
T	s
V	t
W	o

six letters is in the child's line of sight you should either remove it or conduct the exercise in another room. Tell the child:

Here are the letters that we have learned so far. The big letters are on the left (point) *and the little letters are on the right* (point). *I would like for you to draw a line between each big letter on the left and each little letter on the right that has the same name.*

Give him a pencil or crayon.

*Now see if you can draw a line between the big **A** and the little **a**.*

Point to the upper-case **A**. If he has trouble, prompt him by saying something like:

*See if you can find the little **a**.*

Point to the proper column. If he finds it, help him draw the line. If he doesn't find it, ask:

Is this an a?

Point to, say, an x.

Is this an a?

Point to the **a** this time. With a little help he should get the drift of the exercise and be able to complete it. Letters which he has problems matching are obviously letters on which he needs extra work.

You should include this activity in each of the remaining lessons, adding the letters contained in each. Suggested variations for subsequent lessons are:

1. Not pronouncing the capital letters for him, but allowing him to complete the task on his own.
2. Mixing up both upper- and lower-case columns.
3. Switching columns.
4. Including untaught or nonsensical letters in one or more columns.

LESSON #10
Teaching the letters **Bb** and **Yy**

If your child doesn't have a baby brother or sister, you may have an acquaintance with an infant or very young child. Use one or the other as the development for the word "BABY," which contains two of the remaining six untaught letters, **B** and **Y**.

Proceed as usual, although we strongly recommend that you use some variation of the Supplementary Activity discussed in the previous review process. Should you have time, or should you perceive a need to vary the menu, there are many games the two of you can play both in fulfilling the need for review and as strategies for learning new concepts. One such game follows.

SUPPLEMENTARY ACTIVITY
Card games using the word cards

Place the word cards from the ten lessons in a stack, written side down like a deck of playing cards. Mix them up thoroughly and explain the rules of the game to your "opponent." The rules are basically as follows:

1. Each player draws one card in turn.
2. The student must spell the word on his card by looking at it and calling out the letters. If he is correct, he may place the card in his pile; if incorrect, he must surrender the card to your pile.
3. You may spell your card either correctly or incorrectly, after which the child (who may look at your card as you spell) tells you whether you were correct or purposefully incorrect. If he is right, the card goes in his pile; if wrong, the card is yours.
4. The "winner" is the person with the most cards at the end of the game (cards in your pile are, of course, being earmarked for review).

Other variations include using the twenty-two letter cards as the deck in the above game, playing a variation of Fish using word cards as each player's hand and the letter cards as the deck.

LESSONS #11–14
Words representing things that are fun to do

The last four words to be considered may be categorized under the label of "things that are fun to do." If your child is like most children, a favorite activity is watching television, so introducing this familiar word (or its even more familiar abbreviation "TV") should present no problem whatever, as should not the other three words: "ZOO" (which your child has probably visited, or would like to); "CAR" (in which he undoubtedly enjoys riding); and "JUMP" (a favorite activity).

Since your child has had a good deal of practice in learning the letter names, and the four letters (**V**, **Z**, **C**, and **J**) to be learned are not particularly difficult and are very similar in their two formats, it may be that you will not need to devote an entire lesson to each. It depends. If your child learns very slowly you may still wish to approach the words separately; if he learns quickly you may want to combine two or more words into a single lesson. If you choose this latter course, however, you will definitely want to devote a final minisession to reviewing the four words and four letters along with their predecessors.

Be sure to include matching exercises (as in the Supplementary Activity in Lesson #9). You should also feel free to invent games using the word and letter cards from all fourteen lessons, since they hold endless possibilities for review. The important thing is to keep the objectives of this chapter in mind and make sure that the child knows the four letters and words in these final lessons before proceeding.

Finishing Touches

You have now taught twenty-six letter names and fourteen words, more words in fact than are contained in some preprimers used in the first grade. In other words, your child has not only learned his letters, he has begun to learn to read as well.

You should have a pretty good idea how well he has mastered the contents of these lessons. If you feel that your child has not mastered some of the letters to the degree that you would like, you should teach some additional lessons using words containing the troublesome letters.

Examples of words that can be used to teach specific letters are (1) the child's name, (2) the names of siblings or friends, (3) names of colors, (4) animal names, and so on. Try to select relatively short words if you choose this course, and remember that if you opt for proper names you must explain the capitalizing of the first letter. If you decide to reteach lessons using the same words over again we suggest that you at least use as many different activities as possible (such as relying more on coloring books and games).

Once you are satisfied that your child has pretty much learned what has been taught, the time has come to administer the following competency tests to find out for sure. Approach these tests as you would the teaching of any other lesson. As far as your child is concerned, in fact, they are just another lesson: he doesn't know what a test is at this point and we hope he doesn't learn about them from anything in this book. If you must approach these materials in the conventional sense of seeing *how well* something was accomplished or *how successful* someone was, consider them as tests designed to determine how successful you have been as a teacher.

COMPETENCY TEST #1
Matching upper- and lower-case letters

Basically this test is only an extension of the Supplementary Activity in Lesson #9 so your child will already be familiar with the overall format. Make a copy of the following chart, supply a pencil or crayon, and instruct the student to:

Draw a line from each letter on the left to the same letter on the right.

Do not help the child in any way and remove all materials from his line of sight that might give a clue to an answer. If he asks for an answer, simply say:

Just draw all the lines you are sure of now and we'll see how many you got right later.

When the child is through with this test go directly to the next one without correcting this one. Again you should give no help. If the child objects, explain it as just a game to see how many answers he can get right without help.

COMPETENCY TEST #1
Matching Upper and Lower Case Letters

B	f
D	h
F	d
H	z
Z	b
X	k
R	o
O	m
M	r
K	x
E	e
C	i
A	c
I	a
P	p
W	l
L	u
S	w
G	g
U	s
J	q
Q	t
N	y
T	v
Y	j
V	n

COMPETENCY TEST #2
Recognizing the upper-case letters

You will need two forms of this test, one for your use (which can be used directly from this book) and one for your child (which you will need to copy).

	COMPETENCY TEST #2	
	Recognizing the Upper-case Letters	
	Your Copy	Your Child's Copy
1. A	A C O	1. A C O
2. K	L K M	2. L K M
3. S	S R G	3. S R G
4. B	D C B	4. D C B
5. D	B D C	5. B D C
6. C	C G D	6. C G D
7. E	C G E	7. C G E
8. M	M N U	8. M N U
9. N	M N U	9. M N U
10. U	M N U	10. M N U
11. R	R S T	11. R S T
12. F	K F L	12. K F L
13. J	J I M	13. J I M
14. G	J M G	14. J M G
15. H	N M H	15. N M H
16. O	D O P	16. D O P
17. I	I J G	17. I J G
18. L	I L M	18. I L M
19. P	P Q G	19. P Q G
20. T	I T S	20. I T S
21. V	W V U	21. W V U
22. G	P Q G	22. P Q G
23. W	W V U	23. W V U
24. Y	Y G P	24. Y G P
25. Z	A Z X	25. A Z X
26. X	M X G	26. M X G

The first letter in each row of *your* copy is the letter your child will be asked to identify (from the field of three) and circle. Do not let your child see your copy of the test. Begin by saying:

I'm going to read one of the letters in this first row out loud.

Point to the **A C O** row on his form.

I want you to circle the letter that I read.
"A."

The child should circle one of the three letters. If he doesn't, repeat the instructions. Do not comment on the answer, but proceed as soon as he finishes.

Now circle the letter that I say in this row.

Point to the **L K M** row.

"K."

Repeat the process for the remaining letters. If you find the child has difficulty staying on line, feel free to place an index card under the appropriate row each time you read a letter.

COMPETENCY TEST #3
Recognizing the lower-case letters

Make another child's copy of the above test, replacing the capital letters with lower-case ones. Use the same order and groupings of letters and repeat the test procedure exactly.

HOW TO EVALUATE THE RESULTS

Once all three tests have been administered you may score them while your child watches. Point out errors and compliment correct answers, but whatever you do don't chide or belittle your child for forgetting letters; that will accomplish absolutely nothing other than make him dislike tests.

If your child achieved a perfect score you may proceed to Chapter Five. If he missed a few items on each test, you should make a note of the problem letters and plan on reteaching the appropriate lessons at another time to correct the deficiencies. If your child missed more letters than you expected, you might consider changing your approach when you review the necessary letters. You can do this by substituting activities, teaching capital and lower-case letters separately, or using exercises like these tests. (If you choose the latter course, mix up the order of the letters to guard against your child's memorizing some of the answers.)

After you have devoted a lesson or two to reviewing the letters that gave your student trouble, give the tests again. Chances are he will do all right this time, in which case you are ready to proceed to Chapter Five. If he continues having problems, use your judgment. If the child shows no signs of boredom studying the letter names, continue; if he gives evidence of feeling frustration at his inability to learn some letters, go on to the next chapter. You will find plenty of opportunities for reinforcing letter recognition there.

HOW TO USE THE RESULTS FOR PLACEMENT IN THIS BOOK

If you have not yet taught this chapter and are using the tests to decide whether or not you should, follow these guidelines if your child needs to be taught any letters:

1. Study the introductory pages and model lesson for this chapter.
2. Teach the lessons for those letter names missed on the test.
3. Readminister the test and file the results in your records so you will know which letter names to reteach in the future. When 80 percent or twenty-one letter names are mastered, proceed to the next chapter.
4. Administer the Competency Tests in Chapter Five and follow the accompanying placement directions.

5

Teaching Letter Sounds, or Beginning Phonics

Phonics is the study of the relationship between common speech sounds and printed symbols. Its purpose is to enable the independent discovery of the pronunciation, and through it, the identity of words during reading. The primary purposes of the lessons contained in this chapter are to teach the child:

    1. to recognize, distinguish, and supply selected initial and final consonant sounds,
    2. an increased sight vocabulary, and
    3. that reading begins on the left side of the page, proceeds to the right, and progresses from the top to the bottom in an orderly progression.

The Importance of Teaching Phonics

If English were a perfectly phonetic language, the teaching of reading would be a simple process. All we would have to do is to teach our children the sounds each letter represents and give them some practice in combining these sounds into words.

Unfortunately, things are not that simple. Most letters have *several* sounds associated with them, depending upon their location in a word and the particular letters adjoining those locations. Teaching a child to apply *all* the language's complex phonetic rules would be as tedious as it would be unrealistic, especially given the fact that every rule has numerous exceptions.

On the positive side, however, English does have a group of very basic, simple letter-sound correspondences which occur so frequently that their learning greatly increases the speed and ease with which a child can learn to read. One of the authors of this book, in fact, has demonstrated that knowing the sounds letters represent is far more helpful to beginning readers than knowing letter names. The reason we chose to have you teach your child letter recognition first was because (1) it is one of the first skills taught in the public school, (2) it is easier to learn than letter sounds (thus helping to ensure a positive initial learning experience for the child), and (3) having something to "call" the letters makes them easier to *teach*.

We are going to tackle only the simplest and most basic letter sounds in this chapter, but given enough practice in their use, even they can be of great value to a child in both learning new words and recalling old ones. Later, after you have completed Chapter Eight, you will extend your child's phonics repertoire to the point where he can actually "sound out" and read words he has never seen before. This skill, when fully developed, signals more than any other the fact that your child has indeed "learned to read."

Format of the Lessons

The lessons are designed in as straightforward and structured a manner as possible to enable you to complete them in a relatively short time. Each lesson contains the following basic steps:

1. Introducing the letter sound, which consists of teaching the child to recognize a sound by listening to words containing it.

2. Distinguishing the sound, which consists of differentiating between words which do and do not contain a particular sound.

3. **Parent-assisted reading,** which introduces words in contexts that contain the sound being taught, introduces the child to actually reading very simple sentences and stories with help, and teaches sight recognition of selected words containing the consonant sounds under consideration.

Materials

Before you sit down with your child, make sure you have all necessary materials handy. The basic ones you will need for teaching this chapter include:

1. 3" by 5" word cards (as in Chapter Four),
2. a felt-tip pen for writing,
3. a box for word cards (such as a greeting card box or 3" by 5" filing box). If you completed Chapter Four, use the same box,
4. crayons,
5. blunt-pointed scissors,
6. pencils,
7. paste,
8. heavy construction paper and/or larger cards (say 6" by 8"),
9. envelopes large enough to hold the cards in (8), and
10. a loose-leaf notebook (if you choose to make a sound book).

General Guidelines

Some general instructional principles which should be kept in mind while teaching your child the initial and final consonant sounds are:

1. Don't spend too much time on this chapter. Phonics are best taught in combination with other reading skills, not in isolation. For that reason, we suggest that you proceed through the lessons in this chapter at a relatively brisk pace, teaching more than one at a sitting. If your child does not master a sound thoroughly or later forgets it, there are ample opportunities built in for review. Even more important, we are going to show you how to reinforce and reteach the consonant sounds in Chapter Six when the child is actually reading stories.

2. Use your judgment. There is still no substitute for your judgment as to how much you should teach at a single session or how fast your child should go. Some children master consonant sounds extremely quickly while others have a great deal of difficulty with them. Since you are in no hurry, take as much time as you think is needed.

3. Do not pressure your child to learn. If you do, he won't.

4. Work within your child's attention span. The lessons in this chapter do not have the intrinsic appeal of many topics taught in this book; therefore it is up to you, the teacher, to attempt to keep enthusiasm and interest as high as possible. There will always be a point at which your child will have had enough, however, and it is your job to try to stop a lesson slightly before that point.

5. Continue reading to your child. No other activity is more pleasant for you both and certainly none is more beneficial.

How to Use This Chapter

The present chapter contains thirty-one lessons divided into two parts, the first dealing with initial consonant sounds, the second with final ones. If you are working with a preschool child, we suggest that you begin with Lesson #1 and proceed straight through the chapter. If your child already reads and you feel that he knows most of the consonant sounds, then administer the competency tests at the end of each part to ascertain which lessons you need to teach, and teach them *after carefully studying the model lesson presented in Lesson #1.* (It might even be wise to teach your child Lesson #1 even if he is familiar with the initial **R** sound to give yourself practice and your child a chance to experience success.)

Given the number of lessons contained in this chapter, we shall present only one detailed lesson plan. We suggest that you study it carefully and apply its script and procedures to the individual lesson outlines that follow.

MODEL LESSON Rr

ACTIVITY #1
Introducing the initial **R** sound

Point to the **R** in the title of the lesson and ask the child,

What letter is this?

If he responds correctly, compliment him. If he does not know, tell him.

R is the name of this letter. R also stands for a special sound. I'm going to read you some words that begin with this sound. I want you to see if you can hear it at the beginning of each word.

Read part of the list below slowly emphasizing, but not distorting, the initial sound. Hold the book so that the words cannot be seen by the child while you read.

red   run   read   radio
rabbit right rope   rain

Do you hear the R sound?

If he doesn't, read the words again, making sure the child watches your mouth as you read.

I thought you would hear it. R makes a rrr sound.

Pronounce the sound heard at the beginning of each word taking care not to drag it out or to couple it with a vowel (don't say "ra" or "ro").

Let's see you make it.

Help the child arrive at a reasonable approximation.

Good. Now I'm going to read you some more words beginning with the rrr (pronounce it) *sound that* **R** *stands for. See if you can hear the sound at the beginning of these words too:*

road   ride   rake
ran   rub   robin

What sound do you hear at the beginning of each word?

Have the child pronounce it.

What sound does the **R** *stand for?*

Now show the child the above words and ask him what is the same about the way they all look (answer: they all begin with the letter "R").

ACTIVITY #2
Distinguishing the initial **R** sound

I'm going to read two words. The first word will always begin with the **R** *sound. I want you to tell me whether the second word begins with the same sound. If it does, say yes. If it doesn't, say no.*

Any time the child has trouble you may remind him of the sound he is listening for. If he obviously can identify the sound, do not feel compelled to complete the list. Hold the book so that the words cannot be seen while you read.

red – rabbit	(yes)	
ride – roll	(yes)	
road – milk	(no)	
rake – make	(no)	If the child misses this pair, you can point out that they end the same but begin differently.

rope	– rain	(yes)
right	– funny	(no)
right	– night	(no) Again the two words rhyme.
ran	– rave	(yes)
robin	– wing	(no)
ring	– wing	(no)
run	– tub	(no)
run	– radio	(yes)

Should the child fail to differentiate the initial **R** from other beginning consonants, you have several options. You may (1) remind him of the sound he is listening for and ask him to make that sound; (2) read words from the above list one at a time and ask the child to say yes (or clap his hands) when he hears the "R" sound; and/or (3) write the words he misses and *show* him that they begin with the letter **R**.

ACTIVITY #3
Parent-assisted reading

O.K. Now that you know the **R** *(pronounce it) sound, let's read a story which has this sound. Listen carefully as I read the story because I want you to read along with me in a minute.*

Read the story slowly but with expression. Allow the child to look at the text and follow along as you read.

My Rabbit

My rabbit can run.

He likes to run.

My rabbit likes to run fast.

WORDS TO LEARN: rabbit, run.

Now I would like you to help me read the story.

Read the story aloud a few times until your child can read most of the words without hesitation. As he gains confidence, lower your voice so that he hears his own as the predominating influence. (It is not necessary, nor expected, that he should read the story unassisted.)

Good, now I would like you to point to all the words that begin with the R sound.

The child should point to the three repetitions of "rabbit" and "run."

Write "rabbit" (in lower case) on a word card in large, clear letters. Do the same thing for "run."

How are these two words alike?

He will, hopefully, either say that they both begin with **R**s or that they both begin with the same sound. If he says the former, read the words again, emphasizing the initial sound and ask him:

How else are they the same?

They begin with the same sound. Make sure that the child can recognize the words on cards as well as in the story. When you are sure he can, place them in the "New Words" section of the Word Box. Continue to review them periodically throughout the next few lessons; when you are convinced that he has mastered them, file them among the other words he knows by sight.

SUPPLEMENTARY ACTIVITIES

The letter sounds and words taught in this chapter will all be given again, so you need not insist that your child master them all at this time. On the other hand, we definitely do recommend that you use the review exercises built into the lesson outlines.

In addition, we suggest that you incorporate *one* of the following two supplementary activities both of which are fun, leisurely activities the child can engage in with you, with another child, or, given a little guidance, by himself. Both employ cutting and pasting, drawing pictures or locating them in magazines, old catalogues, or newspapers. And since these activities take a considerable amount of time, we suggest that they be done after your formal instructional sessions.

SUPPLEMENTARY ACTIVITY #1
Sound cards

Get a folder or manila envelope and label it **Rr** in large letters. Have the child locate pictures of objects which begin with **R**, cut them out, and paste each to a separate card about 6″ by 8″. (The child may also draw his own pictures, or you may wish to draw some yourself.) Write the word representing each picture on the back of its card and place the cards in the folder/envelope. Searching for appropriate pictures is an excellent way to secure knowledge of the newly learned sound. Once made, the cards will also serve as an enjoyable review item to bring out for fun, or when a sound has been forgotten or misrepresented.

To use the sound cards for review, you might simply pull out the appropriate folder and say:

Let's look at the sound cards for r and see if you can remember the sound r makes. What is this card?

Show him the first sound card, perhaps containing a picture of a rabbit. If he guesses correctly, ask him what the next card represents.

Good, now what sound do all these words begin with?

If he pronounces the **r** sound, compliment him. If not, say all the words for him, emphasizing the first sound (but not distorting it) and ask him again. If he still does not know the sound (which is unlikely), give it to him and make sure you review this particular sound at the next lesson as well.

There are any number of ways these sound cards can be used for review. You may, for example, slip a picture which does not represent a given sound into a folder and tell the child:

There's a picture in this folder that does not belong to the **R** (pronounce the sound) *family. See if you can find it.*

Other activities involve mixing all the cards from the different folders and having the child sort them, or going through magazines and picture books pointing out other pictures that represent a given sound.

SUPPLEMENTARY ACTIVITY #2
Making a sound book

This activity is quite similar to the previous one except 8½″ by 11″ paper will be used instead of cards, and a loose-leaf notebook to hold the pages. The upper right-hand corner of a page will have the initial consonant being represented and the rest of the page (and the back as well, if you like) will be devoted to pictures containing objects whose names begin with the appropriate sound.

These pictures may be found in magazines, newspapers, comic books, and pasted or taped on the page, or drawn or traced on the paper by you or your child. (The page representing **R**, for example, might have a red line drawn in crayon, a rabbit traced from the picture for Lesson #3 in the first preprimer, a picture of a radio, and so on.) Most children love the idea of making up their own books and the design of each page becomes a creative activity in its own right.

The sound book can be used to review specific sounds in much the same way as the cards in the first supplementary activity were used. If your child does not remember a particular sound, you may have him look up the page representing that sound in his book and "read" the objects represented by the pictures (you may even label each picture if you like, thereby possibly teaching him some words incidentally). By the time he has accomplished this he will undoubtedly remember the sound and be able to "pronounce" it. If not, help him arrive at it. Like the sound cards, this activity can be used long after you have finished with Chapter Five because the initial and final consonant sounds learned here will be applied throughout the book.

PART ONE
The Initial Consonant Sounds

LESSON #1 Rr (see model lesson)

LESSON #2 Mm

ACTIVITY #1
Introducing the **M** sound

As in Lesson #1. Words to be used to illustrate the **M** sound:

my   mother   monkey   mail   mean   may   middle
milk   money   make   mask   mole   Monday   mud

Have the child listen for the beginning sound while you read these words. Then pronounce the Mmm sound together.

ACTIVITY #2
Distinguishing the initial **M** sound

Pairs of words to be used to accomplish this skill:

moon—match   Mother—middle   mask—roll
mole—may   mail—nail   money—honey
my—red   mean—moon   mud—bird
may—Jay   make—rake   mad—bad

He is to say yes if the second word begins with the sound **M**, no if it doesn't.

ACTIVITY #3
Parent-assisted reading

Mother

Here is Mother.

Here is my mother.

My mother is here.

I like Mother.

WORDS TO LEARN: mother, my.

Your objective is to familiarize the child with the two new words (which he will be expected to learn later in Chapter Six) and to give him practice with the **M** sound. Place "my" and "mother" in the "New Words" section of his word box.

SUPPLEMENTARY ACTIVITIES

Use either the sound cards or sound book activity described on page 77. You do not have to do it right after the lesson or even before you proceed to Lesson #3. Save it for leisure time rather than instructional time.

LESSON #3 S s

ACTIVITY #1
Introducing the **S** sound

sun	so	silly	simple	sing	sorry	same
song	sink	sign	soon	suit	super	sat

ACTIVITY #2
Distinguishing the initial **S** sound

silly—game	sun—the	sun—fun
sign—sat	soon—with	sand—van
simple—sorry	sat—hat	super—Sunday

ACTIVITY #3
Parent-assisted reading

Sun

Here is the sun.

See the sun.

The sun is yellow.

I like the sun.

WORDS TO LEARN: see, sun.

ACTIVITY #4
Review

As the child is introduced to more and more letter sounds, it becomes increasingly important to review those previously introduced. One way to do this is to simply ask him to either give you a word beginning with a particular letter or to pronounce the sound which a letter stands for:

Can you think of a word which begins with R?

If he does not remember, you may ask him if he can make the "R" sound. If he cannot, then go back to Lesson #1 and read him some of the words beginning with "R" and ask him again. If he

82 / Teach Your Child to Read

still has trouble go through a couple of exercises with him. The sound cards and/or book are also an excellent mechanism for this sort of review.

Repeat the process for **M** and **S**.

SUPPLEMENTARY ACTIVITIES (AS DESIRED)

LESSON #4 F f

ACTIVITY #1
Introducing the **F** sound

Father	fun	funny	fair	fire	find
fish	foot	four	fall	feel	fix

ACTIVITY #2
Distinguishing the **F** sound

fish—baby	fall—feel	fix—that
fat—fair	fire—tire	find—fox
four—funny	fun—zoo	feel—very

ACTIVITY #3
Parent-assisted reading

Father

Here is Father.

Here is my father.

Father and I have fun.

I like Father.

WORDS TO LEARN: father, fun.

SUPPLEMENTARY ACTIVITIES (AS DESIRED)

LESSON #5 Hh

ACTIVITY #1
Introducing the **H** sound

house	his	horn	hat	here	hard
he	hill	hit	hop	hope	hut

ACTIVITY #2
Distinguishing the initial **H** sound

him—his	horn—torn	hat—sat
hid—my	hay—wake	hop—hat
had—mad	hope—think	hit—hug
huddle—rake	house—bird	here—hard

The child is getting to the point where he knows enough initial sounds to review some of the previously taught sounds as part of this activity. In the pairs above, for example, if the child were to consistently fail to differentiate the **H** and **M** sounds, you could review "M" before completing the activity by reading some words beginning with **M** and pronouncing the **M** sound for him.

ACTIVITY #3
Parent-assisted reading

House

Here is a house.

It is my house.

I like my house.

See my house.

WORDS TO LEARN: here, house.

ACTIVITY #4
Review

Read the following word list to your child (emphasizing the initial sound) without letting him see the words. Say:

*I'm going to read you some words. After I say each word, tell me the name of the letter it begins with. If I would say "here," you would say **H**. Ready?*

moon   red   house   fun   father   mother   my   here

If he has trouble with a word, give him some more words beginning with the same letter. If he still fails, write the word in question on a sheet of paper for him, pronounce the word, and then ask him what letter it begins with.

SUPPLEMENTARY ACTIVITIES (AS DESIRED)

LESSON #6 Dd

ACTIVITY #1
Introducing the **D** sound

doll   dog   do   does   did   duck
day   dear   day   dark   dish   down

ACTIVITY #2
Distinguishing the initial **D** sound

dog—day   dark—coat   dish—down
duck—make   do—does   did—hid
Dick—like   day—may   down—duck
deck—dark   does—day   doll—bed

ACTIVITY #3
Parent-assisted reading

Dog

Here is my dog.

My dog is big.

I like my dog.

I do like my dog.

Do you?

Do you like my dog?

WORDS TO LEARN: dog, do.

ACTIVITY #4
Review

On a sheet of paper reproduce the following answer sheet for your child.

1. d m f
2. d m f
3. r s h
4. r s h
5. d m h
6. d m s
7. m f s
8. r s d
9. h s f
10. h m d

I'm going to read you some words. After each word I want you to draw a circle around the letter it begins with.

Give the child a pencil and indicate which group of three letters he is to choose from after you read each word.

1. mother
2. day
3. red
4. house
5. moon
6. sun
7. father
8. so
9. fun
10. dirt

Review each sound the child misses. If he misses the same sound twice you should reteach that sound using activities from the original lesson.

SUPPLEMENTARY ACTIVITIES (AS DESIRED)

LESSON #7   Ll

ACTIVITY #1
Introducing the **L** sound

leaf   little   look   light   love   like
lady   laugh   lid   lick   lie   land

ACTIVITY #2
Distinguishing the **L** sound

large—little   leaf—love   little—look
lay—may   love—silly   lie—land
learn—sun   lick—monkey   like—Father
look—land   light—little   laugh—Mother

It may be helpful to pronounce those letter sounds which your child has trouble distinguishing by themselves.

ACTIVITY #3
Parent-assisted reading

Leaf

Here is a leaf.

It is little.

It is a little leaf.

Look at the leaf.

Do you see the leaf?

Do you see the little leaf?

A little, little leaf!

WORDS TO LEARN: little, look.

SUPPLEMENTARY ACTIVITIES (AS DESIRED)

LESSON #8 Tt

ACTIVITY #1
Introducing the **T** sound

toy	Tom	top	tag	to	today
tug	tiger	tongue	tooth	touch	turn

ACTIVITY #2
Distinguishing the **T** sound

tuna—Tom	tiger—touch	tooth—turn
tunnel—rabbit	today—to	turn—burn
ten—top	tag—Tom	tug—hug
tell—fair	to—toy	tongue—dog

ACTIVITY #3
Parent-assisted reading

Tom

Here is Tom.

Tom has a toy.

Tom's toy is a top.

WORDS TO LEARN: Tom, toy.

ACTIVITY #4
Review

Can you tell me a word that begins with F?

If he cannot (and also produce the sound), go back to Lesson #4 and read him some words beginning with **F**. Repeat for **H, D, L,** and **T**.

SUPPLEMENTARY ACTIVITIES (AS DESIRED)

LESSON #9 Nn

ACTIVITY #1
Introducing the **N** sound

| nest | not | no | name | nail | November | never |
| net | new | night | North | number | need | needle |

ACTIVITY #2
Distinguishing the initial **N** sound

nose—new	North—neat	nest—new
neat—make	no—not	not—never
need—needle	never—bird	nail—sing
night—light	net—tight	November—no

ACTIVITY #3
Parent-assisted reading

Nest

Here is a nest.

A nest is big.

A nest is little.

A nest is a house.

Do you live in a nest house?

I do not.

My house is not a nest.

WORDS TO LEARN: nest, not.

This long story will enable you to review some of the words introduced previously. If you are working with a very young child, you may wish to tackle this story a few lines at a time.

SUPPLEMENTARY ACTIVITIES (AS DESIRED)

LESSON #10 Bb

ACTIVITY #1
Introducing the **B** sound

Bill	big	be	boy	banana	bell	bake
ball	bang	bird	baby	book	bed	boat

ACTIVITY #2
Distinguishing the initial **B** sound

ball—boil	Bill—nail	bang—dog
big—wig	boat—bed	be—see
boy—bull	bake—cake	bird—voice
baby—bunch	banana—key	book—poor

ACTIVITY #3
Parent-assisted reading

The Ball

Bill has a ball.

The ball is big.

Bill plays with the ball.

The ball is yellow.

Look at the yellow ball.

WORDS TO LEARN: ball, big.

ACTIVITY #4
Review

Tell me the name of the letter that each word begins with.

Read the following word list, emphasizing the initial sound of each word, and pausing long enough for the child to supply the letter.

love   dog   no   Bill   toy   little   night   bull

If there is trouble with a word, give the child some more words beginning with the same letter. If he still fails, write the word in question on a sheet of paper for him to look at, pronounce the word, and then ask him what letter it begins with.

SUPPLEMENTARY ACTIVITIES (AS DESIRED)

LESSON #11 Jj

ACTIVITY #1
Introducing the J sound

---

jump	jar	Jello	job	Jack	jug	join
jumping	joy	Jip	jaw	juicy	joke	Jane

ACTIVITY #2
Distinguishing the initial **J** sound

jump—Jill	joy—toy	juicy—joke
jar—Jim	jar—car	joke—choke
Jip—Jerry	Jello—hello	Jane—zoo
Jack—pack	job—juicy	join—jug

ACTIVITY #3
Parent-assisted reading

Jump

Jump up!

Jump down.

Do you jump up?

Do you jump down?

I jump up.

I jump down.

I jump and jump.

I jump the jumping rope.

WORDS TO LEARN: jump, jumping.

ACTIVITY #4
Consonant substitution

One excellent means of giving a child practice in both hearing and differentiating spoken sounds is to help him construct words by simply substituting the initial letter. Within the word lists above, for example, "lump," "bump," and "hump" can all be made from "jump" by substitution of a letter sound the child has already learned. A similar situation exists with "jug" which can make "mug," "tug," "hug," and "dug."

To use this activity with your child, approach it as a game, telling him that you are going to show him how to make some brand new words just by changing the first letter in one word. He may have some trouble doing this unassisted, but with your help will soon become quite proficient at it. For each example write the new words in a column below the word he knows.

SUPPLEMENTARY ACTIVITIES (AS DESIRED)

LESSON #12 Kk–Cc

When the letter **C** is followed by the vowels "O," "A," or "U" at the beginning of a word, it represents the same sound as the letter "K." With an older child you should probably explain this at the onset; with a younger child you may wish to allow him to arrive at this fact himself through experience. For now, show him the words in Activity #1 as you read them. We suggest that you refer to the sound in question as the **K** sound, simply making sure that the child understands that *under certain circumstances* a "C" can represent this **K** sound.

ACTIVITY #1
Introducing the **K–C** sound

comb   coat   key   cup   cat   kangaroo   cold
kite   cap   card   curtain   can   keep   color

ACTIVITY #2
Distinguishing the **K–C** sound

comb—kitchen   curtain—king   cold—Jane
cup—cone   cat—hat   coat—cold
keep—pair   can—gang   kangaroo—will
key—he   keep—color   cap—tap

ACTIVITY #3
Consonant substitution

"Cat" is an excellent word for this activity (see the previous lesson for more detailed instructions). Words that can be created by replacing the c are "rat," "mat," "sat," "fat," and "bat" from the sounds already studied.

One method of helping your child generate these words, incidentally, is to have him go through the alphabet and try out each consonant in order. (If he does not know his ABCs you may write them out for him, thereby giving him practice in learning them.) The two of you can have a good time with nonsense words generated in this manner, and they give excellent practice in learning the initial sounds.

ACTIVITY #4
Parent-assisted reading

The Cat and the Kitten

Here is a cat.

Here is a kitten.

The kitten is a baby.

The cat is a mother.

Come, Mother cat.

Come, baby kitten.

The kitten is little.

A little cat is a kitten.

WORDS TO LEARN: cat, come.

SUPPLEMENTARY ACTIVITIES (AS DESIRED)

LESSON #13 Pp

ACTIVITY #1
Introducing the **P** sound

| pet | pig | puff | pond | park | piece | point |
| Peter | pair | pan | pack | pick | pillow | Pam |

ACTIVITY #2
Distinguishing the **P** sound

pet—pop	Pam—ham	puff—Peter
pan—pot	piece—puddle	pan—Pam
pick—kick	point—bite	pair—fair
pillow—perfect	pond—dog	Peter—pig

ACTIVITY #3
Consonant substitution

"Pet" is an excellent point of departure for this activity: "met," "set," "let," "net," "jet," and "bet."

ACTIVITY #4
Parent-assisted reading

My Pet

Peter Rabbit is my pet.

My pet is big.

My pet is white.

My pet can hop.

Hop, Peter Rabbit, hop.

WORDS TO LEARN: pet, Peter.

ACTIVITY #5
Review

SUPPLEMENTARY ACTIVITIES (AS DESIRED)

LESSON #14 Gg

ACTIVITY #1
Introducing the **G** sound

girl	get	give	gold	guy	good	garden
go	gate	gave	gum	goose	gas	game

ACTIVITY #2
Distinguishing the **G** sound

girl—gold   good—gas   gate—Kate
game—tame   garden—game   goose—garden
go—row   give—get   gold—game
guy—girl   get—set   gate—guy

ACTIVITY #3
Parent-assisted reading

The Girl

Here is the girl.

She is a little girl.

She can go.

She can go home.

She can go home with Mother.

WORDS TO LEARN: girl, go.

SUPPLEMENTARY ACTIVITIES (AS DESIRED)

LESSON #15 Ww

ACTIVITY #1
Introducing the **W** sound

wig	we	was	with	water	walk	wash
wear	were	will	wing	wall	watch	wax

ACTIVITY #2
Distinguishing the **W** sound

wear—week	was—wet	wash—wig
were—her	wing—leaf	wax—watch
with—weigh	wall—hall	will—Bill
watch—toy	walk—thin	with—worm

ACTIVITY #3
Consonant substitution

"Will" can be used to form "mill," "fill," "hill," "sill," "dill," "Bill," "Jill," and "pill."

ACTIVITY #4
Parent-assisted reading

A Wig for a Pig

A wig for a pig?

Will a pig wear a wig?

Will a pig like a wig?

A wig for a pig?

A pig with a wig?

WORDS TO LEARN: wig, will.

ACTIVITY #5
Review

Read the following word list to your child, emphasizing the initial sound, and ask him to name the letter that each word begins with:

wig   jump   cat*   kangaroo*   catch*   Jack   pig   will   girl   go

SUPPLEMENTARY ACTIVITIES (AS DESIRED)

LESSON #16 Zz

Since there are relatively few words beginning with "Z" in most children's vocabularies, we will not introduce as many words in the first two activities as usual. The other side of this coin is that the **Z** sound is not as important as the ones introduced to date, so it does not deserve as much instructional time.

ACTIVITY #1
Introducing the **Z** sound

| zoo | zipper | zero | zone |
| zebra | zoom | zany | zigzag |

---

* Since the child does not yet know how to spell, it is enough that he recognizes the **K** sound for these words.

ACTIVITY #2
Distinguishing the initial **Z** sound

| zoo—zone | zoom—zigzag | zero—hero |
| zany—game | zebra—see* | zipper—zoom |

ACTIVITY #3
Parent-assisted reading

The Zoo

We like the zoo.

We have fun at the zoo.

We like the animals at the zoo.

We like the zebra.

The zebra is a zoo animal.

WORD TO LEARN: ZOO.

SUPPLEMENTARY ACTIVITIES (AS DESIRED)

LESSON #17 Qq

This is another sound not often encountered and one very easily mistaken for the initial **K–C** sound. ("Q" is always followed by a "U" at the beginning of a word and makes a **KW** sound.) To

---

* Make sure that you enunciate the difference between the **Z** and **S** sounds clearly.

introduce this particular sound you might want to use the following dialogue to ensure that your child knows the meaning of some "Q" words.

Make a card that says "QUIET" using all capital letters and show it to the child. Say:

Sometimes you see this quiet sign in hospitals. It means that visitors are not to make any noise. Can you guess why?

ACTIVITY #1
Introducing the **Q** sound

> quiet   quarrel   question   quit   queen
> quack   quarter   quart   quick

ACTIVITY #2
Distinguishing the **Q** sound

> quack—question   quack—duck   quiet—quack
> quarrel—question   quart—go   quick—Rick
> quarter—kite*   queen—quiet   question—queen

ACTIVITY #3
Parent-assisted reading

The Duck

This is a duck.

The duck said, "Quack."

The duck said, "Quack, quack."

WORD TO LEARN: quack.

* This is one of the most difficult sound pairs to differentiate. Enunciate carefully, but don't worry too much if your child still has trouble.

SUPPLEMENTARY ACTIVITIES (AS DESIRED)

LESSON #18 Vv

The letter "V" is not used very often in children's readers. Since it looks like a "W" and sounds somewhat like an "F," it is often difficult for children to remember.

ACTIVITY #1
Introducing the **V** sound

valentine	voice	vegetable	vinegar	vine	visit
violet	very	village	view	vitamin	

ACTIVITY #2
Differentiating the **V** sound

valentine—vacuum   very—berry
voice—wing   village—vine
vest—vinegar   vinegar—question
vine—fog   vitamin—vinegar
view—vitamin   voice—juice
very—view   village—valentine

ACTIVITY #3
Parent-assisted reading

Valentine

Here is a valentine.

It is my valentine.

It is a red valentine.

It has violets on it.

WORD TO LEARN: valentine.

SUPPLEMENTARY ACTIVITIES (AS DESIRED)

LESSON #19 Yy

ACTIVITY #1
Introducing the **Y** sound

yellow	yes	yak	year	young	yet
yo-yo	yell	yard	you	yawn	yesterday

ACTIVITY #2
Distinguishing the **Y** sound

yellow—year	yet—net	yawn—dawn
yes—me	yesterday—yo-yo	yard—hard
year—yak	yak—back	yo-yo—yesterday
yawn—yard	yell—yellow	you—yard

ACTIVITY #3
Parent-assisted reading

The Yellow Yo-Yo

Here is a yo-yo.

It is yellow.

It is a yellow yo-yo.

I like it.

It can go up.

It can go down.

Up and down.

Up and down.

It is fun.

WORDS TO LEARN: yellow, yo-yo.

ACTIVITY #4
Review: **Z**, **Q**, **V**, and **Y**

Read the following word list to your child (emphasizing the initial sound) and ask him to name the letter that each word begins with:

yes   quiet   zebra   valentine   zipper   yellow   violet   quack

COMPETENCY TEST
Initial consonant sounds

Listed below are twenty short "words," some real and some nonsense. Each word begins with a consonant sound which was introduced in Part One of this chapter. To create a relaxed atmosphere, approach the test as you would any ordinary activity, and avoid using the word "test." Afterwards use the section "How to Evaluate the Results" to decide which sounds your child still needs to be taught.

HOW TO ADMINISTER THE TEST

The materials you will need are (1) an index card with a small window cut out of the center in which one word on the test can be framed without exposing the words immediately above or below (see illustration), and (2) a worksheet upon which you can record the results of the test (a model is included for you to copy).

Sit side by side at a table or desk. If you are right-handed, have the child on your left with the test in front of him and the worksheet on your right for easy access.

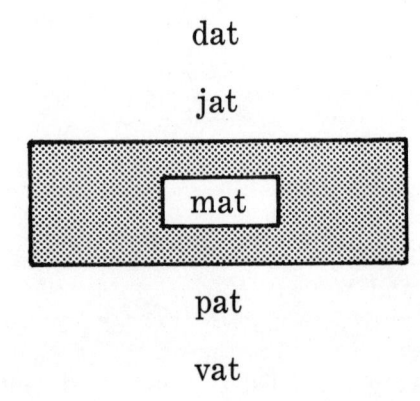

dat

jat

[mat]

pat

vat

Starting at the top of the list, expose one word through the window for several seconds. Ask the child to say the sound made by the first letter of the word or say the word itself. When he has done so, mark the worksheet and slide the window down to the next word. Mark the worksheet on the basis of the initial consonant sound only. Therefore, if he says "mad" instead of "mat," the answer is correct because the **M** sound was given. You may find it convenient to use the following symbols to mark the worksheet:

Correct response : +
No response : −
Wrong sound : write the answer that was given

To use the test you should say something like this:

I am going to show you a list of words one at a time through a little window. Some of the words will be real and some will be silly words that don't mean anything. Tell me the first sound of the word, or say the word. Let's practice together so you will know what to do.

Frame the word "mat" at the top of the test with the word window.

Can you think of the sound made by the first letter in this word or can you say the word? (Give the child a chance to respond.) *You could say "mmm" for the sound, or you could say "mat."*

Practice using the sample until the task is understood; then go ahead to administer the test. For each item say:

Tell me the sound the first letter makes or tell me the word.

Initial Consonant Sounds Competency Test

Sample   mat

1. dat
2. jat
3. zat
4. mat

5. tat
6. pat
7. vat
8. hat
9. bat
10. wat
11. rat
12. lat
13. kat
14. quat
15. sat
16. nat
17. gat
18. yat
19. fat
20. cat

Initial Consonant Sounds Competency Test Worksheet

Date _____

___# correct ÷ 20 = ___% correct

PART ONE
LESSON #

1. d_____		6
2. j_____		11
3. z_____		16
4. m_____		2
5. t_____		8
6. p_____		13
7. v_____		18
8. h_____		5
9. b_____		10
10. w_____		15
11. r_____		1
12. l_____		7
13. k_____		12
14. qu_____		17
15. s_____		3
16. n_____		9
17. g_____		14
18. y_____		19
19. f_____		4
20. c_____		12

HOW TO EVALUATE THE RESULTS

Count up the number of correct responses (the number of plus marks on your worksheet) and record it at the top of your worksheet. You now have a record of how many and which initial consonant sounds are in your child's *functional phonics repertoire*. These are the sounds you can expect your child to use in unlocking unknown words. Those letters marked with a minus will need to be retaught. In cases where the wrong answer was given, *both* sounds should be retaught.

No matter how many sounds your child knew, tell him you are pleased with his performance. Always think positively in terms of what he knows. Regard what he doesn't know as your next teaching assignment. Learning letter-sound correspondences is no easy task and what is learned one day may easily be forgotten the next. Keep in mind that learning sounds is just one tool in recognizing words—and leads to the ultimate goal which is reading itself.

If you have gone through all the lessons we recommend that now, no matter how many sounds your child does not know, you proceed. Included next to every test item on your worksheet is the lesson in which it was introduced. When you start teaching Chapter Six, "Reading the First Book," you should come back to reteach the lessons for the sounds your child missed *as those sounds come up in his reading.* Your job is an ongoing one which lasts until the child can tell you the consonant sound in any new word he encounters in his reading. Going through Parts One and Two the first time is a mere introduction to the study of sounds. You will continue to refer to it as your child learns to read.

HOW TO USE THE RESULTS FOR PLACEMENT IN THE BOOK

If you are not using this book from cover to cover, but want to know where in the book to start working with your child, follow these guidelines. If a perfect score was attained proceed to administer the next Competency Test; otherwise:

1. Study the introductory pages and the model lesson in this chapter.
2. Teach only the lessons for those sounds missed on the test.
3. Readminister the test and file the worksheet in your records. Proceed to the next section of the book, coming back to reteach certain lessons.
4. Administer the next Competency Test and follow the same placement procedures.

PART TWO
Ending Consonant Sounds

By now your child has been introduced to, and is probably thoroughly familiar with, most of the initial consonant sounds. The purpose of the second part of this chapter is to demonstrate that letters also represent sounds at the ends of words *and* that in many cases these ending consonant sounds are nearly identical to beginning ones.

Since the usefulness of this knowledge lies largely in its application to the learning of the new words presented in later chapters and as a review for some of the sounds taught in Part One, we don't recommend that you spend more than two or three sessions on the lessons in this section.

Furthermore, since all nineteen initial consonant sounds taught in Part One unfortunately do not have equivalent ending sounds, we recommend that if you are dealing with a very young child, or one that seemed to have a great deal of trouble learning the initial sounds, you concentrate your instruction on those consonants that are equivalent: **B**, **D**, **F**, **K–C**, **M**, **N**, **P**, and **T**. If you are dealing with a school-age child, or if you think your child will not be easily confused, you may teach **R** and **ll** (which represent slightly different sounds at the end of a word than at the beginning) and **S** (which doubles for both the S and the Z sounds). If you do adopt this latter course, make sure that you point out their differences, by saying, for instance:

Did you know that an S can sometimes sound like a Z? or *What other letter does an S at the end of a word sometimes sound like?*

Lesson Format

We are going to present the instructional contents of this section in more compact fashion than was done for Part One since the lessons will be taught in the same way as those for initial sounds. Also, we recommend that *less* instructional time be spent on this section. If you did not go through Part One, study the model lesson presented at the beginning of the chapter before proceeding.

Other changes to be found in this section are:

(1) Instead of supplying you with pairs of words to give your child practice in discriminating, we are going to present some words containing the appropriate ending sounds and let you make your own combinations.

(2) Instead of presenting formal stories for your child to read (with your assistance), we are going to supply sentences, which you can read together, comprised of words containing appropriate endings. You should feel free to construct more sentences, possibly with the child's help, if you perceive a need or interest in the task. Often the "sillier" a sentence is the more enjoyable to the child.

(3) You shouldn't feel compelled to require your child to learn to recognize new words in this section, although if he picks one or two up quickly there's certainly no harm in adding them to his repertoire. Since the teaching of a sight vocabulary is the chief purpose of the next chapter, however, we suggest that you do not spend a great deal of time doing this here.

The general sequence for ending sounds can, therefore, be quite similar to that used for the beginning ones:

(1) ensure that the child can hear the sound by reading an appropriate word list to him,

(2) help him discriminate the sounds by composing pairs of words, some containing the same ending sounds, others ending differently (you may vary this exercise by asking the child to name the ending consonant or by seeing if he can think of words or find pictures of words which end similarly),

(3) read some sentences to him which contain several similarly ending words followed by his reading them with you in unison, and

(4) practice some supplementary activities, such as the sound cards and sound book suggested for previous lessons, as needed.

Ending Consonant Word Lists Plus Sample Sentences

LESSON #1. b

Bob   tub   rub   scrub   cab   cob   mob   sob   cub

Bob rubs and scrubs in a tub.
Rob put his sub in a cab.

LESSON #2. d

did said red fed head dead sad mad bad

Jed said, "Does that dog have a red head?"
Mother was mad because Ted was bad.

LESSON #3. f

leaf chief if off puff loaf calf half cuff

If I can I'll eat half a loaf.
The calf ate half a leaf.

LESSON #4. k–ck

look sick quack duck Dick book hook luck kick

"Quack, quack," said the duck.
Look at Dick kick the sock.

LESSON #5. g

wig big dog pig bag rug bug hug rag tag

Can a pig have a wig?
Is that a big bug on the rug?

LESSON #6. m

Tom am him ham gum drum Pam Sam

I am Sam.
Pam chews gum and beats the drum.

LESSON #7. n

green fun down can in tin on son

Jan can run.
Jan saw a green tin can.

LESSON #8. p

up hop top jump stop cup tap nap

Hop up on top.
Stop, then jump and hop.

LESSON #9. t

not   it   at   pet   get   hat   cat   sat   fat   met

We met a wet pet.
The fat cat sat on a hat.

Slightly Irregular Ending Consonant Sounds

LESSON #10. l (ll)

Bill   will   ball   call   hill   pull   pencil   fill

Bill will throw the ball up the hill.
I will call Jill.

LESSON #11. r

tear   air   hair   for   color   Peter   sooner   fair   door

Air has no color.
Peter went to the fair four times.

LESSON #12. s(s) and s(z)

Explain to the child that the letter has two different final sounds and you want him to learn both of them.

(a)   yes   dress   us   less   miss   likes

Yes, she likes my dress.

(b)   has   is   ours   as   runs   days   his

Is his the same as ours?

COMPETENCY TEST
Final consonant sounds

Listed below in random order are the thirteen letters for which sounds were introduced in Part Two of this chapter. After giving the test to your child, note which sounds were missed and incorporate them in your lessons as you teach the next chapter.

To use the test you should say something like this:

I am going to read you a list of words. Listen carefully for the sound you hear at the end of each word. Then look at the row of letters on your paper. Draw a circle around the one letter that stands for the last sound in the word. Let's practice together so you will know what to do.

Frame the row of letters at the top of the test paper where it says "Sample."

Listen carefully while I say this word: "cat" . . . "cat."

Emphasize the **t** sound at the end without distorting the word.

What sound do you hear at the end? (answer: **t**). *Look at this row of letters. Do you see a letter that stands for that sound?*

Help the child arrive at the right answer, repeating the process if necessary.

*Yes, the **t** stands for the sound you hear at the end of the word "cat." Circle the letter **t**.*

Show the child how to do this.

Proceed with the test items sliding down the window and dictating the words below.

1. Circle the letter that stands for the sound at the end of the word "came" . . . "came."

2. Circle the letter that stands for the sound at the end of the word "huff" . . . "huff."

Repeat the directions as long as they seem to be helpful.

    3. "sob" . . . "sob"
    4. "tan" . . . "tan"
    5. "bog" . . . "bog"
    6. "trap" . . . "trap"
    7. "red" . . . "red"
    8. "sick" . . . "sick"
    9. "pet" . . . "pet"
   10. "ball" . . . "ball"
   11. "for" . . . "for"
   12. "miss" . . . "miss"
   13. "has" . . . "has"

Final Consonant Sounds Competency Test

Sample	r	g	t
1.	d	m	t
2.	f	g	r
3.	b	p	m
4.	t	n	k
5.	r	f	g
6.	p	m	s
7.	s	n	d
8.	ck	d	p
9.	m	t	r
10.	l	s	b
11.	f	r	n
12.	g	t	s
13.	p	s	r

Final Consonant Sounds Competency Test Worksheet

Date _____   ___# correct ÷ 13 = ___% correct

	PART TWO LESSON #
1. m_____	6
2. f_____	3
3. b_____	1
4. n_____	7
5. g_____	5
6. p_____	8
7. d_____	2
8. ck_____	4
9. t_____	9
10. ll_____	10
11. r_____	11
12. s_____	13
13. s_____	13

6

Reading the First "Book": Preprimer #1

The overall objective of the forty-five lessons in this chapter and the next two chapters is quite ambitious. It is to enable the child to read and comprehend simple prose materials. This objective will be accomplished primarily by teaching the child sight recognition of over 150 words common in speech and print, words he will be able to recognize immediately without having to stop and think. Although the possession of a reasonably large sight vocabulary is undoubtedly the single most important reading skill you can give your child, many other skills are taught in these chapters as well. Some of the more important are:

    1. the recognition of unfamiliar words through phonics, structural, and context clues,
    2. the appropriate use of capitalization,
    3. the role of punctuation in the meaning of a story,
    4. hearing and recognizing identical elements in words,
    5. silent as well as oral reading, and
    6. the use of root words to form new constructions by adding **s**, **ed**, and **ing**.

Your child is ready to master the skills taught in this chapter if he shows interest in being able to read simple stories and if he:

1. has a reasonable command of oral language from talking and listening to others,
2. has developed some appreciation for the pleasures and satisfaction of having printed material read to him,
3. knows that reading is basically "talk written down" and that what he and others say and think can be written down *and* read,
4. knows from watching you read that one begins on the left side of the page and proceeds to the right, as well as that one starts at the top of a page and progresses toward the bottom in an orderly progression,
5. is able to recognize all the capital and lower-case letters by name,
6. knows the sounds associated with most of the letters of the alphabet, and
7. is able to recognize a few words (although the stories in this chapter are written so that no specific word recognition knowledge is assumed).

The key factor here is motivation; your child may have mastered none of the last six skills but may still learn to read if he *wants* to learn to read. The best way to determine whether or not he is ready for the "books" in these chapters, which are referred to in the first grade curriculum as preprimers, is to attempt to teach him the first couple of lessons. If he shows interest, then proceed. If he does not, continue the less structured activities suggested in Chapters Two and Three.

Before you begin any instruction in the preprimers, however, we would like to suggest that you study carefully the lesson plans and instructional activities below. The better prepared you are, the more relaxed and fun your lessons will be.

Format of the Lessons

Each lesson has been planned to include the following basic steps:

1. Laying the groundwork, which usually consists of looking at the picture accompanying the lesson and discussing questions that will be answered in the story. The purpose of this activity is twofold. In the first place it develops the child's curiosity and desire to read the story. Secondly, it helps make him a *reflective* reader (that is, someone who thinks about and comprehends what he is reading). Subsidiary purposes are the introduction of concepts contained in the story which lend themselves to discussion and to fostering oral communication skills.

2. Reading the story, which you yourself will do only in the first few lessons, after which the child will read and reread each story with you supplying the words he does not know. This will be a rewarding experience for both of you because you will realize—as will your child—that he is actually starting to read.

3. Discussing what has been read, which consists of briefly reviewing the discussion preceding the reading of the story. Although this step need take only a very short time, it is essential in the effort to make your child a reflective reader. It reviews the purpose set for reading the story and it shows the child that reading can accomplish certain objectives.

4. Word study, which consists primarily of activities using the word cards, can be conducted in a gamelike fashion but actually comprises the backbone of the entire chapter; it is these activities which foster the all-important word recognition skills so essential to early reading.

Materials

We suggest that you be prepared with all the materials and aids needed for a particular lesson *before* you sit down to teach. The basic materials needed for this chapter include:

1. 3″ by 5″ word cards, constructed identically with those used in previous chapters,
2. a felt tip pen, for writing words on the cards, among other things,

3. a box for the word cards. A candy box, greeting card box, or 3" by 5" filing box may be used. If you have completed Chapters Four or Five, use the same box, retaining the same words and filing system,

4. a "word window" which consists of a 3" by 5" index card with a rectangular slit cut in the center large enough to bracket individual words in the preprimer stories,

5. crayons,
6. blunt-point scissors,
7. pencils,
8. paste, and
9. wide-lined paper.

General Guidelines

Some very general teaching principles that should be kept in mind while helping your child to learn to read the preprimers are:

1. Use your judgment. Even though we have not written *detailed* lesson plans for each individual story and review session, the suggested outline in each case is quite explicit. As with the lessons in the preceding chapter, however, there is no substitute for your judgment with respect to how closely you follow these plans with your child. If he reads a story well during a first or second reading and already knows most of the new words in it, there may be no need for the subsequent rereadings often indicated. If he is experiencing difficulty, however, you will definitely find all the activities necessary as well as the possible addition of extensive review of relevant content contained in previous lessons. (If you are not sure of how quickly you should proceed, we suggest that you err on the side of conservatism, since learning as many new words as are presented in the preprimers can be a tall order for some children.)

You must also not hesitate to vary the procedure if you perceive that the suggested routine is beginning to bore your child. As always, you have a great deal of control over your child's level of interest through the amount of enthusiasm you can bring to the task, but don't hesitate to substitute activities your child seems to enjoy especially for those he does not appreciate as much. It is, in other words, perfectly all right, even desirable, to exhibit a great deal of flexibility as long as you *keep the objectives of each lesson clearly in mind and make sure you teach everything that needs to be learned.*

2. Work within your child's attention span. Wide variations in attention span exist both between children and for any given child from day to day and lesson to lesson. If you have worked your way through Chapters Four and Five you have probably noticed a definite increase in your child's attention span and have undoubtedly developed strategies for maintaining his interest level. You are aware, however, that there is always a point in every lesson at which further work is counter-productive. Thus what you must do is structure your teaching sessions in such a way that your objectives for a particular lesson can be met as quickly and efficiently as possible. Doing this will require your controlling the direction your sessions are taking as well as the pace at which they proceed. Strive to get as much accomplished as possible, but strive always to *quit just before your child's interest begins to flag* so that he will look forward to the next session. We realize that this can sometimes be difficult to do, so in order to ease the task, each lesson contains several natural stopping places (for example, after the initial reading attempts, or after any of the word study activities).

3. Continue reading to your child. Regardless of how your formal lessons are progressing, the single most important teaching activity you can perform for your child at this stage is to *continue reading to him.* This practice, along with all its other advantages and benefits, provides an excellent opportunity to reinforce the very words being taught in the preprimers. Many of the small words that give children the most trouble will appear again and again in practically any story you read and your child will delight in being able to pick some of them out. You should encourage this sort of activity by saying something like:

Here is that word (point to the word and call it by name) *we had in our last story. Do you see another word we had?*

Your child will soon become so alert to this exercise that he may spontaneously point out which word says "bird," "rabbit," and so on, whenever you read about something in one of the preprimer lessons. If he enjoys this sort of activity, let him actually pull out the preprimer story involved and show you where the word in question is. As usual, show your delight if he is correct; help him if he is wrong.

4. Help your child become a reflective reader. Even though the primary purpose of the lessons and activities presented in this chapter is to give your child a sufficiently large sight vocabulary to enable him to begin to read simple books, we must never lose sight of the fact that being able to recognize words is not the same as reading. Reading is a language skill involving *communication* (from the author to the reader); reading is also a comprehension process involving *meaning*, or understanding the written message. Your ultimate goal in teaching your child to read is to enable him to understand the meaning communicated by the written word.

At first glance it might seem reasonable that if a child can recognize all the words in a passage, he should be able to read that passage. Nothing could be further from the truth. Educators have made a distinction between "word calling" and reading for years for the simple reason that many children simply do not comprehend the message in the words they recognize. To prevent this from happening to your child, we are going to suggest activities which will encourage him to become a *reflective* reader, a reader who thinks about what he is reading, who reads for a purpose.

5. Keep careful records. You will be teaching your child 50 words in this chapter, some of which he may have considerable difficulty learning, some of which he may continually forget. It is absolutely essential that you keep track of both the words he has trouble with and the words he knows.

The Word Box is an invaluable tool in this regard. In addition, the review activities suggest forms for recording troublesome words for later work. All of these strategies are helpful and should be carefully followed, but you may prefer to simply take notes at each lesson to remind yourself which words and concepts require extra work. It is also a good idea to note which activities work best for your child and which he finds the most fun. Whenever possible you should tailor your instruction to fit your child's individual needs and preferences.

6. Keep your instruction low-key. It is extremely easy for you as a teacher to get so involved in what you are trying to accomplish that you begin to apply a bit of pressure to force your child to learn more quickly, forgetting that it will have exactly the opposite effect. You must always keep your perspective by remembering that your child's happiness and the rapport the two of you share is far more important than anything taught in this book. With time and patience any child will learn. Certainly you should have no lack of either.

Using Chapters Six, Seven, and Eight

The three preprimers in these chapters contain a number of lessons followed by a Word Recognition Competency Test. If you are dealing with a preschool child you will, of course, begin with the first preprimer and proceed from there. If you are dealing with a school-age child and are not sure with which preprimer you should begin, we suggest that you administer the Word Recognition Test for Preprimer #1 at the end of the first preprimer. If your child performs satisfactorily, then proceed to the Word Recognition Test at the end of Chapter Seven, and so forth. (If your child is too advanced for any of the three preprimers then Chapters Nine and Ten will show you how to use the lessons in this chapter with more advanced reading material.)

In any case, we would like to suggest again that you read through Chapters Six, Seven, and Eight before actually beginning your teaching. This is especially important for anyone beginning instruction with other than the first preprimer (Chapter Six), because only it contains complete lesson plans and only the first lesson ("The Kite") contains a detailed teaching script. Later preprimers (Chapters Seven and Eight) contain only supplementary activities designed to add variation and to teach specific concepts introduced for the first time in any given lesson.

Preprimer #1

The purpose of this preprimer is to teach sight recognition of fifty words which will enable your child to begin reading simple prose material. Eleven stories are presented, along with suggestions for steering him through each of the four steps outlined earlier (laying the groundwork, reading, discussion, and word study). In addition, a detailed sample lesson plan is presented for the first story to serve as a model for the teaching of all subsequent lessons.

The stories themselves are, of necessity, very simple. No assumptions are made with respect to previous reading vocabulary, so the first two stories contain only four words, the third adds two more, and so forth. What these stories lack in content, however, can be more than made up for by discussion with your child of their accompanying pictures and the enthusiasm you communicate at the fact that *he is actually beginning to read his first book*! This is as big a developmental landmark as his first spoken words or his first steps, but it has the advantage of being an experience *both* of you will remember.

Model Lesson Plan for "The Kite"

Since there are so many lessons contained in the Chapters Six, Seven and Eight, and since they all use the same basic teaching format, we shall present only one detailed lesson plan, which will serve as a model for the reading of all subsequent stories. Rather complete outlines are given for the rest of the first preprimer, which should ease your mastery of the teaching routine, but should any questions arise you may always refer back to this model.

LESSON #1
The Kite

NEW WORDS: is, kite, the, up.

(These words, introduced for the first time in this story, are listed each time for your reference only. They are not to be read by the child in isolation.)

A. Laying the groundwork

Make sure you are comfortably seated side by side. Tell your child that today the two of you will read the first story in this, his first book. You might introduce the story as follows:

Today we're going to learn to read the first story in this book. Look at the picture and tell me what you see.

He may attend to any number of things about the picture including either the child or the sky. Your job is to direct his attention to the kite.

The story is called "The Kite," so what do you think it's about?

The child will probably answer correctly.

That's right! A kite! Have you ever seen a kite before?

Other questions you might ask are:

What can you do with a kite?
Did you ever fly one?
Would you like to fly a kite?

Obviously you do not need to follow this or any script *verbatim*. Communicate naturally with your child by asking him anything you please in the language the two of you usually use. What you should try to accomplish by this introductory activity is to:

1. stimulate as much verbal interaction as possible,
2. generate interest in reading the story, and
3. direct his attention to the story.

Once these objectives are accomplished the next step involves giving the child a reason to read (in this case to listen to) the story, such as:

I'm going to read you this story about a kite. Listen carefully because when I'm finished I want you to tell me where the kite is.

B. Reading the story

Read the story slowly but fluently with natural expression. Let your child look at the story while you read but do not point to any words yet. (You will actually read the story first only during the first few lessons; from then on your child will be doing all the reading.)

Now, where is the kite?

The child should answer that "the kite is up." If he gives any answer based on the picture, however, such as "up in the sky" or even "flying," he is of course correct.

O.K. That's good! Now I'm going to read the story again. This time watch carefully because when I'm finished I want you to help me read it.

If he wants to help read it right away, let him.
Read the story slowly but fluently again, this time sliding your finger under the words as you read them so your child can visually connect written with spoken words. Try to keep your tone natural and avoid jerky word calling.

Now I want you to help me read the story.

Read the story aloud together a couple of times until your child can read most of the words without hesitation. As he gains confidence lower your voice so that he hears his own as the dominating one. (Be careful not to continue this activity to the point at which he memorizes the story.)
Use your judgment with respect to how much help your child needs on this and subsequent initial readings. We will eventually completely phase out your reading of the story, so if you believe he can read without this extra help, stop doing it even sooner.

Are you ready to read the story by yourself?

Participate in the reading only when your child needs help with a word, at which time you can simply supply it. On later tries you can give him a phonics cue (such as *What sound does k make?*) pointing to the initial letter in "kite," for example, or a context cue for a word like "up" (such as *Where is the kite?*).

You may have the child read the story several times in this fashion, but there is a limit to how many times a ten-word story can be read before tedium or memorization sets in. Go to the word study activities before that happens. Also remember to be highly complimentary. This is his first official story, the first time he has read independently. Don't hesitate to point that out. Don't ever forget our primary rule either. Never, never demean or criticize your child because he isn't learning as fast as you would like him to. If your child isn't meeting your expectations, just be positive and keep trying, if you can't do that, your only other constructive choice is to leave his education to someone who can.

If your child can read "The Kite" fluently by the end of this series of reading attempts, you shouldn't assume that he will be able to recognize in a different context the four new words in it. On the other hand, if he cannot read the story after multiple attempts you should *definitely* not assume that he has some kind of "learning problem" or is a "slow learner." Beginning reading is often difficult for even the brightest children and we can offer some tricks to help get your child through this crucial period.

Thus whether the child can read the story at this point, or whether he cannot, he definitely needs more practice recognizing and using his new words, which is the purpose of the word study activities.

(This is a natural breaking point if in your judgment the child needs a rest.)

C. Word study

1. Introducing the word cards. You are now going to write the new words on index cards if you haven't already done so (the instructions assume you have not). As always, write carefully and clearly in the style advocated in Chapter Four.

I'm going to write the words from the story now and I want you to read each word as I write it.

Write "kite" (lower case) on the first index card. The child will probably recognize and call out the word before you finish writing it. If he does, compliment him; if he doesn't, you have several alternatives:

1. supply the name yourself,
2. discuss the initial sound, or
3. find it in the story and see if he can read it in context (that is, if he can read the sentence in which it is found).

As always, praise him when he is correct and help him encouragingly if he is not.

Next write "Kite" (capitalize the "K") on another word card and place the two index cards together, one under the other.

> Kite
> kite

Do you see any difference in these two words?

If he notices the difference in the two k's, go on to the next word. If not, point out the difference (using the "large" and "small" terminology introduced in Chapter Four) making sure that he realizes that both represent the same word. Remind him that every letter has an upper- and lower-case counterpart.

Proceed to the other three words in exactly the same manner:

> Up   The   Is
> up   the   is

2. Sentence construction using the word cards. In this activity you are going to help the child construct sentences by physically arranging word cards. This will give him needed practice in word recognition via a different medium than simply rereading the story over and over.

You may begin by holding the story so that he can look at it.

Give him the four word cards he will need (the capitalized version of "The" and the lower-case versions of "kite," "is," and "up") and say:

I want you to make the first sentence in the story with these word cards.

Point to the sentence and read it.

Can you put the cards down to make this sentence?

If he needs some help in doing this you can point to the first word while he finds the right card. Be sure to talk to him about the "first word," the "second word," and so on, so that you'll help him develop his numerical concepts at the same time.

When the sentence is laid out correctly have him read it, then point to the period in the story and say something like:

Oops! Something is missing! We need a period because it's the end of the sentence.

Give him the period and question mark cards and ask him:

Which of these cards is a period?

If he answers correctly, say:

Good. Why don't you put it at the end of your sentence?

When he complies, say:

This other one is a question mark. It comes after a question. Let's see if we can make your sentence into a question.

Help him arrive at the question "Is the kite up?" verbally, and then encourage him to rearrange his word cards appropriately.

Can you read this question?

Have him read it.

Good. Now that you have a question what do you need at the end instead of this period?

He should point to the card with the question mark written on it. Have him place the question mark card at the end of the sentence.

You should point out that sentences with question marks also begin with "large" letters, just like sentences which end in periods. Don't be surprised if he has difficulty distinguishing between sentences which ask questions and those which do not. If you wish to give him some practice in making the distinction you may dictate some sentences to him orally and ask which will end with question marks and which with periods. (The story itself contains exclamation marks. At this point you should simply use these to add emphasis to your own reading. If your child asks about them, simply say that they are used to show excitement or to point something out.)

The next step is to see if your child can construct a sentence without benefit of the story as a guide. To accomplish this, simply take the story out of his line of sight and ask him to form a sentence with any of the eight words and two punctuation cards. Given the fact that he only has four words with which to work, the two previous sentences are probably the only ones he will offer. As more words are introduced in subsequent lessons, this activity can become much more varied and interesting.

If he arranges the word cards in some kind of random order have him read them and ask him *if it makes sense*. This is one way of teaching your child to read for meaning right from the start. That is, after all, what reading is all about.

You should now be ready to begin the second lesson the next time the two of you sit down for a session. Put his word cards in the same Word Box you used for the two previous chapters and tell him that next time you will see if he can remember both these and learn some new ones.

A Note About the Word Box

Although the Word Box has been discussed previously, it takes on such an important role in this chapter that we would like to review its function and use. It is basically a recording device, a record of the words your child has been taught. The chief purpose of this record is to serve as a convenient form of review by which recognition of words once taught can be reinforced. Although formal, periodic review sessions are suggested throughout the chapter, the Word Box can and should be used whenever you feel your child needs some extra practice by simply withdrawing the relevant words and presenting them to the child to read.

Since over 150 words will be taught in the three preprimers, it is important that you record faithfully new words introduced in each lesson. We suggest that immediately following a lesson you place the new words together in a "new word" envelope and only file them with previous words once the child has demonstrated his recognition of them at the next session, either by reading them without help in the new story, or through presentation of the cards themselves as review.

We further suggest that you write the words in lower-case format (with the exception of proper names, of course) and that you record on the card the page number of the story in which the word was first introduced as a reference strategy (review activities often suggest that the child read a sentence containing a given word). When activities such as the ones presented above require a capitalized version of a word, it is probably best to simply make the card especially for that purpose.

As a final note, make sure that (1) you print each word legibly using letters at least as large as the ones contained in the preprimers, (2) you review the entire contents of the box periodically, and (3) you always replace word cards pulled from the box after each use. The time you spend keeping the Word Box current and in good order will pay off in the long run.

New Words Introduced in Preprimer #1

Lesson #1: is, kite, the, up
Lesson #2: down
Lesson #3: and, ball
Lesson #4: balloon, red
Lesson #5: big, my, rabbit, white
Lesson #6: baby, little, Mother, one, rabbits, two

Lesson #7: a, I, nest, tree, green, see
Lesson #8: brown, in
Lesson #9: Bird, blue, four, eggs, Here, on, she, sits
Lesson #10: Father, fly, for, food, has, he, to, will
Lesson #11: all, are, day, eat, need, They, with

LESSON #1
The kite

NEW WORDS: is, kite, the, up.

A. Laying the groundwork

1. Use prompts and questions to encourage verbal interaction plus interest in the story such as:
   a. *Today we're going to learn to read the first story in this book. Look at the picture and tell me what you see.*
   b. *The story is called "The Kite." What do you know about kites?*
   c. *Have you ever seen a kite before?*

B. Parent-assisted reading

1. Read the story to the child giving him a reason for listening, such as: *Listen carefully because when I'm finished reading I want you to tell me where the kite is.*
2. Discuss the story briefly with respect to relevant questions raised prior to reading.
3. Follow this by allowing the child to read with you in unison.

C. Reading by the child alone

1. Allow the child to read the story, supplying words he does not know so that the flow of the story is not interrupted. Do this as many times as necessary.
2. Later use an initial consonant cue for "kite" if it is not

LESSON 1

The Kite

The kite is up.
Up! Up! Up!
The kite is up.

kite

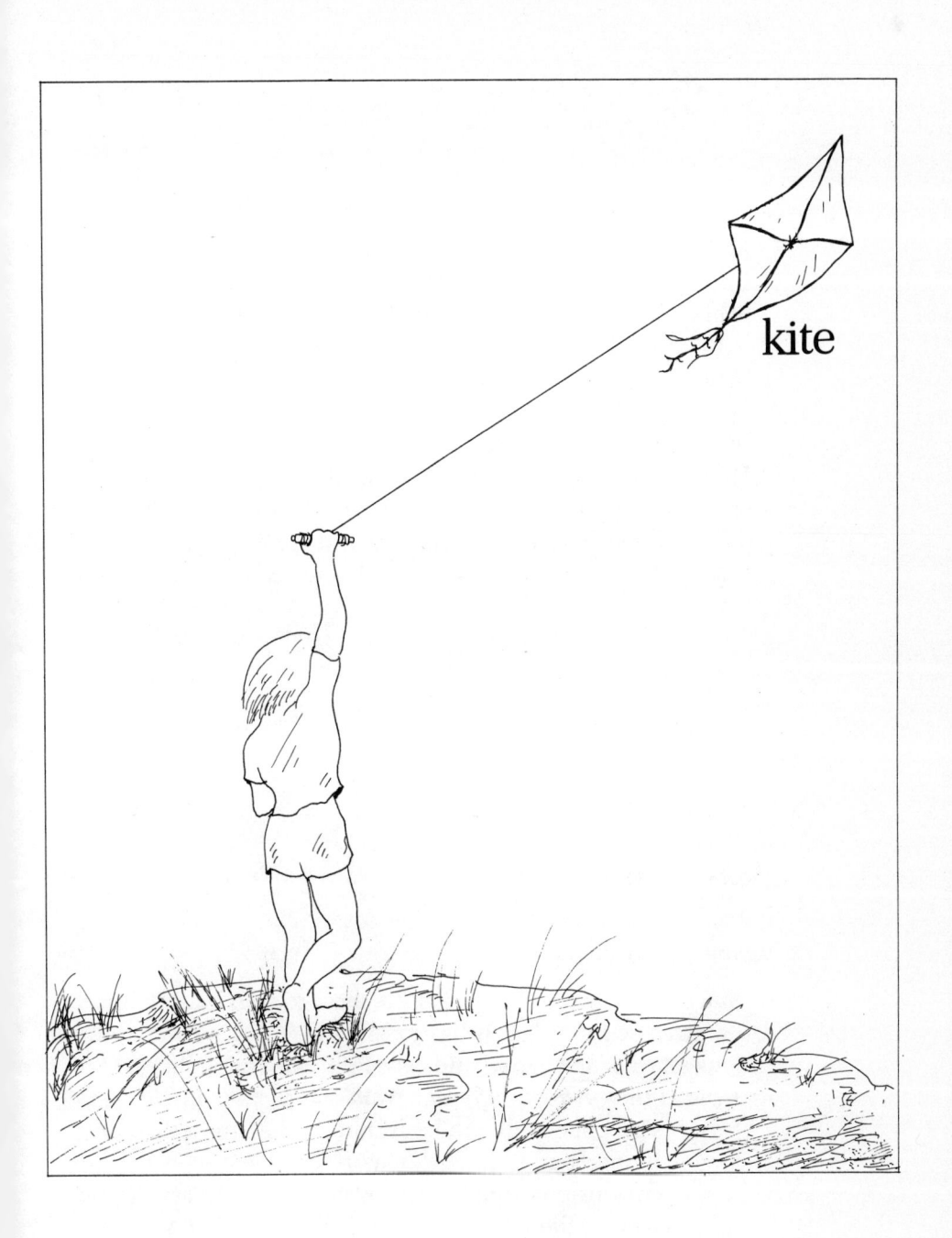

known (for example, *What sound does a k make?*) or a context cue for "up" (*Where is the kite?*).

D. Word study

1. Make a capitalized version of each of the word cards and then point out distinctions between capitalized and non-capitalized words, making sure that the child realizes that both formats represent the same word.
2. Have him construct simple sentences using his four new words, pointing out the role of capitalization and punctuation in sentence construction.
3. Have him read each sentence he makes with his word cards, asking him if they make sense. (Remember our ultimate objective of making him a reflective reader.)
4. File the four words in his Word Box for future study and review.

LESSON #2
Down

NEW WORD: down.

A. Laying the groundwork

1. Since this story is so similar to the previous one it must be discussed in relationship to "The Kite." Have the child look at the first story and ask him something like this: *How is this picture different from the picture in the first story?* The child will probably notice that the kite is no longer flying, but is now down. If he doesn't, lead him to that conclusion using the word "down." You may discuss how he thinks the kite came down. Tell him that *We now have a new word that says the kite is down.* Show him the word by pointing to it and telling him that it is the title of the new story.

2. Tell the child that you are going to read the story to him. Ask him to listen carefully for the part which tells where the kite is.

B. Parent-assisted reading

Read the story to the child, then ask where the kite is. Reread it, encouraging the child to read in unison.

C. Reading by the child alone

*1. Same as in Lesson #1 except you may not need to have the child read the story quite as many times, given the fact that only one new word is introduced. Supply any words he misses. If trouble is encountered with "down" you might remind him what sound a **d** makes. Be sure to discuss what he found out about the kite by reading the story.

D. Word study

*1. Construct two word cards (capitalized and noncapitalized) for "down" as in Lesson #1. Take out the eight word cards made for the previous lesson and place all ten face down on the table. Instruct the child to draw a card, and after reading it correctly, place it in his pile. If he misses one he has to give it back *after* you tell him what it represents. Mix the cards again and proceed until all cards have been read. The game is over when all the cards are in his pile and he has "won."

*2. Place all the cards on the table face up. Let the child draw a card and read it, then draw another card which has the same word written on it. Continue until all five pairs of words are properly matched.

3. Allow the child to use the word cards to make sentences as he did in Lesson #1. If he constructs a sentence such as "the Kite is down," all you really need say is: *This sentence must begin with a capital letter and kite does*

---

* An asterisk indicates a new activity.

LESSON 2

Down

The kite is down.
Down, down!
The kite is down.
Down! Down! down!

kite

not have a capital letter unless it is at the beginning. Have him read each sentence he has made, ask him if it makes sense, then break the sentence up and have him construct another. Examples of some of the sentences he could build are: "The kite is up." "Is the kite up?" "Is the kite down?" "The kite is down." If he can't think of a sentence to make, give him the first word.

LESSON #3
Up and down

NEW WORDS: and, ball.

A. Laying the groundwork

1. After some discussion of the positions of the ball and the kite, as well as about balls in general, playing with them, and so on, you might say: *Let's read the story and see if it tells what we saw in the picture.*

*B. Reading by the child alone

1. Allow the child to read the story himself, giving him whatever help is needed. Immediately following the reading ask him a few questions based on the story, such as, *Where is the ball?*, *Where is the kite?*

COMMENT: You will note that we did not suggest that you read the story to your child this time. The reason for this lies in the need to gradually phase out your reading of the pre-primer stories and phase in your child's reading of them. If you believe that he still needs this step, feel free for a couple more lessons to continue reading the story prior to his attempting it.

---

* An asterisk indicates a new activity.

*C. Review activities
   1. Have the child read all the word cards contained in Lessons #1–#3.
   2. Play the matching (capitalized vs. noncapitalized) game with all the words and/or make sentences using all seven words if interest is high. To vary this exercise you could construct the sentences this time and let the child read them. (If there are other words from previous chapters in the Word Box that your child has thoroughly mastered, you may add them to the pool, thus making far more varied sentences possible.)
   *3. You may, at this stage, begin keeping a "book" of sentences which you and your child construct. This can be done quite simply by using a loose-leaf notebook and writing each sentence down carefully. If you decide to engage in this activity make a big production out of the fact that a book is being written based on the child's sentences. Let the child decorate the cover of the book, put his name on it, and give it a title.

---

* An asterisk indicates a new activity.

Up and Down

The kite is up.
The ball is down.
Kite, up!
Ball, down!
Up and down!
Down and up!

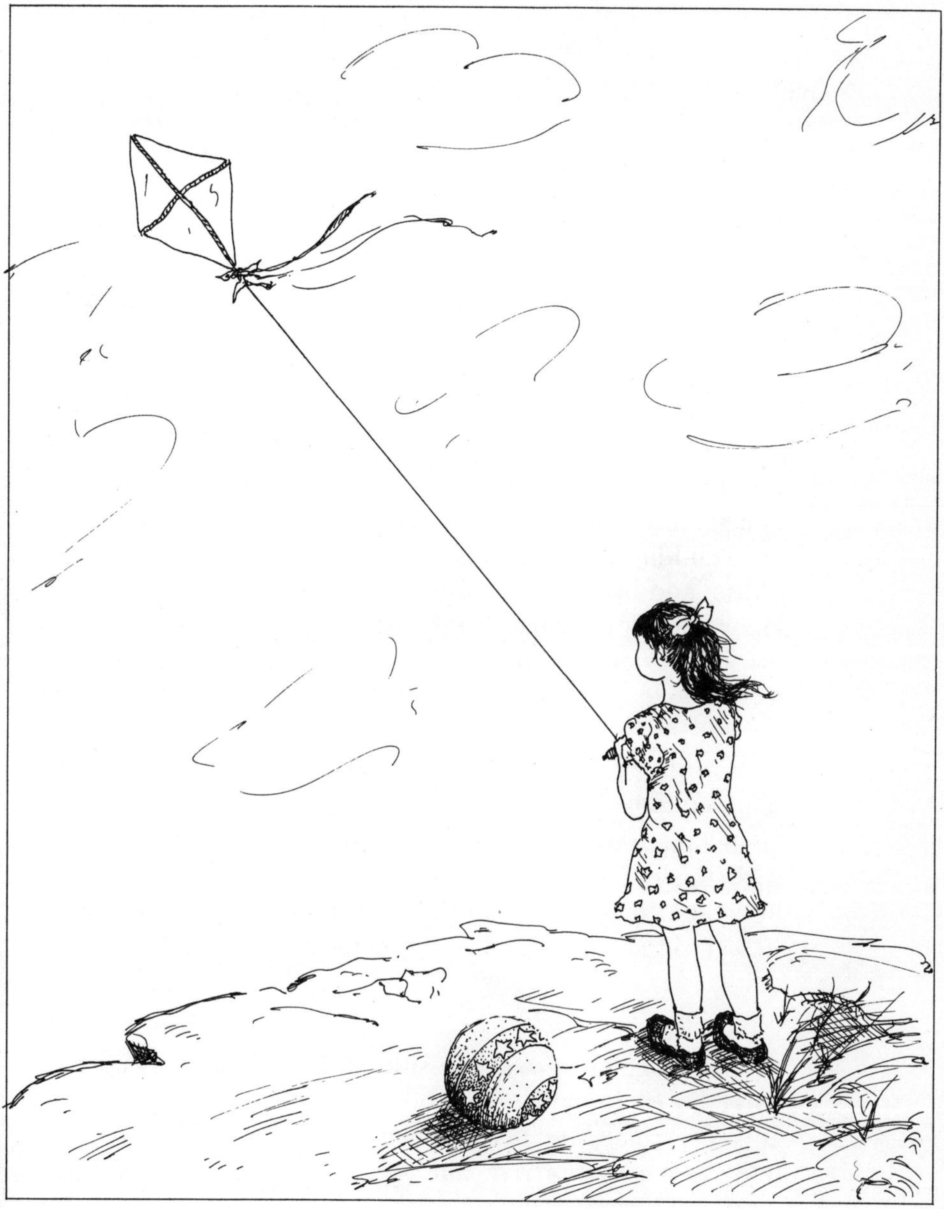

LESSON #4
The balloon

NEW WORDS: balloon, red.

A. Laying the groundwork
1. Two characteristics of the balloon should be discussed prior to reading the story: its position and its color. After asking the child *where* the balloon is (try to elicit "up" or "up in the air"), ask if he can guess from the picture what is about to happen to the balloon. You might say, *The balloon is up now but where do you think it will be in a minute?* Next ask the child what colors balloons can be. Tell him this balloon is the same color as a fire engine, a rose, and lipstick, one of his red toys). If he doesn't yet know his colors by name, take out a packet of crayons and ask him to choose the color of crayon that matches the hints you gave him. Explain to him that the color represented by this crayon is called "red." (It probably has "red" printed on it.) If he is interested, teach him the names of the other major colors.
2. Have him draw both a fully inflated and a deflated balloon with the red crayon.
3. Suggest that he now read the story to find out: what happened to the balloon, and what color it was in real life.

B. Reading the story
1. Allow the child to read the story; supply help as needed. After he is through ask him:
   a. *What color was the balloon?*
   b. *Where was the red balloon at the beginning of the story?*
   c. *Where was it at the end of the story? Can you point to the word that tells where?*
2. Have him reread until he does so fluently.

C. Word study
   1. Use any of the techniques employed in previous lessons that appear fruitful. Also mix up the word cards for all words learned thus far and practice reading them.
   *2. Another good activity is to let the child draw a picture and "write" his own story to illustrate it (he will of course dictate the story to you). If he wants to use words he doesn't have in his Word Box, don't worry about it. Write the story on large-lined paper and have him read it as he does the preprimer stories. These stories can later be collected in his own "picture book." You might also allow the child to try to copy the story he has just written. Visualize this activity, however, as completely independent of the preprimers; actually *we recommend it only if your child is progressing relatively easily* from story to story. If he is experiencing difficulty, save this for later.

---

* An asterisk indicates a new activity.

LESSON 4

The Balloon

The balloon is red.
The balloon is up.
Up, up, up!
The red balloon is up.
Down, down, down!
The balloon is down.

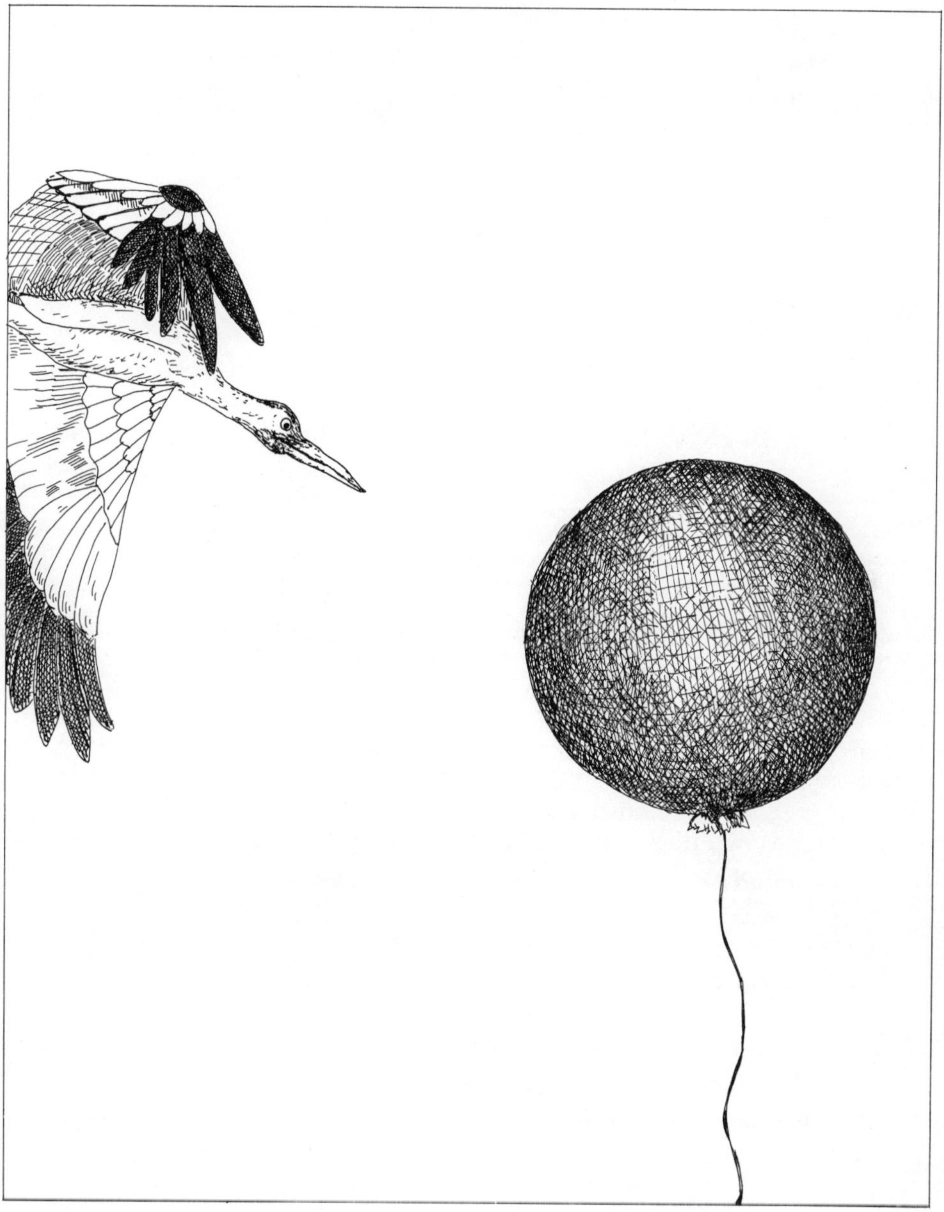

LESSON #5
My rabbit

NEW WORDS: big, my, rabbit, white.

A. Laying the groundwork
1. Look at the picture and discuss the rabbit. The two of you could talk about what he eats, the color of other rabbits, and the color of this one.
2. In giving the child a reason for reading this story you can suggest finding out what color the rabbit really is and who he belongs to.

B. Reading the story
1. Have the child read the story as usual, asking him the above-mentioned questions (or others) upon completion.
*2. This time you might have him locate the new words in the story, point to each, and read it as you write it on an index card. If he puts his finger under a word that has been previously introduced, ask him to try to find it in his Word Box. Have him read it if he finds it. If it isn't known, find the story in which it was introduced and have him reread it.

*C. Word study

COMMENT: The child now knows enough words to continue a more intensive study of sounds begun in Chapter Five. The following activities are designed with this in mind.
1. Place the following word cards in front of the child:

      rabbit   ball
      red   balloon
                big

---

* An asterisk indicates a new activity.

Say them so that the child can hear the sound that each beginning letter represents.

2. Give the child cards with both upper- and lower-case r's and b's written on them: **Rr, Bb**. Next have him hold up the proper letter card each time you read one of the five words listed above. In other words if you say "ball," the child should hold up the **Bb** card to indicate that "ball" begins with the sound of the letter **b**.
3. Next point to "rabbit" and "red" in the first column of word cards. *These words are alike in one way. What is it?* Hopefully he will say that both have a **r** in the beginning. If he doesn't, lead him to this conclusion, possibly by covering all the letters in both except the **r**'s. *Now I'm going to say some words that begin like rabbit. Listen carefully and see if you can hear the **r**.*

Read the following pairs of words:

    rabbit   red
    red   ride
    ride   rabbit
    ran   rabbit
    rabbit   Ricky

Let the child repeat each pair after you.

4. *Now look at the second column of words* (in [1] above): *ball, balloon, big* (read them). *Do they begin with the same letter?* After the child responds affirmatively, *Let's say them and see if the letter makes the same sound.* (Repeat the words.) *Do they make the same sound? What is the name of the letter that stands for the first sound in ball, balloon, big?* (Emphasize the initial sound as you read the words.)

*Now I'm going to say some more words that have the sound that **b** stands for just like ball, balloon, and big. Listen carefully. Baby, bat, boy, bang, boot, Ben, Billy.*

(It might be helpful to write these words out so that you can point to each as you say it.)

LESSON 5

My Rabbit

My rabbit is big.
My rabbit is white.
My rabbit is big and white.
White and Big!
Big and white!

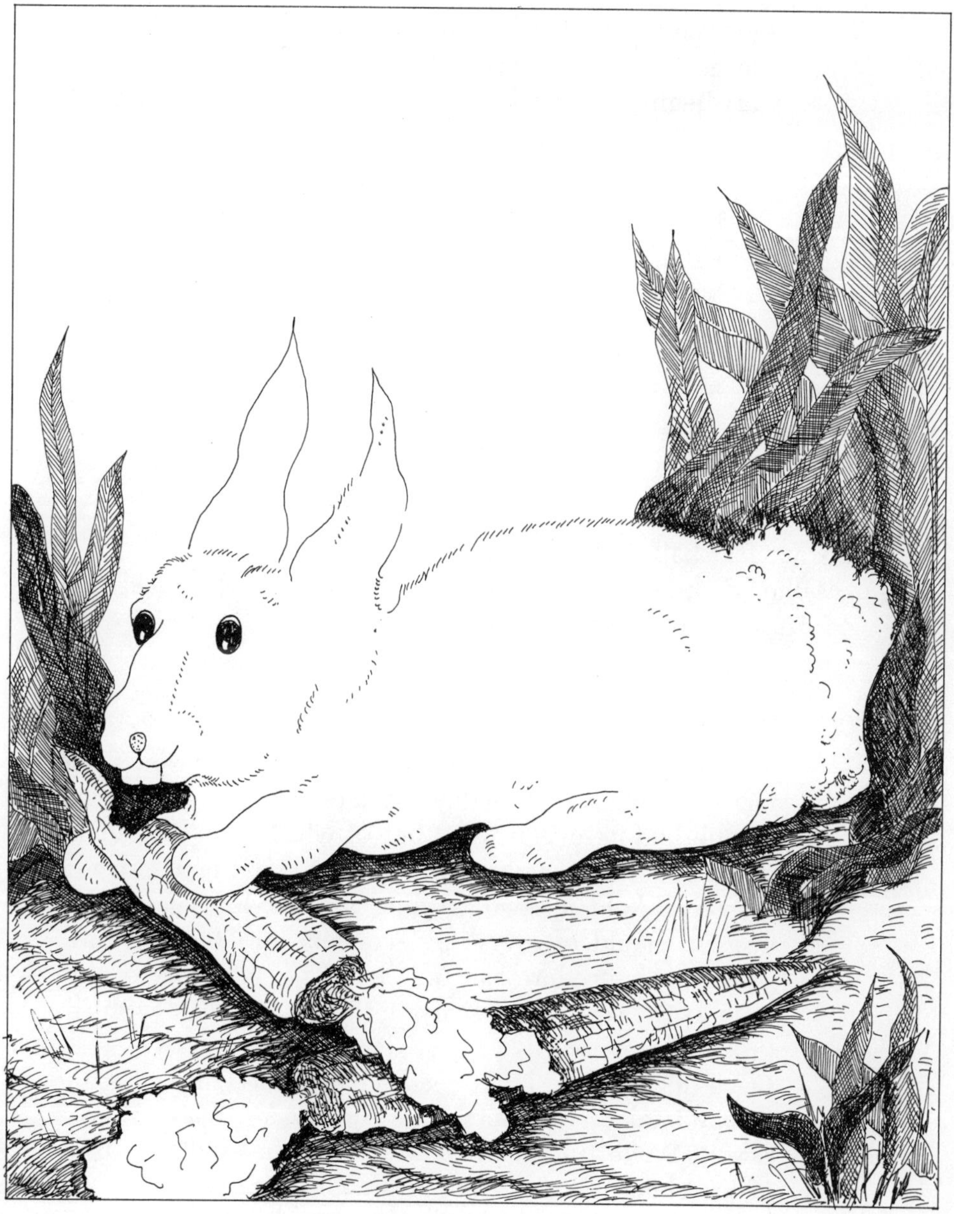

Next have him say the words in pairs with you or after you as in the previous exercise. Each time ask if these pairs begin alike. (Obviously the answer will be yes.)

ball	Ben
ball	Billy
big	baby
balloon	bat
balloon	boy

LESSON #6
The two rabbits

NEW WORDS: baby, little, Mother, one, rabbits, two.

(Although listed as new words you will note that *one*, *two*, and *Mother* have been used in previous chapters.)

A. Laying the groundwork

*1. You should develop the concept of plurality if your child has not already thoroughly mastered it. This can be accomplished in several ways, one of which is to hold up an object like a crayon and ask the child what it is. Once he responds, hold up two crayons and ask him again. The answer should of course be "crayons" or "two crayons." The same procedure can be repeated using other objects such as blocks, toys, pencils, until he is familiar with the oral plural of words.

*2. Once the above task has been accomplished, ask what the first animal in the picture is. He will recognize it as a rabbit. Write "rabbit" on a word card and put it in front of the child. Next, ask him: *How many rabbits are in the entire picture?* Undoubtedly by now he will say either "two rabbits" or "rabbits." (If he is not yet comfortable with number concepts, help him.)

---

* An asterisk indicates a new activity.

Write "rabbits" on a card and place it under the other one.

rabbit
rabbits

Do you see any difference between these two words?
(If he doesn't notice the s, point it out.) Explain that more than one is denoted by simply adding an s to many words.

*3. Write the word "big" on a piece of paper or a chalkboard if you have one. First ask the child, *Look at the big rabbit in the picture. Now look at the other rabbit. Is he big?* The child will answer no. *What is he?* Elicit the word "little."
That's right. This rabbit is little.
Write the word "little" under "big."
What else could you call a little rabbit? (The word you're looking for is "baby.") Write it as above. Now show the child the cards with "one," "two," and "Mother" written on them. Hopefully, they will be recognized. If not, review them.

B. Reading the story

Let's read the story to find out the names of the big and little rabbits.

Have the child read the story several times with you supplying words as needed. Discuss the story with respect to the above questions.

C. Word study

1. Have the child point out the new words as you write them. Ask him to read them if he does not do so spontaneously. (You can also ask the child to find and point out each new word in the story.)
2. Place the word cards used for this and the previous lesson on the table.
Do you see a word that begins like big? (Point to the b.) The child should respond with "baby." If he encounters problems, reteach the section of Lesson Five which dealt

* An asterisk indicates a new activity.

LESSON 6

The Two Rabbits

One rabbit is big.
One rabbit is little.
Mother Rabbit is big.
Baby rabbit is little.
Little rabbit is a baby.
Big rabbit is a mother.

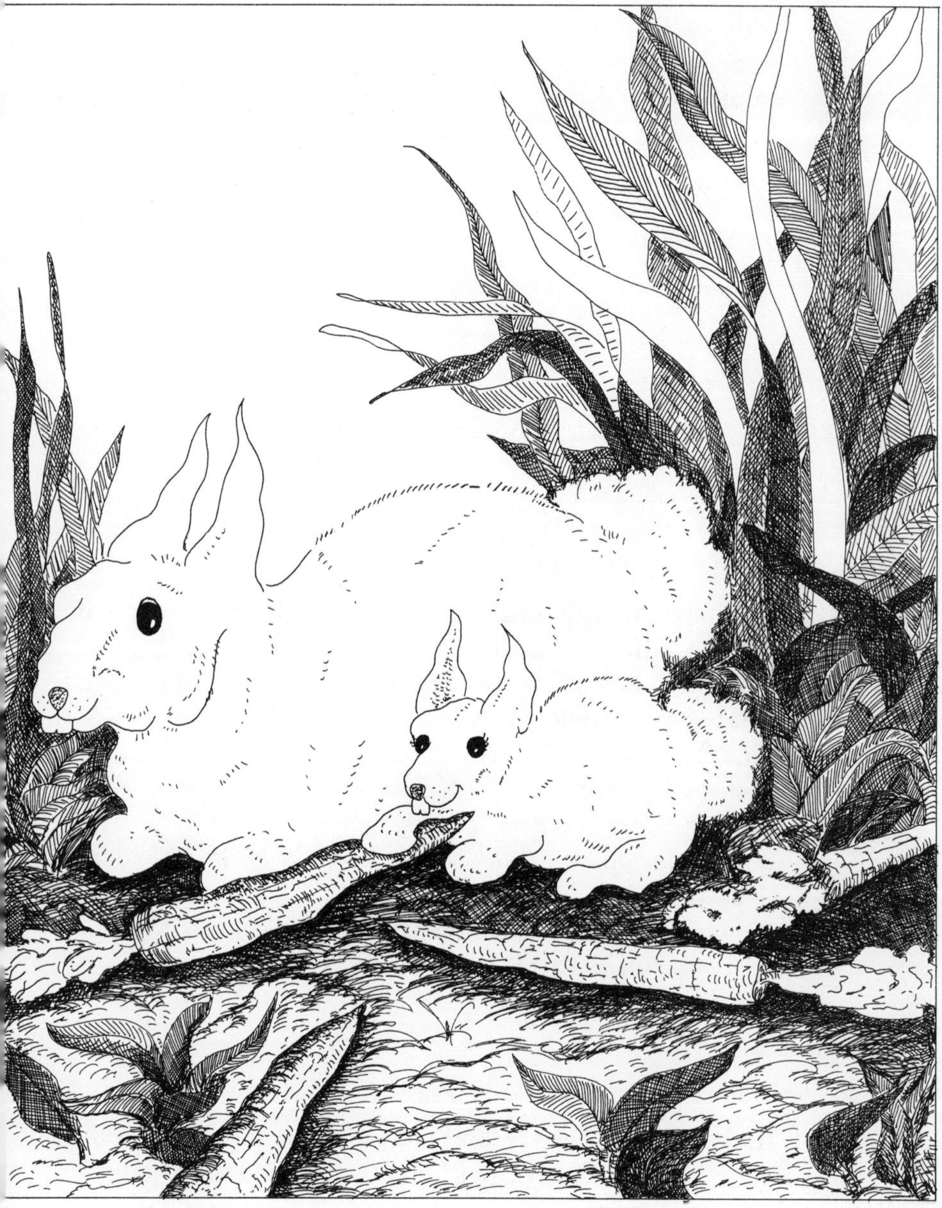

with words beginning with **b**. (Be very careful not to include words with blends like black, brown, in your examples.)
Now find two words that begin with the same letter and the same sound as "red." "Rabbit" and "rabbits" should be identified. Again, if problems are encountered, refer to the relevant section in Lesson Five.

LESSON #7
The tree

NEW WORDS: a, green, I, nest, see, tree.

A. Laying the groundwork

1. Have the child describe the picture. Ask him to compare the size of the tree to that of the nest. *Is the tree big?*
2. Ask him to talk about the tree. Is it big or small? (It's big.)
Is there something in this tree?
What? (A nest.)
Is the nest big?
If it isn't big, what is it?
What color do you think the tree would be in real life?
If he doesn't know his colors by name let him choose a crayon that matches the color he would expect a tree to be. Point out that this color is green. Show him the word written on the crayon.

B. Reading the story

1. Have the child read to find out more about what the child in the picture can see. Let him take the lead in reading the story, but supply words as he needs them. Have him point out the words that tell the size and color of the tree, the size of the nest, and other facts.

2. Ask him to try to read through the entire story now that he has had some help with the words. If he does well, compliment him. If not, just say that *"Perhaps we need some more work on this long story."* Give him as much additional practice reading the story as you deem appropriate, as long as he does not become frustrated.

C. Word study

1. Have the child point out the new words introduced in the story. Write each on a word card as he reads it. If he fails to read one, say, for example,
This is "nest"; look carefully as I write it. It begins with an n. What sound does n make? (Remind him if necessary.)
2. When the new words have all been written, have the child read them and then read the story again.
*3. Call attention to **I** and **a** used in this story. They were first learned as letters, but now also function as words. Make sure the child understands this distinction. You should also point out the fact that **I**, when used as a word referring to the speaker, is always capitalized.

---

* An asterisk indicates a new activity.

LESSON 7

The Tree

I see a tree.

I see a big tree.

I see a green tree.

I see a nest.

I see a little nest.

159

REVIEW

If you stop to think about it, your child has been required to master a great deal of new material in the last few sessions. Besides teaching capitalization, punctuation, sentence construction, plurality, phonics, color, number, and a host of subsidiary concepts, we have presented him with twenty-five new words plus seven stories of varying complexity. This is a tall order by any reckoning, and, given the nature of learning, we have to expect that our pupil will have forgotten a good deal of what he has learned by now.

Since forgetting is a natural human function, you as a teacher must build review activities into your instruction to counter its effects. Basically all that is entailed in review is ascertaining what has been forgotten and reteaching it. Since forgetting is an ongoing, continuous process, review must keep pace. Fortunately, relearning a concept is never as difficult as original learning. Although there is no guarantee that the same concept won't be forgotten twice, the probability decreases each time it is reviewed.

Some children need more review than others, but there is danger of boring a child if the same lessons are retaught in the same way too often. We have therefore avoided a formal review session until this point and have attempted to make it as different from the original lessons as possible. If, after conducting the exercises below, you believe your child would profit by more frequent reviews than we have provided, feel free to do so. We suggest, however, that you structure them similarly to ours: both by using our record-keeping devices and by varying them from the regular lessons.

Materials

You will need twenty-four word cards from the Word Box plus the following form:

Date _____

Lesson #1	Lesson #2	Lesson #3	Lesson #4	Lesson #5	Lesson #6	Lesson #7
___is	___down	___and	___balloon	___big	___baby	___a
___kite		___ball	___red	___my	___little	___I
___the				___rabbit	___Mother	___nest
___up				___white	___one	___tree
					___rabbits	___green
					___two	___see

ACTIVITY #1

Test the child on all twenty-five words by presenting the word cards one at a time for his recognition. Lay the ones he knows in one pile and the ones he doesn't in another. Record the missed words by simply checking the appropriate words in the chart above. Do not act as though this is a test, just tell the child you will go over all his words to see which ones he knows best and which ones need practice.

ACTIVITY #2

Find the missed words in the preprimer and have the child read the stories containing them. Have the child point to the word in question each time it is used in the story.

ACTIVITY #3

Reread each of the originally missed words.

ACTIVITY #4

The following games will provide valuable practice on all the words. Your child will enjoy them if you do. Be sure not to chide him or suggest that he could "do better than that." If he misses something point out the answer as though you only just then located it yourself. Spread the twenty-four word cards out in front of him and ask him to:

a. *Find three words that have only two letters.* (Answer: my, is, up) Always have the child read the words in this and the following exercises as he finds them.

b. *Find four words that begin with the letter b.* (Answer: big, ball, baby, balloon)

c. *Find three words that begin with the letter r.* (Answer: red, rabbit, rabbits)

d. *Find a word that names something big and green.* (Answer: tree)

e. *Find two words that begin with the letter a.* (Answer: a, and)

f. *Find two color words.* (Answer: red, green)

g. *Find a word that is the opposite of big.* (Answer: little) The child may not know what opposite means, but he has the concept, so simply explain in words that he will understand. You might gesture and say, "If it's not big, it's _____."

h. *Find two words that name something that can fly.* (Answer: kite, balloon)

i. *Find a word that is the opposite of up.* (Answer: down)

j. *Find two words that name the same animal.* (Answer: rabbit, rabbits)

k. *Find two words that name a number.* (Answer: one, two) The child may feel more comfortable with terminology such as "tell how many."

l. *Find the name of a bird's home.* (Answer: nest)

m. *Find and read all three-letter words.* (Answer: the, and, big, one, two, see)

This is only a sample of the types of questions you can ask to encourage your child's sifting through and reading his word repertoire. If he enjoys activities such as this, or if you judge that he needs more practice in working with his words, feel free to make up your own review activities and engage in them at any time. It certainly would be a good idea if you tested the child on the words checked as not known on the review form above a couple of days following this session. A good way to do this is to simply place them in the "New Words" envelope and keep them there until you are sure they have been relearned.

LESSON #8
A nest

NEW WORDS: brown, in.

A. Laying the groundwork
   1. This story is very similar to the one in Lesson #7 and may be introduced as a continuation of that episode. You might tell the child that you are going to learn some more about the nest.
   2. Talk about nests—what they are made of, what color they are and where they are found.
   Let's read the story to find out.

B. Reading the story

   (As in previous lessons) After the child reads the story ask him what he found out about the color of the nest and where it was.

C. Word study
   1. *Find the two new words* (**brown** and **in**) *and read the sentences in which they are found.*

LESSON 8

A Nest

I see a nest.
A nest in a tree!
The nest is little.
The nest is brown.
Little and brown.
The nest is in the tree.

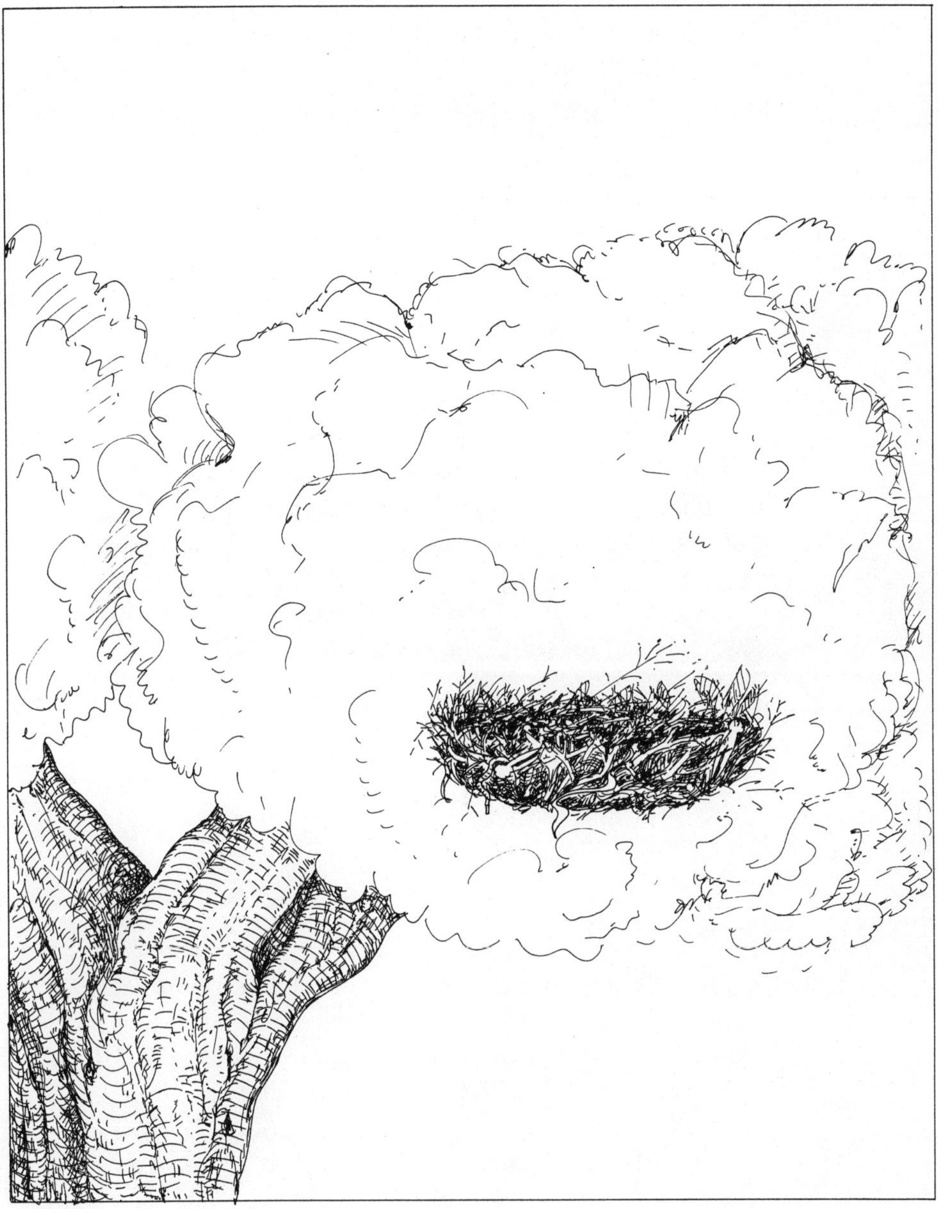

2. Have him make sentences from the word cards involving the sentences he read plus any other words that were missed during reading. Examples of some of the sentences he might make are:

>I see brown.
>I see a brown nest.
>The nest is little.
>I see a baby in the nest.
>The brown kite is in the tree.

As always, have him read the sentences he makes and ask him if his "nonsentences" make sense.
3. Test the child again on the troublesome words. If he still has difficulty, use any of the activities discussed so far to give him extra practice.

LESSON #9
Mother bird

NEW WORDS: bird, blue, four, eggs, here, on, she, sits.

A. Laying the groundwork

1. As you will note, the child's sight vocabulary is increasing to the point where the stories have more substance and intrinsic interest. It would be a great error not to capitalize on this state of affairs. You have already discussed the nest, where it's located, and perhaps its function. The present story affords an opportunity for an even more extensive discussion.
2. Questions you might use to give the child a reason for reading the story are:
Who do you think is sitting on the nest?
That's right, and she's the same color as the nest. Do you remember what color that was?

What do you think is in the nest?
What is the mother bird doing to the eggs?
How many eggs do you see? (Remember you have been working on number and counting concepts. If the child still can't count, help him.)
Is Mother Bird big or little?
The eggs are the same color as the sky. What color do you think they are?
Convey enthusiasm with these questions. Try to build a sense of anticipation to make the child want to read the story. You don't need to correct the child if he guesses incorrectly. Simply say, *We'll find out when you read the story.*

B. Reading the story

Proceed as in previous lessons, except that you should bear in mind that the vocabulary load in the present story is very heavy even though the child should be familiar with many of the "new" words from previous chapters. If a great deal of difficulty is encountered in the reading of this story, proceed to the word study activities to familiarize him with the words. Once he is more familiar with the eight new words you can go back and have him work on his reading fluency. Discuss all the questions raised prior to reading the story and ask him what he found out.

C. Word study

1. Ask the child to give you the new words (or to point to those he does not know) as you write them.
2. Have him read the new words from the word cards. As he does so make the capitalized version of each word.

He reads:	*You write:*
here	Here
bird	Bird
and so on.	

LESSON 9

Mother Bird

Here is Mother Bird.
She is a big bird.
She is a big brown bird.
She is on the nest.
Mother Bird has four blue eggs.
Mother Bird sits on the four eggs.
She sits on the four blue eggs.

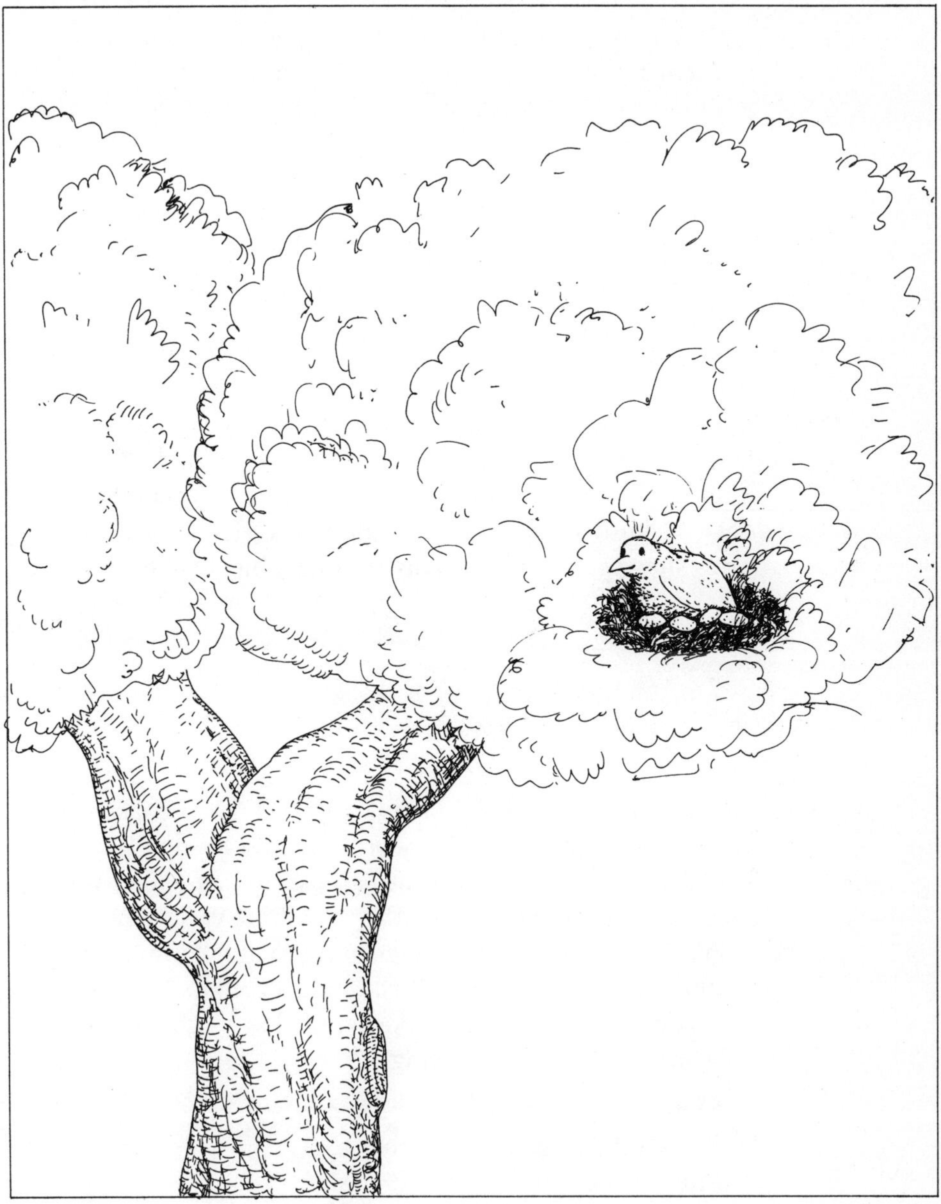

Place them together and have him tell you how they differ. Mix them up and have him match them.

3. For those words with which he has had difficulty, hold up the version (capitalized or not) which appears in the story, pronounce it, and have him find the word in the story and read it to you. (This seemingly dull exercise can be a fun activity if it is done in a lively gamelike fashion.)

*4. A variation on this theme with the word cards is to mix the cards thoroughly, draw one without allowing the child to see it, pronounce it, and ask him to find the matching word in the stack.

*5. Have him match the numbers with the words by connecting the proper pairs with a line. (He hasn't had "three" yet but will be able to do the exercise if he can match the others. If he doesn't know the numerals give him a hint such as showing him how many of some object each stands for.)

1	two
2	three
3	four
4	one

6. As always, if needed you may allow the child to construct his own sentences from the words in this lesson. If you do not supplement the words he can use, his sentences will be very similar to the ones in the story, but variations are possible. In fact it might be interesting to allow him to use only the words in "Mother Bird" and see if he can construct new sentences that make sense. He might, for example, make up the following:

> Mother Bird sits on the brown nest.
> The nest is brown and blue.
> Mother sits on the brown nest.
> The brown nest has blue eggs.

If this is too complicated for him you can construct the first half of a sentence and ask him to make up a suitable ending.

* An asterisk indicates a new activity.

LESSON #10
Father bird

NEW WORDS: Father, fly, food, for, has, He, to, will.

A. Laying the groundwork
   1. A new character is introduced into our saga, the identity of which the child probably will guess immediately. Questions that might be asked to give the child a reason for reading the story are:
   Who do you think the other bird in the picture is?
   What do you think he has in his mouth?
   Who do you think the food is for?
   Where is Father Bird flying?
   2. As always, suggest that the child read the story to find out the answers. Topics of discussion may be the reason Father Bird must bring food for Mother Bird, why Mother Bird must sit on the nest, and so on.

B. Reading the story

   As in Lesson #9, eight new words are introduced. The two of you may have to concentrate a little harder than usual on the word study activities. If a great deal of trouble is encountered in the initial reading phases, go to work with the word cards and return to reading the story when the child is more comfortable with the words. Even on the initial reading attempts always try to structure the session so that the reading moves along briskly by supplying unknown words to keep interest in the story high. Also be sure to continue to follow up on the questions which constituted the purpose for reading the story.

C. Word study
   1. Select whichever activities you deem appropriate for using the word cards.

Father Bird

Here is Father Bird.

He has food.

He has food for Mother Bird.

He will fly to the nest.

He will fly to Mother Bird.

The food is for Mother Bird.

See the food for Mother Bird.

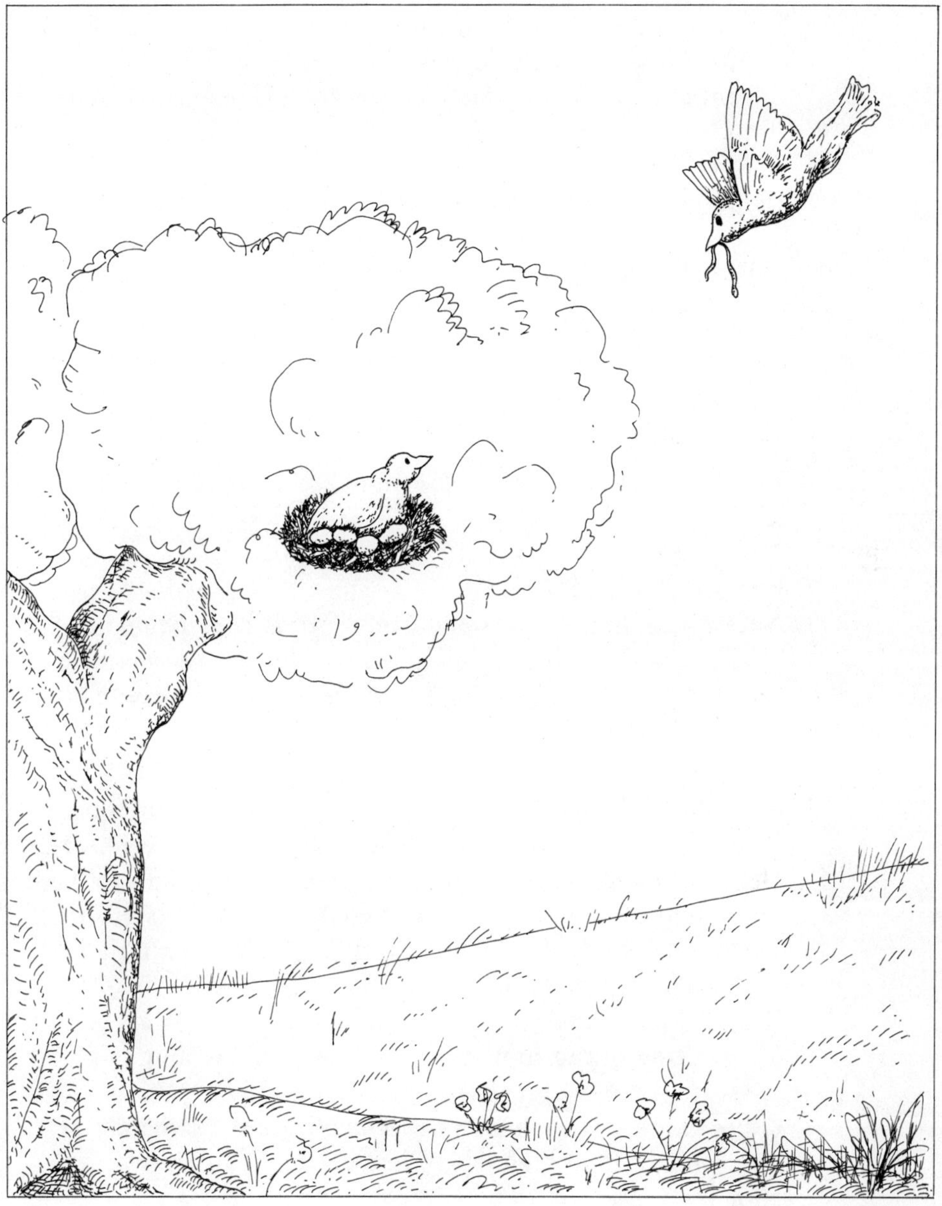

*2. Three words in this lesson begin with the initial f consonant sound, so naturally we are going to have to take advantage of the situation. Note that "fly" begins with an initial consonant blend and should not be included in the following phonics exercises. You may of course point out that fact to the child, making the **fl** sound, and asking him if he hears the difference between it and the initial **f** sound. Write the three words on a sheet of paper or place the word cards in a column:

>   for
>   food
>   Father

Look at these words and tell me how they are alike. (They all begin with **f**.)
Now read them and tell me how they sound alike. (They begin with the **f** sound.)

*3. *Now I'm going to say some other words that begin like "for," "Father," and "food"* (stress the initial sound). *Listen carefully and see if you can hear the same sound at the beginning.*
You read: **fig   fog   five   fin   fun   fur   furniture**

*4. Give the child the opportunity to supply some words beginning with the **f** sound if you like, but be sure to reject any consonant blends (such as "free," "flop," "flame"). You might also encourage him to look back at the story in Lesson #9 to find another word beginning with the **f** sound ("four").

*5. Repeat 2. and 3. above with **he** and **has** by asking the child (or pointing out to him) how they: look alike, and sound alike.
Other words to give him orally which have the same initial sound might be: **high   his   horse   hill   hurry   hungry   Henry   house**.

---

* An asterisk indicates a new activity.

LESSON #11
The baby birds

NEW WORDS: all, are, day, eat, need, They, with.

A. Laying the groundwork
   1. This story will have a great deal of intrinsic interest to your child so capitalize on that interest to the fullest possible extent. Discuss with him the fact that the birds have grown in the eggs because Mother Bird kept them warm with her body heat. Describe how the baby birds pecked the shell and came out when they were ready. Recall how many eggs there were originally and ask how many baby birds there are now. (Answer: four, one for each egg.)
   2. Some questions to give the child a reason for reading the story might be:
   What do you think is in the nest now?
   How many baby birds are in the nest?
   Mother Bird was a big bird. Are the baby birds big?
   What are they then?
   What do you think they want?
   What do you think Mother Bird is bringing them?
   Is anyone else bringing food?

B. Reading the story

   Again, many new words are introduced, so you will need to help supply them in the initial phases before proceeding to the word study activities. (Be sure to discuss the story after it is read with respect to the above-mentioned questions.)

C. Word study
   1. Write the new words on word cards as they are pointed out and read to you.

LESSON 11

The Baby Birds

The baby birds are in the nest.
Four baby birds are in the nest.
They are little.
They need food.
Here is Father with food.
Here is Mother with food.
The baby birds eat and eat.
They eat all day.

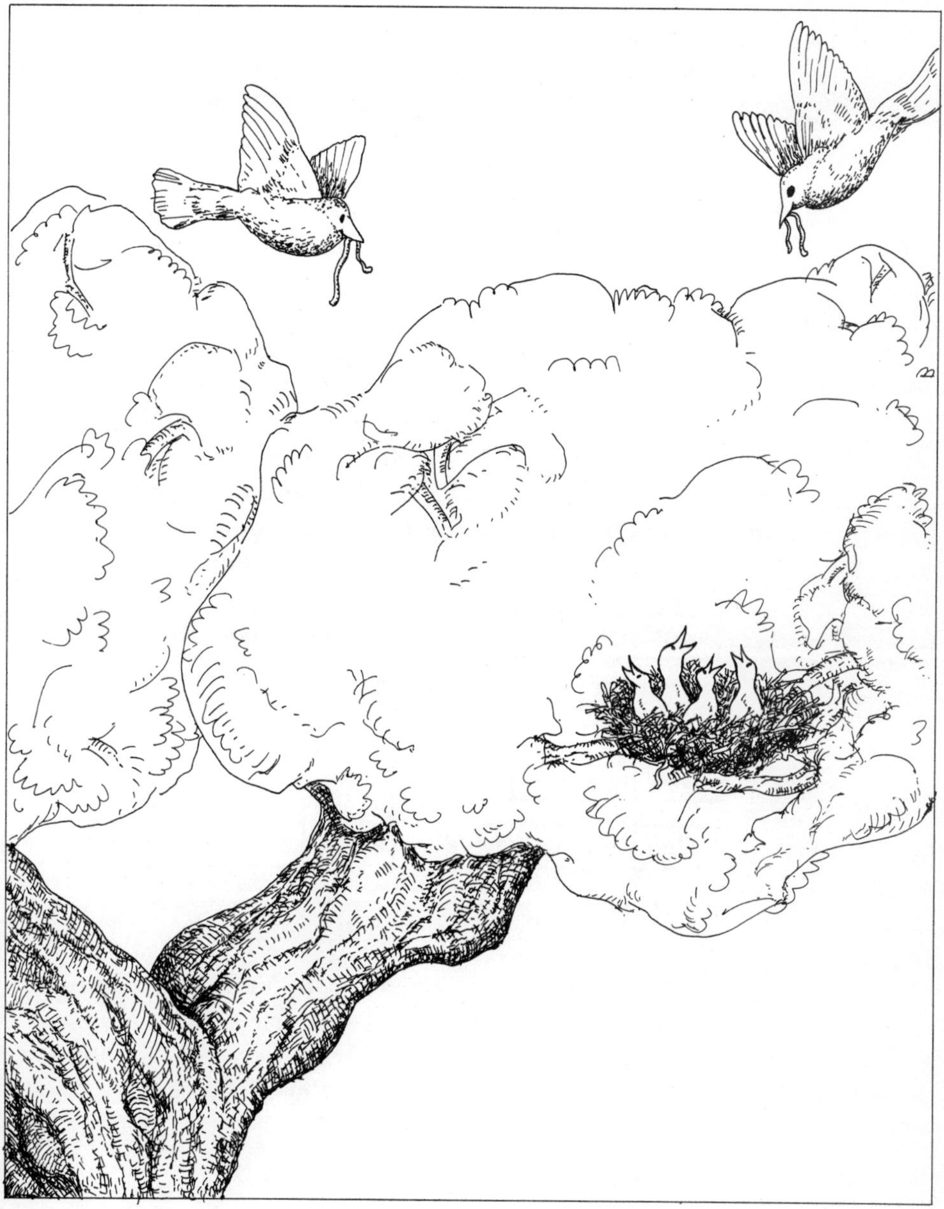

2. Take the "down" and "nest" cards out of the Word Box and ask the child to find a new word from the present story that begins with the same sounds. (Answer: day and need)
*3. Do the same thing for "the." (Answer: they) Discuss or call attention to this **th** sound, which is heard in so many words we use every day (for example, this, them, that, there, those).
*4. Work with the new words until you feel that your child has mastered them, perhaps using one of the games developed earlier which he enjoys, or by making his own sentences. If either of you feel ambitious you might let him construct his own "story" from an assortment of word cards. Since he may need to use the same word more than once you can construct word cards for him on demand. A story he might construct could look something like this:

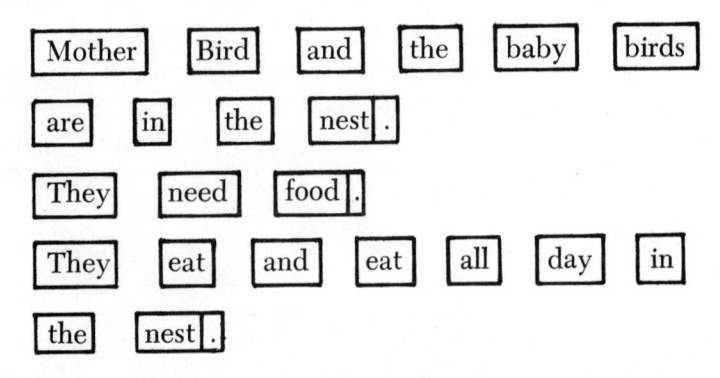

| Mother | Bird | and | the | baby | birds |

| are | in | the | nest | . |

| They | need | food | . |

| They | eat | and | eat | all | day | in |

| the | nest | . |

Have him read his story, discuss it with him, and of course be very supportive. If he makes a sentence which does not make much sense, try to find out what he was attempting to say and help him construct a better sentence.

---

* An asterisk indicates a new activity.

WORD RECOGNITION COMPETENCY
TEST FOR PREPRIMER #1

The fifty words introduced in the first preprimer are listed below. The purpose of this competency test is to find out which of these words are recognized on sight by your child. After giving the test you will be better able to decide whether your child needs to go back through the preceding lessons in Preprimer #1 or has sufficient word knowledge to proceed to Preprimer #2.

There is no need to approach this task any differently than any other study activity or game. The more relaxed your child is, the better indication you will have of what he knows. (The mere idea of a test is enough to intimidate many children.)

HOW TO ADMINISTER THE TEST

The only materials you will need are (1) an index card with a small window cut out of the center in which a single word on the test can be framed without exposing any part of the words immediately above or below it (as in previous tests), and (2) a worksheet upon which you can record the results of the test (one is included for your convenience). You should sit side by side with your child at a table or desk so that he can look at the test and you can record the results.

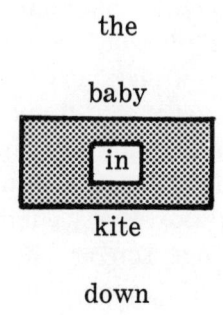

the

baby

[in]

kite

down

Starting at the top of the list of test words, "flash" each word through the word window for about three seconds. When the child says the word or the time limit has expired, proceed to the next word marking your worksheet accordingly. You may find it convenient to use the following symbols to mark the worksheet:

correct response   : +
no response   : −
wrong word   : write the actual word that was said
correct but time exceeded : +T

To use the test you should say something like this:

I am going to show you a list of words one at a time through a little window. Just like in the game shows on TV, tell me each word as soon as you can. If you can't think what the word is by the time I go on to the next one, don't worry about it. We'll learn those words later.

HOW TO EVALUATE THE RESULTS

Count up the number of words your child recognized within the three-second exposure (the number of plus marks on your worksheet). These words constitute his "sight vocabulary." Those words marked minus (−) will need to be retaught and those marked +T will require review and practice. In cases where your child gave the wrong word, *both* words should be retaught.

Regardless of how many words your child knew, tell him he has done well. Be pleased with what he remembered as opposed to disappointed with what he forgot. Let the test results be a learning experience for *you*. You may be surprised that he seemed to know a word in a story, yet now did not recognize it in the test. Maybe you did not spend sufficient time on the word study activities or perhaps your child needed more frequent reviews of all the words in his Word Box. Every child has his individual rates of learning and forgetting. You are in the unique position to learn just how much teaching, repetition, and review he requires.

Included next to every test word on your worksheet is the lesson in which it was introduced. We recommend that at some point you go back and reteach or review those he missed. You may do this before proceeding or, if not too many words were missed, you may choose to slip them in while you are teaching the subsequent lessons. Vocabulary is repeated in all the pre-

Word Recognition Competency Test for Preprimer #1

the	has	Father	little
baby	day	Here	I
food	bird	brown	blue
on	nest	a	will
in	balloon	see	two
green	is	ball	for
Mother	tree	big	sits
kite	They	rabbits	with
down	My	she	need
and	rabbit	four	all
red	white	fly	to
up	one	eat	
he	are	eggs	

Word Recognition Competency Test
Preprimer #1—Worksheet

Date _____ __# correct (+) __% correct = $\frac{\text{\# pluses}}{50}$

Word	Lesson #	Word	Lesson #
the ____	1	are ____	11
baby ____	11	Father ____	10
food ____	10	Here ____	9
on ____	9	brown ____	8
in ____	8	a ____	7
green ____	7	see ____	7
Mother ____	6	ball ____	3
kite ____	1	big ____	5
down ____	2	rabbits ____	6
and ____	3	she ____	9
red ____	4	four ____	9
up ____	1	fly ____	10
he ____	10	eat ____	11
has ____	10	eggs ____	9
day ____	11	little ____	6
Bird ____	9	I ____	7
nest ____	7	blue ____	9
balloon ____	4	will ____	10
is ____	1	two ____	6
tree ____	7	for ____	10
They ____	11	sits ____	9
My ____	5	with ____	11
rabbit ____	5	need ____	11
white ____	5	all ____	11
one ____	6	to ____	10

primers so whichever path you choose there will be many more occasions to learn those words.

A final note: When you are going back to reteach and review, please don't make it a "failing" experience or a boring one for your child. Use activities from the word study sections that he enjoys, and let him practice reading some of the stories he remembers and can show off with, as well as those he has forgotten. Learning to read is not easy, so do your best to reassure him of his ultimate success and to make it a rewarding experience.

HOW TO USE THE RESULTS FOR PLACEMENT IN THE BOOK

If you are not using this book from cover to cover, but want to know *where* in the book to start working with your child, follow these guidelines:

1. If the child knows 45–50 words (90–100%) he does not need to study the first preprimer. Give him the Word Recognition Competency Test at the end of Preprimer #2 (Chapter Seven). Keep a record of the few words he missed so you can teach them later.

2. If the child knows 40–45 words (80–90%) go back only to those lessons in Preprimer #1 (Chapter Six) that present the missed words and pay particular attention to the word study activities. Then administer the Word Recognition Competency Test at the end of Preprimer #2 and follow the accompanying placement directions.

3. If the child knows fewer than forty words (less than 80%) begin teaching him with Preprimer #1 proceeding from the beginning to the end. Then go on to teach Preprimers #2 and #3 (Chapters Seven and Eight).

7

Reading the Second "Book": Preprimer #2

The purpose of Preprimer #2 is much the same as its predecessor's—to increase the child's sight vocabulary, to foster his word attack skills through the use of simple phonics exercises, and to help make him a reflective reader. These objectives will be accomplished basically in the same manner as in Preprimer #1, although Preprimer #2 contains more stories (twenty) and introduces more new words (seventy). One other difference will be immediately apparent as well. These additional words, together with the fifty learned previously, give the stories greater range and intrinsic appeal. They are more like "real" stories and your child will undoubtedly enjoy reading them more.

The stories themselves are divided into two sections, one dealing with a family of five with its pets and another describing their trip to the zoo. If you have worked your way through the first preprimer, you will be well equipped to teach the lessons in Preprimer #2. The routine is basically the same:

1. First, the story is discussed in terms of its probable contents as shown in the accompanying picture. This is done to give the child a *reason* for reading the story.

2. Next, the story is actually read by the child with you supplying words when necessary. Remember as well to discuss the story after it is read, basing this discussion on the questions raised before reading the story.

3. Reread as necessary.

4. Finally, the two of you will engage in word study activities designed to make the child so familiar with the new words introduced via the story that they become part of his sight vocabulary.

Although we suggest that you continue to follow this general framework, we are suggesting considerably greater freedom in selecting the specific activities both for laying the groundwork and for word study. Feel free to improvise in both cases, to use any combinations of the strategies presented in Preprimer #1 to teach lessons in this one, or to employ one of the supplementary activities presented below. If you are working with a more advanced child and skipped Preprimer #1, we strongly recommend that you study both the detailed lesson plan presented at the beginning of Chapter 6 as well as the more abbreviated suggestions for the lessons contained in Preprimer #1 before proceeding.

SUPPLEMENTARY ACTIVITIES FOR
Unit 1—The family

The following activities are designed both to help familiarize your child with the new words presented in each story and to help him review troublesome words already encountered. We suggest that you add these activities to your teaching in order to make your sessions more varied and thereby more interesting. Some activities will be more effective with your child than others and these, of course, are the ones you will use most frequently.

1. Discussing the Picture

The large picture of the family on page 193 affords an excellent opportunity both to stimulate interest in reading the stories in the first preprimer and to familiarize the child with the names of the family members. You will note that we said *familiarize*, not teach. The purpose of this activity is only to make the learning of the names easier once they are introduced in the stories.

Write the names appearing on the introductory drawing, "The Family," on individual cards. Have the child draw the appropriate character on the back of each. Mix the cards and present them one at a time to the child. If he doesn't recognize a name, turn it over and see if he recognizes the drawing. If he is correct in guessing the name the first time, turn the card over and say, for example: *You're right. That's Jim!* Continue as long as interest warrants.

2. Sentence Completion

Using the word cards make some simple sentences by leaving out a new word introduced in any given story. Let the child supply an appropriate word card for the blank and then have him read the sentence to be certain that it "makes sense." You may start with actual sentences used in the story and progress to new ones. (This is also an excellent review activity for words that consistently prove troublesome). Since several words will often logically fit a blank, it may be wise to structure the activity by giving the child only three word cards with which to work, only one of which makes sense. Another variation consists of actually seeing how many words the child can find which will grammatically complete the sentence. In either case, have him read the sentence once he has completed it.

Examples might be:
The _____ live here. (children)
This is a little white _____. (house)
I see all the _____. (family)
Father, Mother, and the children _____ here. (live)

3. Third Person Singular, Present Tense

The child has encountered the convention of adding an s to a word to denote plurality with "rabbit"–"rabbits." In Lesson #2 of this preprimer he will encounter a somewhat different situation with "live"–"lives" where the s serves another function entirely. This is not an easy concept for most very young children to grasp, but one which they do acquire in their speech patterns at an early age. Therefore, you can use the child's knowledge of grammar in the following way. Ask him,

>   *Which is right:* "*Mary play*" or "*Mary plays*"?
>   *Which is right:* "*He run*" or "*He runs*"?
>   *Which is right:* "*I sleep*" or "*I sleeps*"?

First do the above exercise orally and then write the two alternate forms of the sentences (or others you make up) and have the child read them and tell you which one is right and fix the one that's wrong by adding or crossing out an s. At this stage it is probably wise not to attempt to verbalize any grammatical rules for this particular point.

4. Filing the Word Cards

As more and more new words are introduced, the finding of a specific word in the Word Box may become increasingly difficult for you and your child. One strategy for saving time and also reviewing the words learned to date is simply to use alphabetical dividers for the Word Box. These can be either purchased in any office supply store or constructed with cards that are larger than those used for word cards yet still fit in your box. At the top of each card write the capital and lower-case version of one letter so that it can be seen above the word cards when placed in the box. (If you purchase dividers you will probably have to add the lower-case version.) From this point on, when your child reads a story with new words he knows, give him the word cards to file in the box (otherwise he will place them in the "new word" envelope as described below). You need not specifically teach the concept of alphabetical order at this point, but help him go through the letters, reciting the alphabet aloud until he finds the right place. It would probably also be a good idea to let him help you file all the cards learned to date. When you do so ask him to read each word and say the letter with which it begins.

5. "Jail"

During the process of having your child file all the words he has studied, you will undoubtedly discover that he has forgotten many of the words he once knew. Many children get a kick out of putting these words in an envelope labeled "Jail" and placing it in the front of their Word Box. To get a word out of "Jail" all he need do is identify the word correctly at another time. This strategy offers an excellent way to review difficult words periodically, or at each session if you wish. A question like *Would you like to see who you can get out of "Jail" today?* will often be met with a great deal of enthusiasm. When a previously unknown word is correctly identified you will, of course, liberate it with a great deal of fanfare and have the child place it in its appropriate envelope.

6. New Words

A similar strategy can be used with new words. You have already marked an envelope "new words" in which all words introduced in a lesson for the first time are placed, regardless of whether or not the child seems to know them. During the next session, if he can recognize the word on the first try, he may file it under the appropriate letter in the Word Box as always. If he cannot, have him place it in "Jail." (When placing a word in the "Jail" envelope do so in a playful manner, as though it is the word's fault, not your child's, for not recognizing it.) The two of you can then work on setting it free at your leisure. (Actually most words are repeated again and again in subsequent stories, so ample opportunities will be afforded over and above review activities. You can also structure your lessons to help teach your child words with which he is having difficulty by reviewing the "Jail" envelope yourself periodically, and making a point of including them in phonics and other word study drills.)

7. Irregular Plurals

Although the child may have mastered plurality by adding "s," some additional help may be needed for irregular formations such as "child"–"children" as introduced in Lesson #5. Whenever such a construction is encountered it should be pointed out. Since most children pick up irregular constructions orally quite easily, approach the problem from an oral perspective such as *Tom, Jim, and Pam are children. If I wanted to speak only of Pam what would I call her?* If the child doesn't answer right away, make a sentence where the child has to supply the construction orally, such as *Pam is a* _____. (If your child answers "girl" you'll have to try again.) You might say, *Could I say you are a children?* This will probably lead him to say that no he would be called a child. Lead him to the realization that "child" is one and "children" is more than one.

8. Reading Specific Sentences for a Purpose

To vary the routine of rereading the story and increase your child's comprehension of what he is reading, you might occasionally give instructions to read specific sentences. If you decided to adopt such a strategy for Lesson Five, for example, you might ask the child to:

    a. *Read the sentence that has Tom's name in it.*
    b. *Read the sentence that tells who lives with the family.*
    c. *Read the sentence that tells who the children love.*
    d. *Read a sentence that has "one" for the first word.*
    e. *Do you see another sentence that begins with "one"? Read it.*

9. Reading with Expression

Eventually you will want your child to be able to read with some expression. Don't rush into this; it's enough that he simply be able to read at all at this stage and to be able to reflect upon what he reads. You might occasionally try to help his reading delivery, however, when you come upon a story that he reads unusually well or seems to enjoy more than usual. When this combination of events occurs you might ask him:

Now read the story again and try to let your voice sound just like you are talking to me.

If he has a great deal of trouble you could demonstrate how the story could have been read with more expression. Do not run this activity into the ground; there are much more important things for him to learn at this stage.

10. Silent Reading

Your child had undoubtedly observed you and others reading silently to yourselves. Eventually you are going to want your child to be able to read silently when he is advanced enough to read books and stories on his own. Not only will he be able to read more quickly, he will also enjoy the story line more by being able to concentrate on one less thing (orally pronouncing the words).

You may begin to foster this skill by occasionally asking him to reread a story to himself. A good way to see to it that he is indeed reading is to give him a reason for doing so, such as *Read this story to yourself and tell me what the mother does* (in Lesson #4, for example). If he does not know a particular word, simply have him point it out and supply it. Don't be concerned if he moves his lips while reading "to himself" or even softly pronounces the words. Most children do this when they start out; they gradually learn to avoid both behaviors.

11. Continued Phonics Training: Similarities and Differences

Each time a new word is introduced you have the option of emphasizing its initial sound. Be especially careful to do this with new words that begin with sounds not commonly encountered up to this point. If the child seems to have no trouble hearing an initial sound, throw in some words with different beginnings and see if he can hear differences as well as similarities. If you are working with the "l" sound, for example, after satisfying yourself that the child hears that "love," "live," and "lives" all begin with the same sound, throw in some word pairs that differ initially. For example you could tell the child:

> *I am going to give you some pairs of words. The first word will always begin with the l sound. If the second word begins with an l, say yes. If it begins with another letter, say no.*

When reading the first word, start out by saying it in a normal fashion but if the child does not hear the differences, exaggerate the first sound in each word and have him watch your lips at the same time.

    live—light   (yes)
    letter—love (yes)
    little—big   (no)
    little—line   (yes)
    love—move   (no)

12. TH

When "this" is introduced in Lesson #6 it might be a good idea to take the opportunity to work on the "th" words again. Ask the child to look in the **Tt** envelope and take out all the words beginning with "th." He should remove "the" and "they." After having him read these words along with "this," construct some sentences with blanks which could be filled with one of the three words. For example:

    Pam is _____ girl. (the)
    _____ children like to play. (The)
    _____ love mother. (They)
    _____ is my house. (This)

Now have the child supply the appropriate word card. If he makes an error, have him read the sentence asking him if it makes "sense."

New Words Introduced in Unit 1

Lesson #1: children, family, house, live
Lesson #2: Jim, Jip, lives, Meow-Meow, Pam, Tom
Lesson #3: love, loves, man
Lesson #4: help, helps
Lesson #5: child
Lesson #6: boy, boys, this
Lesson #7: girl, play, plays

UNIT 1
The Family

Father   Mother

Tom   Pam   Jim

House

LESSON 1

The Family

The family lives in the house.
They all live here.
Father and Mother live here.
The children live here.
They live in the little white house.

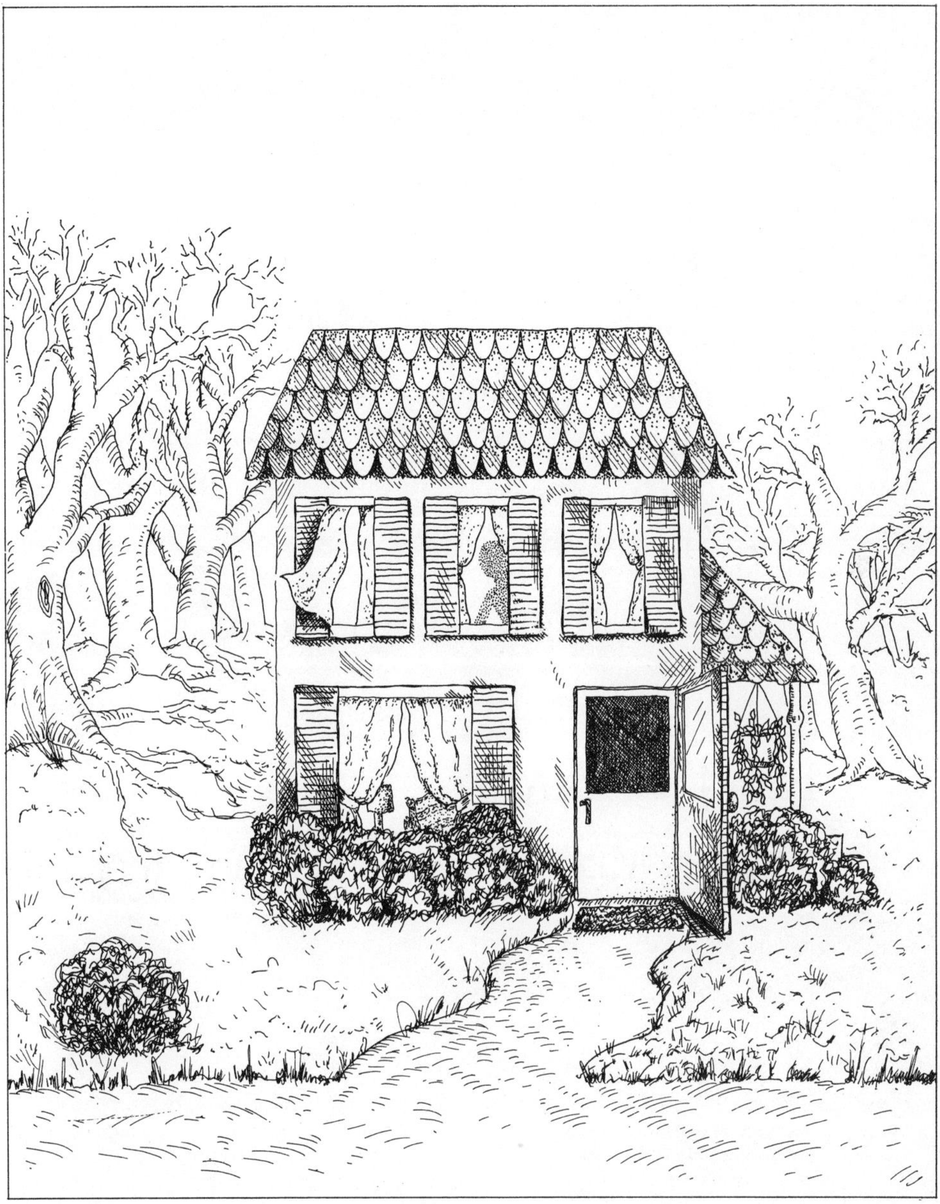

LESSON 2

The House

The house is little.

It is white.

The family lives here.

Mother and Father live here.

Jim and Tom live here.

Pam lives here.

Jip and Meow-Meow live here, too.

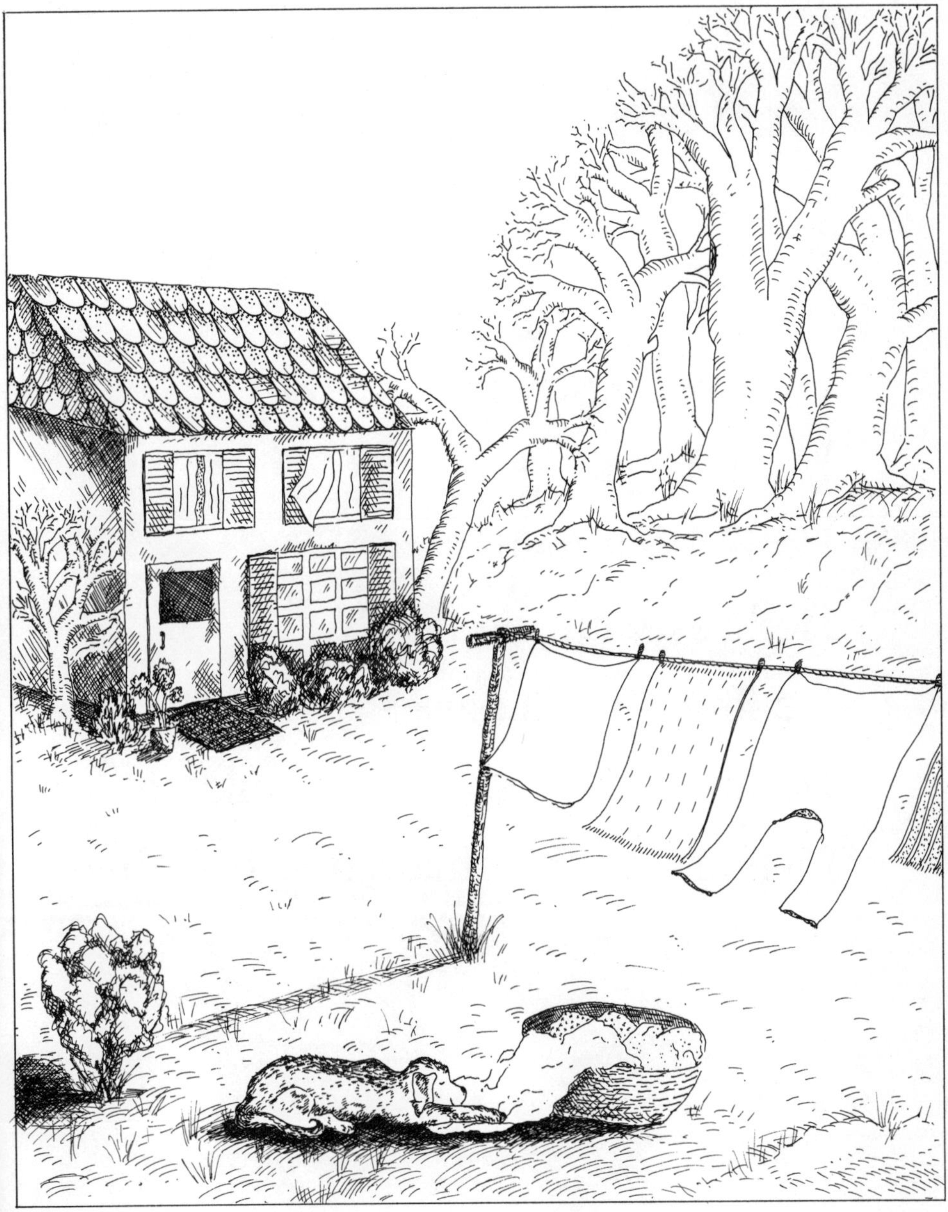

LESSON 3

Father

Here is Father.

He is a man.

He is a big man.

He lives with the family.

He loves the family.

He loves Mother and the children.

Mother and the children love Father.

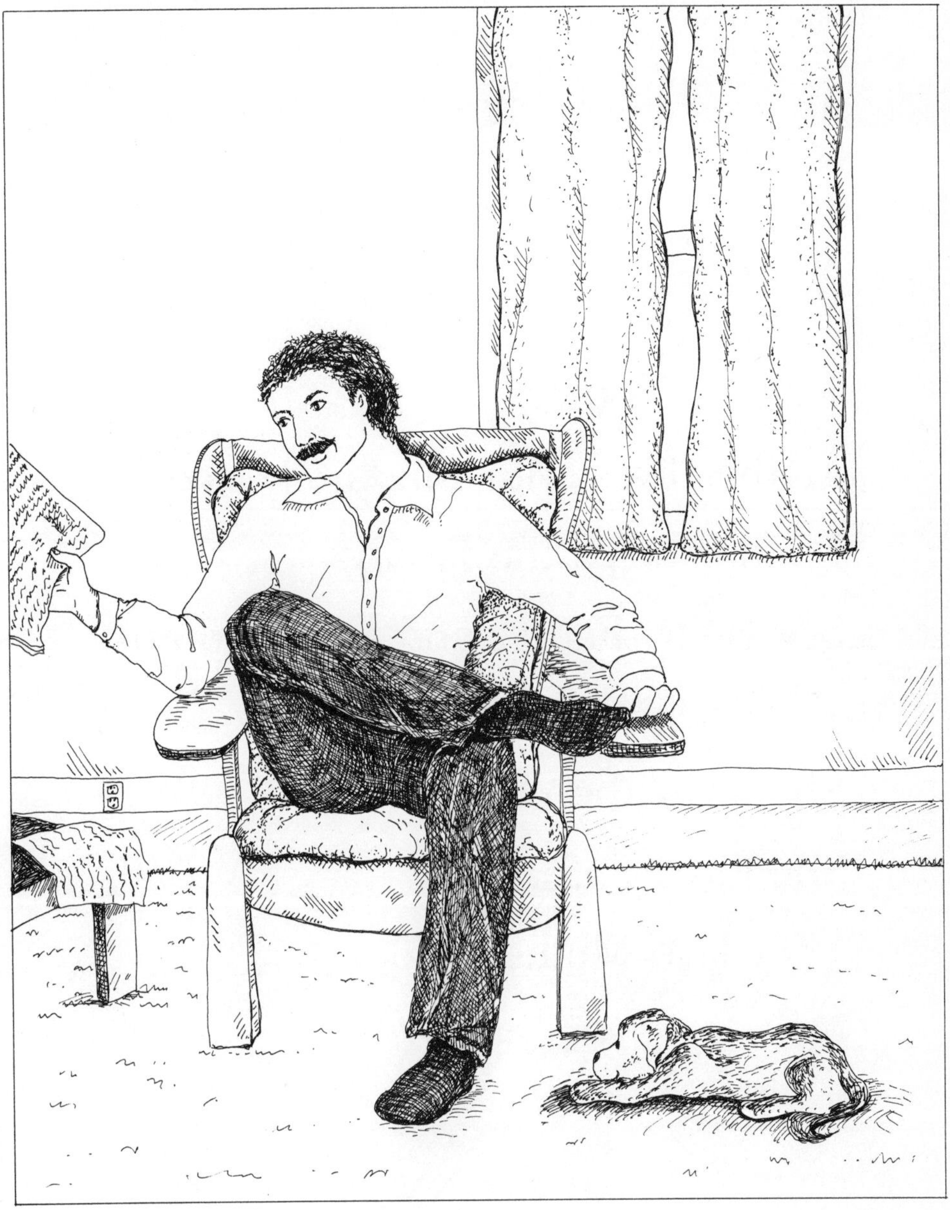

LESSON 4

Mother

Here is Mother.
Mother lives with the family, too.
Mother helps the family.
She helps Father and the children.
They help Mother.
She loves the children.
She loves Father.
They love Mother.

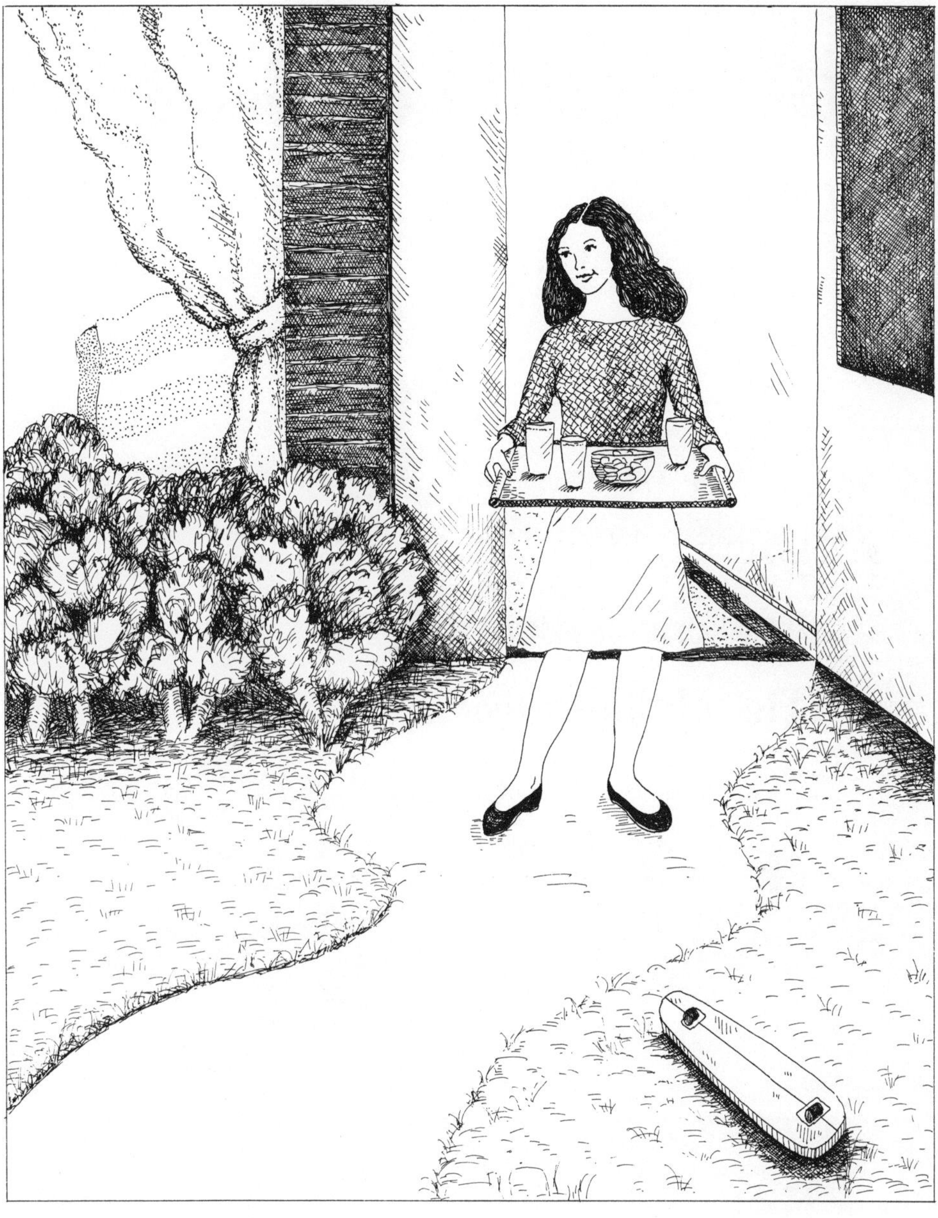

LESSON 5

The Children

Here are the children.
One child is Tom.
One child is Jim.
And one is Pam.
The children live with the family.
They love the family.

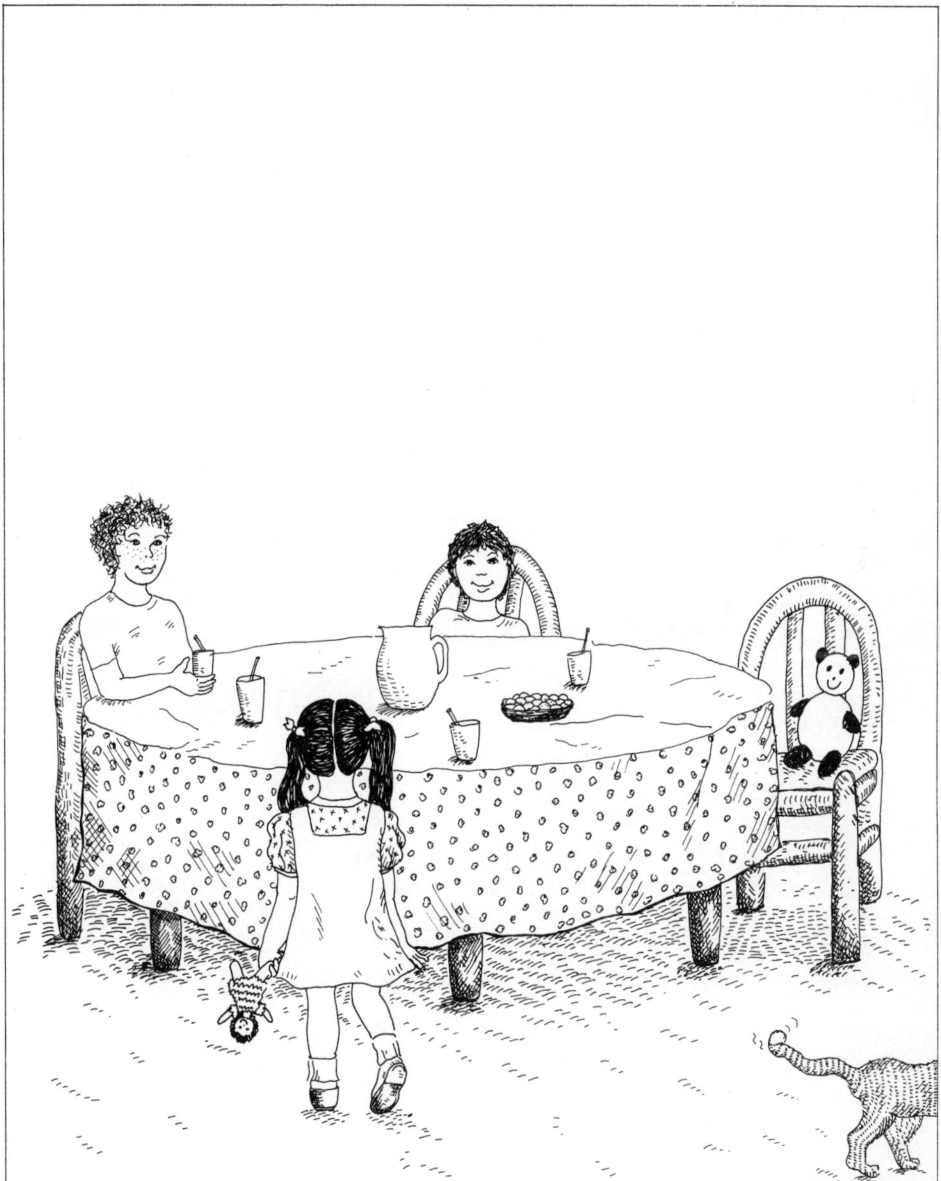

Boys

Here are the boys.

Two boys are in this family.

Tom is a big boy.

Jim is not big.

The boys like to live here.

They love the family.

They help the family.

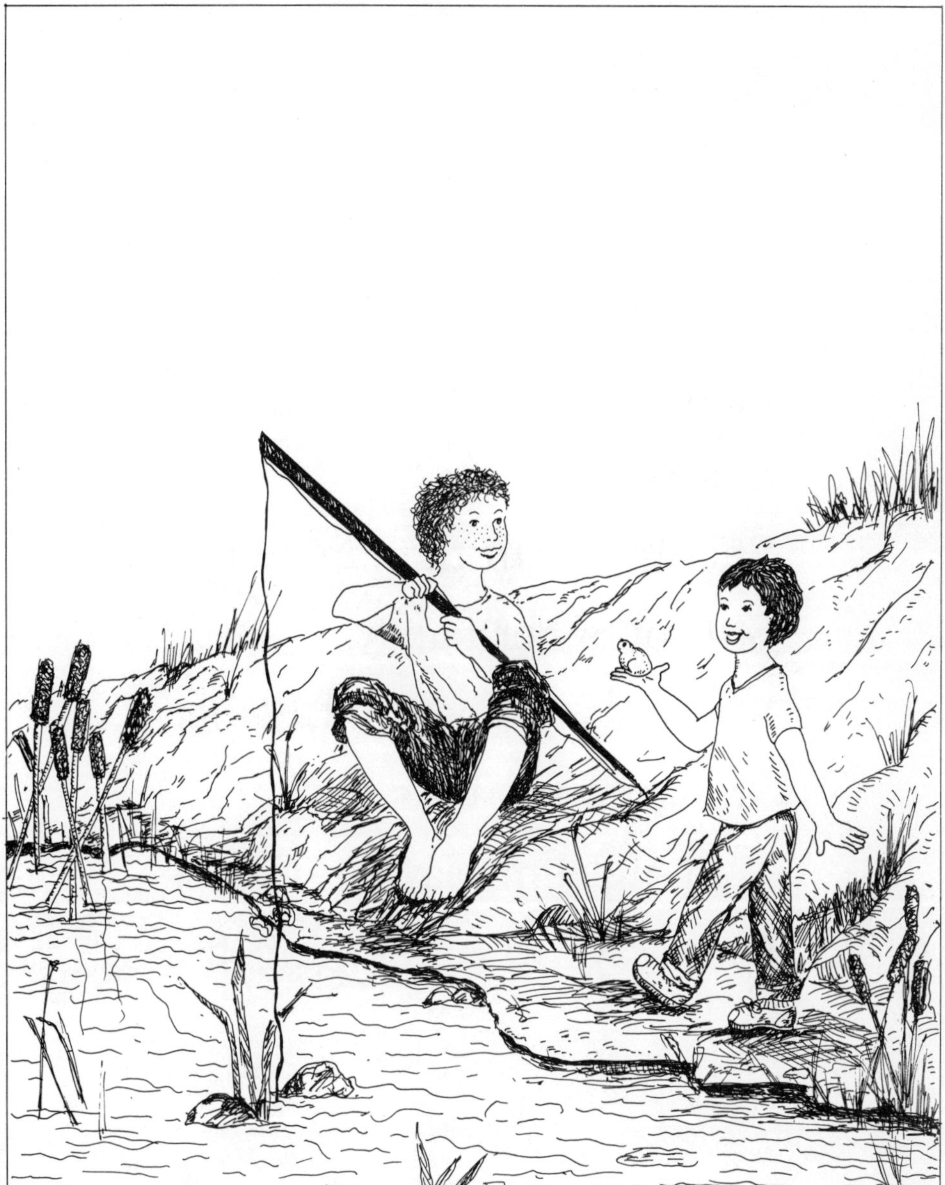

LESSON 7

Pam

Pam is a girl.
She is little.
She lives with the family too.
She loves her family.
She loves Mother and Father.
She loves the boys too.
Tom and Jim play with Pam.
Pam plays with Tom and Jim.

REVIEW

1. Twenty-two new words have been presented in the preceding seven lessons of Unit 1. Remove all twenty-two from the Word Box, mix them up, and present them to the child, one at a time, at a relaxed pace. Put those words he does not know in a separate pile, and mark them off on the form provided below. Then take each troublesome word and discuss it together to try to find a way in which the child will recognize the word in the future. (If there are several such words don't work on all of them the same day.) Here are some suggestions:

   a. Ask him what sound it starts with. Have him apply any additional phonics skills he possesses.

   b. Have him go back to the story in which it was introduced (the page number should be marked on the word card) and try to read it in the story (and repeat any word study activities that are applicable).

   c. Help him identify any features that physically distinguish the word, such as its length and its shape.

   d. Have him see if any part of the word could be broken off and a new word formed (such parts would be endings such as **-s, -ed, -ing**).

   e. Ask him to think of any other words he knows that are similar in the way they look or sound. Write the words down and have him compare spellings and sounds.

2. Below is an alphabetical list of the words introduced in this unit. We suggest you copy the list, mark the words which gave your child trouble, and keep it handy so that you can conduct extra practice in their use as you continue with other lessons in this chapter.

___boy	___girl	___Jip	___man	___this
___boys	___help	___live	___Meow-Meow	___Tom
___child	___helps	___lives	___Pam	
___children	___house	___love	___play	
___family	___Jim	___loves	___plays	

3. Count the number of words your child identified correctly and divide it by the total number of words shown (twenty-two) to compute the percentage of success. Record the figure with your other performance records. If the percentage is unusually low this is a good indication that you are trying to go too fast. Take more time in the future to read the stories and work through the word study activities.

4. After working on the words your child missed, test him on them again. If he misses any again, make a special note of them so that you can work on them in the future, or put them in the "Jail" envelope.

5. Here is an activity that will foster the use of context clues in word recognition as well as develop visual discrimination of fine differences between words. You can conduct it orally by reading the sentences and having the child choose between three word cards, or by writing out the sentences and word choices as we have below. The directions are: *Read* (or, *listen to*) *the sentence and circle* (or, *point to*) *the right word.* (If difficulty is encountered have the child say the sentence aloud with each of the choices and decide which one sounds the best and makes the most sense.)

a. Jim is a   boys / girl / boy

b. Jim, Tom, and Pam are   boys / children / child

c. The children   help / helps / fly   in the house.

d. Baby bird   live / sit / lives   in the nest.

e. Jip plays with Meow-Meow.
       white
       play

f. Tom little to play.
       loves
       love

SUPPLEMENTARY ACTIVITY FOR
Unit 2—The pets

This part of Preprimer #2 introduces the children's pets. The primary purposes of the introductory drawing on page 215 are to (1) motivate the child to want to read the stories which follow, and (2) familiarize him with some of the names to be introduced in those stories.

Actually both goals can be accomplished at the same time. Whatever techniques you use to familiarize the child with the pet names, use this time and this opportunity to build anticipation for reading the subsequent stories about them. Almost all children love animals so tell the child that just as the last eight stories told about the family and their activities, these stories tell all about the children's pets. Discuss what each pet looks like, its characteristics, and what it probably likes to do.

In addition to the routine detailed previously, as well as the suggested activities listed for the first preprimer and Unit 1 of the present one, you may wish to incorporate some of the following suggestions in your teaching of the stories in Unit 2:

1. Familiarizing the Child with the Pet Names

You may use the same techniques used with the cover picture in Unit 1, or you can make up some sentences for the child to read involving the names:

> Jip is a pet.
> Meow-Meow is a pet.
> Yellow Duck and Red Hen are pets.
> Little Chick is a pet.
> Red Hen and Little Chick are chickens.
> Is Jip a chicken?

2. Phonics

As always, phonics activities are beneficial for any lesson:

Find a word that begins like "down." (duck)
Find a word that begins like "house." (hen)

The child's word repertoire is getting large enough so that just about any new word can be matched with one already learned with respect to beginning sounds. (We still recommend that you stay away from blends such as "black.")

3. Miscellaneous Facts

These stories contain a wide assortment of facts and relationships which you can teach your child if time and interest allow. For example, if your child hasn't had a lot of experience with farm animals you may need to explain that a baby chicken is often referred to as a chick. Show him that "chick" is really just a shortened version of "chicken." Or, these stories use direct quotations or conversation for the first time, so you might explain to the child that a quotation mark (") indicates that a character is actually talking, and that there are always two: the first tells when the character begins to talk and the second one tells when the conversation is over. Again, feel free either to explain or not to explain these matters. Use your judgment. Sometimes such explanations can add interest to a lesson, sometimes they are merely distracting. (The same is true for the comma. If the child expresses interest, tell him its function is to tell the reader when to pause. If it remains unnoticed, use your judgment when to introduce it.)

4. Using the Context to Guess Words

The stories are becoming complex enough for the child to be able to use context clues to figure out unknown words. If upon reading the first sentence in the first story, for example, the child reads: "Jip is a _____," you might ask him *What is Jip?* Hopefully he will answer "dog," in which case you should tell him to try it and see if the word fits in the sentence. If he should answer that "Jip is a pet," say *Yes, but this word begins like "down." Now what is Jip?* A child can get a great deal of mileage out of using context clues coupled with initial letter sounds. It will definitely be worth your while to try to foster this skill.

5. Word Characteristics

Many words have obvious characteristics which, when pointed out to a child, make them easier to remember. With a little thought you can identify these characteristics and use them in your teaching. For example, when "did" is introduced in Lesson #4 you can ask the child to find a word that begins and ends with the same letter. ("Sits" is another.) Similarly, you can ask the child to find a word that rhymes with "me" (he, she, see, and tree) or with "fun" (run) in Lesson #2. (If the child doesn't have a clear concept of rhyme you may introduce it by simply asking for words that "sound the same way at the end.")

6. Continuing to Help the Child Become a Reflective Reader

As a variation of the recurring necessity to ask the child questions about the stories he reads, try having him simply hold up a word card to answer a question (rather than requiring him to verbally answer or read an entire sentence). Taking Lesson #5 as an example, you might instruct him:

Hold up the word cards that answer my questions:

   a. *What does Yellow Duck like to do?* (swim)
   b. *Can Pam swim?* (no)
   c. *How can Yellow Duck swim?* (fast)

7. The Same Technique Applied to Word Study

What word told that Pam didn't know how to swim? (cannot)
What word in the story is the opposite of yes? (no)

New Words Introduced in Unit 2

Lesson #1: cat, chicken, dog, Little Chick, pets, Red Hen, Yellow Duck
Lesson #2: fun, jump, run
Lesson #3: black, can, fast, high, runs
Lesson #4: come, did, me, played, said
Lesson #5: cannot, no, swim
Lesson #6: chickens, cluck, comes, eat, feed, get, look, pen, Thank you

UNIT 2
The Pets

Red Hen　　Little Chick

Meow-Meow　Yellow Duck　　Jip

LESSON 1

The Pets

Jip is a dog.
Meow-Meow is a cat.
Yellow duck is a little duck.
Red Hen is a big chicken.
Baby Chick is a little chicken.

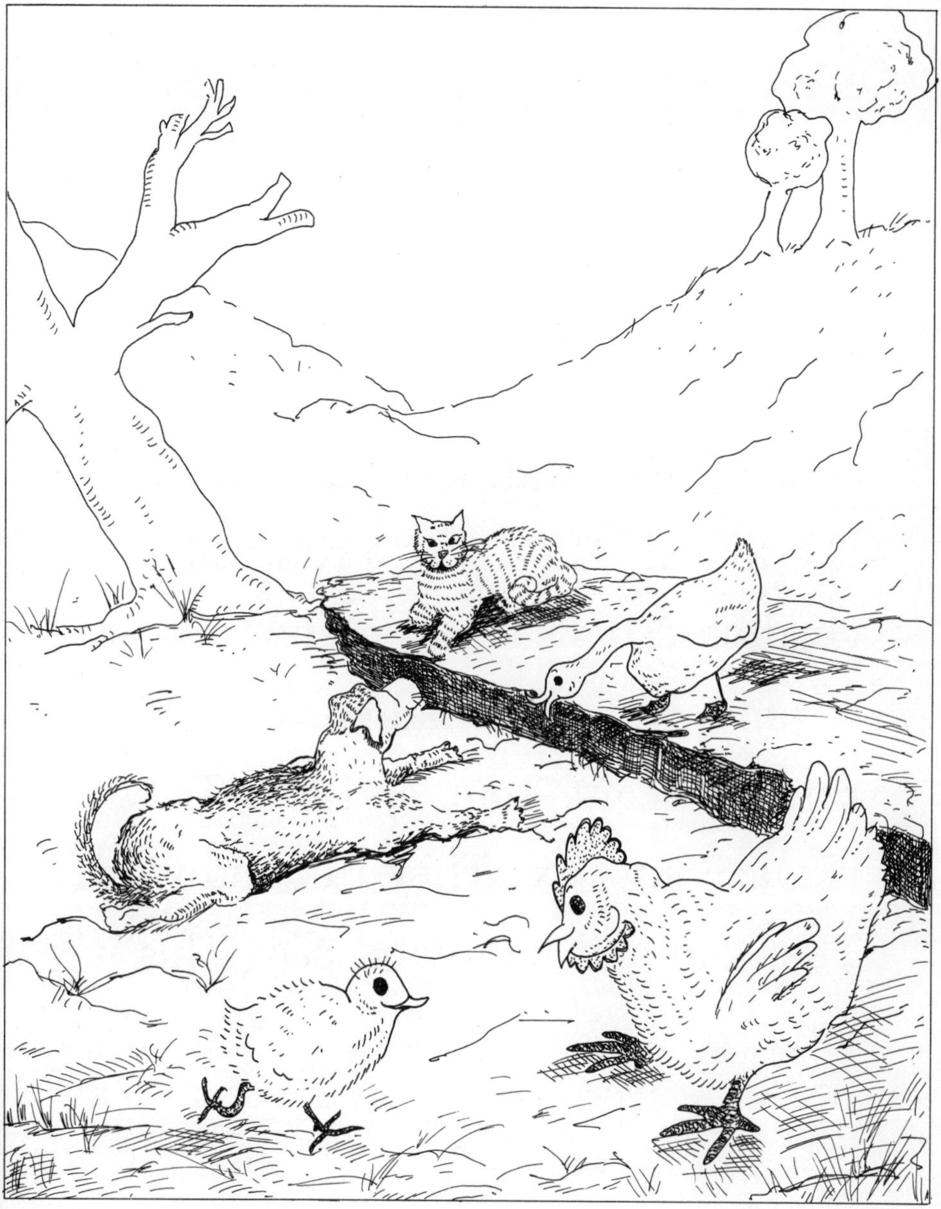

LESSON 2

Fun

The pets play with the children. The children play with the pets. The pets like to run. They like to run with the children. They like to jump. They like to jump with the children. They like to run with Pam, Tom, and Jim. They like to jump, too. They run and jump. They run and jump and play. This is fun.

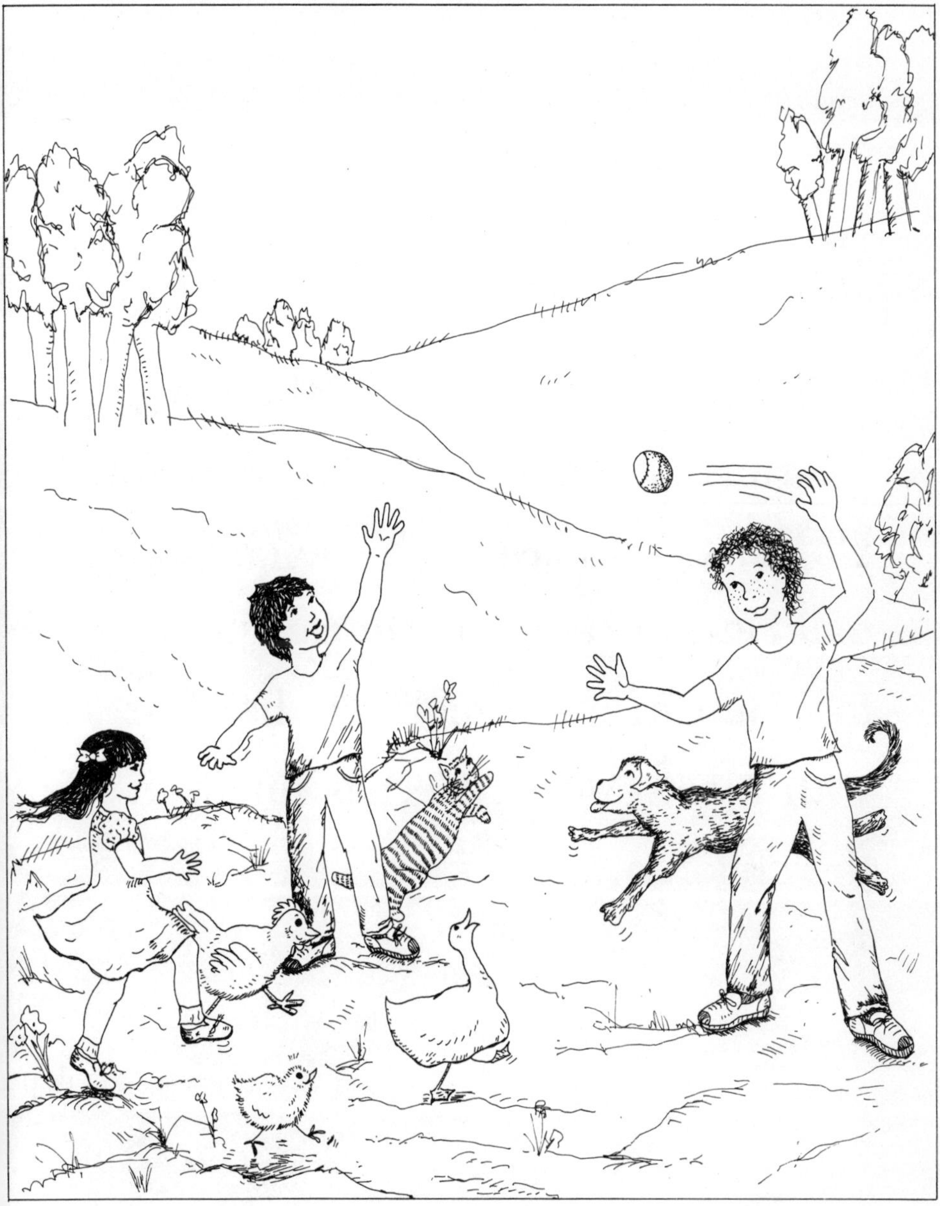

LESSON 3

Jip

Jip is a little black and white dog. He runs and plays with Meow-Meow. He runs and plays with the children, too. He can run fast. He can jump too. He can jump high. He has fun with Meow-Meow. He has fun with the children too.

221

Meow-Meow

"Come, Meow-Meow! Come, Meow-Meow," said Pam. "Come and play! Come and play with me! Come and play with Jip and me!"

"Meow-Meow," said the cat. "I like to play. I like to play with Jip. I like to play with Pam. I will play."

And she did.

She did play with Jip and Pam. They played with the ball. They played with the balloon. They played and played. The cat, the dog, and the little girl played all day.

223

Yellow Duck

Yellow Duck is here. She can swim. She can swim fast. She likes to swim.

Yellow Duck ran to Jip. She said, "Come Jip. Come and swim." Jip said, "No, no! I cannot swim."

She ran to Meow-Meow and said, "Come and swim." Meow-Meow said, "No, no! I cannot swim."

Yellow Duck ran to Pam and said, "Come, Pam. Come and swim." Pam said, "No, no Yellow Duck! I cannot swim. You swim."

And she did.

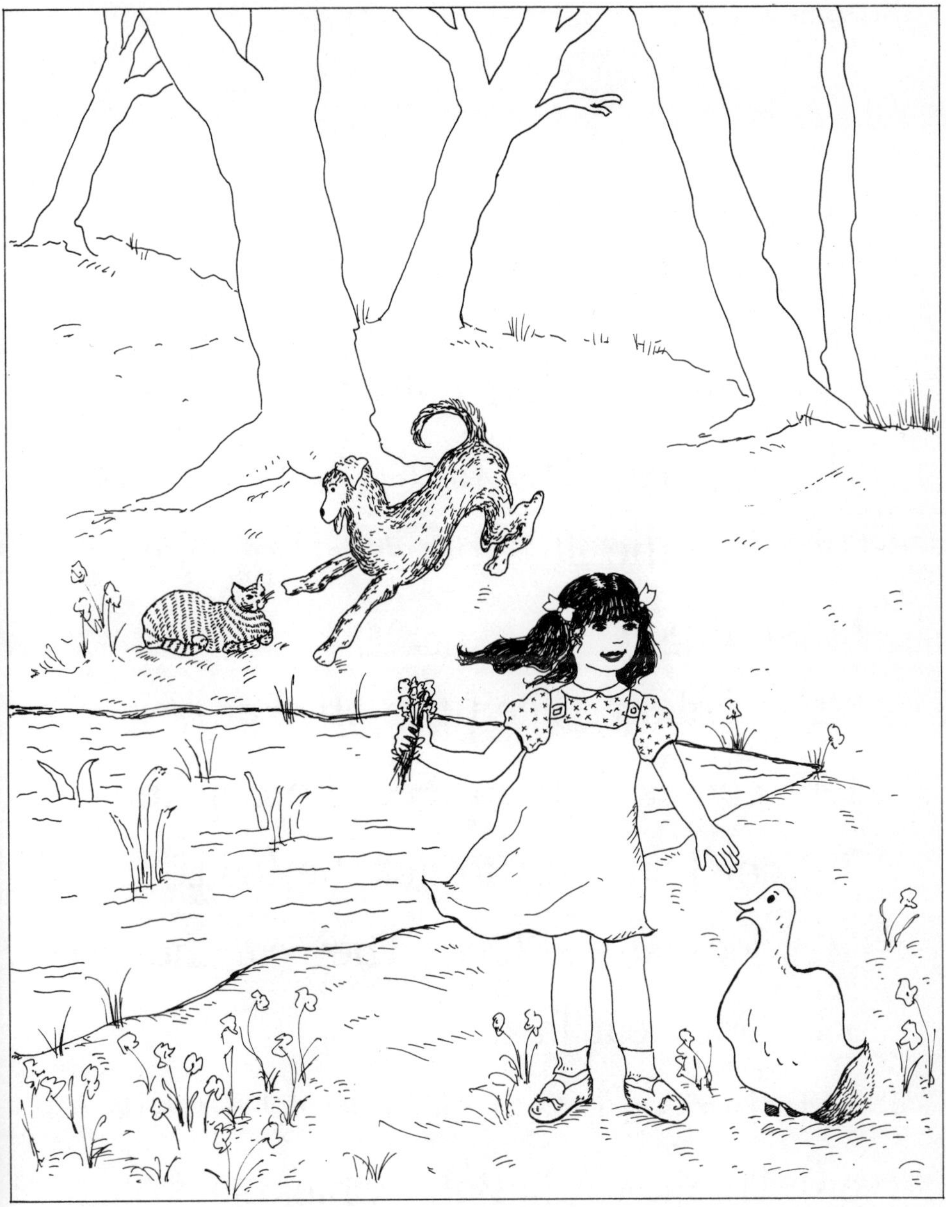

LESSON 6

Mother Hen and Baby Chick

Mother Hen and Baby Chick live in a little house. The house is a little pen. They like the little house. They like the little pen.

The children feed the chickens. Here comes Jim to feed the chickens. The chickens run to get the food. They look at the food. They eat the food. They eat fast.

Mother said, "Cluck! Cluck! Thank you! Thank you!" Baby Chick said "Thank you" too.

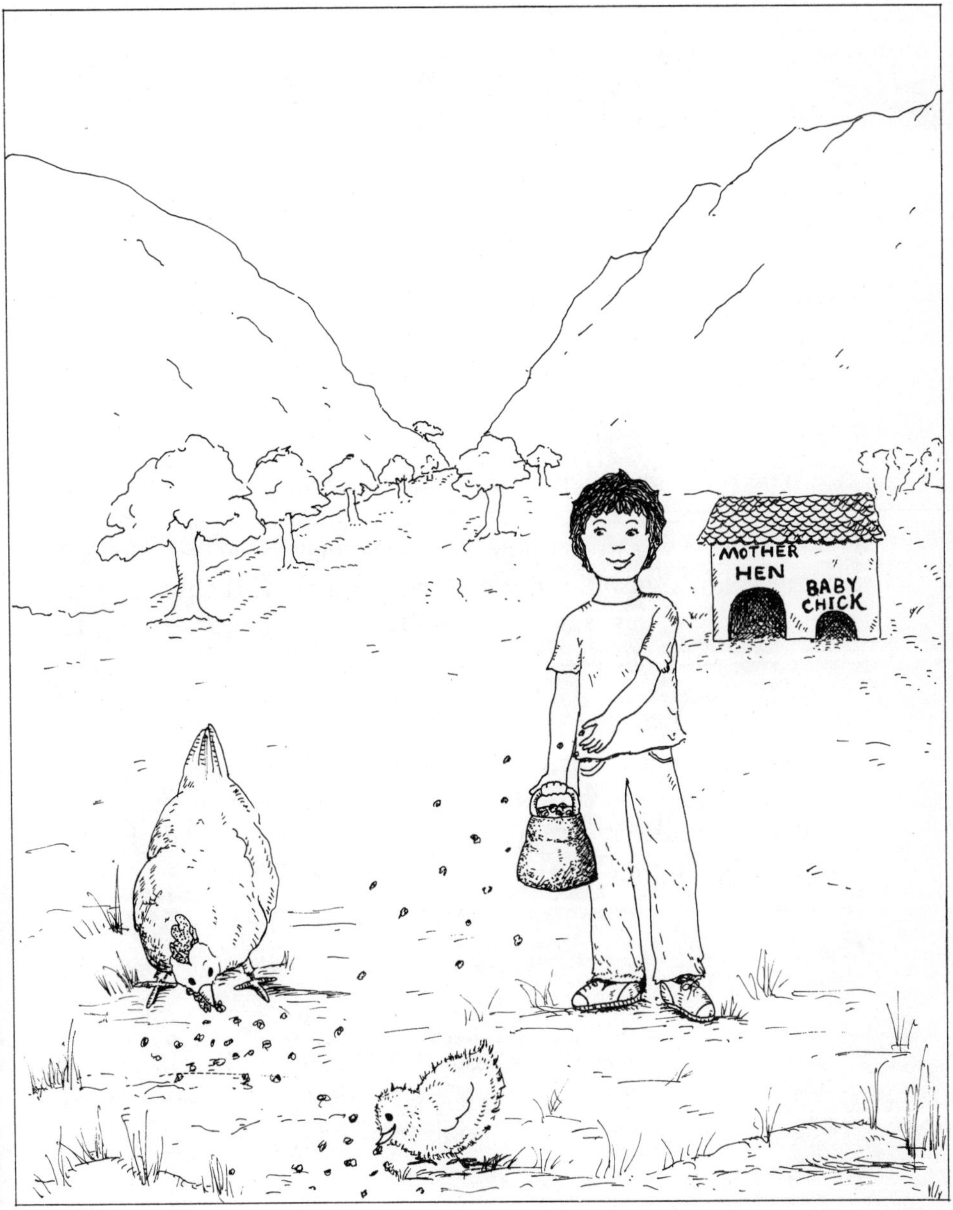
MOTHER
HEN
BABY
CHICK

REVIEW

1. Take the thirty-five word cards representing the words introduced in Unit 2 from the Word Box. Show them to the child, one at a time, giving him enough time to identify each without feeling pressured. Place all the words with which he has trouble in a separate stack.

When he doesn't know a word tell it to him and ask him to look at it carefully. If it has some unusual characteristic, call attention to it. If not, identify a word that he does know which either begins or ends with the same sound.

2. When you have finished, count the number of words he identified correctly, and divide it by the total number of words shown (thirty-five) to compute the percentage of success. Record the figure with your other performance records. If the percentage is unusually low this is a good indication that you are trying to go too fast. Slow up and add more word study activities in the future.

3. Below is an alphabetical list of the words introduced in this unit. We suggest you copy the list, mark the words which gave your child trouble, and keep it handy so that you can administer extra practice in their use as you continue with other lessons in this chapter.

___black	___cluck	___fast	___look	___run
___can	___come	___feed	___me	___runs
___cannot	___comes	___fun	___no	___said
___cat	___dog	___get	___pen	___swim
___chick	___did	___hen	___pets	___Thank
___chicken	___duck	___high	___played	___yellow
___chickens	___eat	___jump	___red	___you

4. Below are some simple sentences for the child to read which contain the words introduced in Unit 2 in new contexts. (Don't have him read them all at the same time.)

I see the pets.

Come black dog.

The chickens eat the food.

Pam will feed the hen and the baby chick.

Here comes Yellow Duck.

Did the pet jump high?

"No no," said Jim.

Black dog said, "Thank you."

I cannot get them.

You can run fast.

Little Duck runs fast, too.

"Swim swim," said little duck.

Here comes a chicken.

The boy cannot get in the pen.

The hen said "Cluck, Cluck."

The pet is not a duck.

Pam will look for them.

The chickens are in the pen.

I can play with them.

Then Little Duck said, "Feed me."

The children play with the pets.

5. After working on these sentences, go through those word cards with which the child had trouble the first time. Place a second mark next to any missed a second time (on the alphabetized list), put them either in the "New Words" or "Jail" envelope, and give extra practice in subsequent lessons.

SUPPLEMENTARY ACTIVITIES FOR
Unit 3—The zoo

The stories in this section deal with our family's trip to the zoo. If your child has been to a zoo his memories of that experience will provide an excellent way of generating discussion and enthusiasm for reading the stories.

The fact that the zoo in this unit contains domestic animals may lend an element of surprise for the child, so we suggest that you do not tell him that during your discussion. If your child has not visited a zoo in person, chances are that he is very familiar with animals from watching television. Use whatever background experiences are available to foster interest in reading the unit.

We suggest that you follow the same routine for teaching the stories that you have in the past, remembering not to skimp on the word study activities, especially if the child missed more than five words in the last review exercise. One change you will notice is the fact that the stories are continuing to grow in length and complexity. If you are dealing with a very young child or one with a limited attention span, you may wish to spend more than one session reading any given story. We have tried to counter this by introducing only nineteen new words in this unit in order to allow the child to consolidate his other skills; but any time you feel that a lesson is too long or too short you should adjust your teaching in any way you please to meet your child's needs. Some other suggestions for the eight stories comprising Unit 3 follow.

1. Using Known Words to Decipher New Ones

Occasionally a new word can be discovered by using existing sounds already in the child's repertoire. It is a good idea to give the child practice in this skill whenever possible. In Lesson #1, for example, when "stay" is introduced you might remind your child that the word begins like "stop" (or ask him what word it begins like) and ends like "play." If he is helped to put the two sounds together he will undoubtedly recognize the word.

2. Opposites

The child's sight vocabulary is expanding to the point where he knows enough words to study the concept of *opposite*. Write two columns of words, one of which contains opposites of the other, and have the child draw a line connecting the pairs. For example,

stay	no
ride	go
yes	walk
up	down

(You can accomplish the same objective by having him use word cards and simply match the appropriate cards.)

3. Consonant Substitution

A word like "car" can be used to generate new words through consonant substitution. Write "car" on a sheet of paper and say:

We can make some new words out of "car" by leaving off the "c" and using another letter instead. Let's try it!

Write "ar" several times in a column, then ask the child to supply another letter to make a new word. As he gives letters, write them in and ask him to read the new word. He will undoubtedly construct some nonsense words, but his reading of them will afford valuable practice in sounding out words. After he reads each word ask him if that is a real word or a "silly" word. Examples of legitimate words which may be constructed in this manner are *b*ar, *f*ar, *j*ar, *t*ar. He may well construct some perfectly good words, such as *m*ar and *p*ar, which he will not recognize.

"May" in Lesson #2 affords an even more fruitful example: *d*ay, *s*ay, *h*ay, *l*ay, *w*ay, *b*ay, *J*ay, *K*ay, *p*ay, *r*ay.

4. Rhyming

Children enjoy words that rhyme and exercises such as the following give the child valuable "sounding" experience as well as affording an opportunity for word study. *Join the words which rhyme with a line.* (You may use cards if you prefer.)

all	so
zoo	ball
go	bat
at	to
we	not
got	see

5. Plurals

Continue to reinforce the concept of plurality occasionally by writing some nouns such as "animal," "duck," and "pet." Have the child read the words, then add an s and have him read them again telling you how the meaning has changed. If you feel adventuresome you might sprinkle a few verbs in the list to demonstrate again that adding an s doesn't always denote more than one.

6. Root Words

When "looked" is introduced in Lesson #7 it might be a good idea to discuss constructions that can be added to words and how these additions change the meaning of the original word. Write a few examples in a column such as "children," "looked," and "animals." (Have the child read them as you write.) Then write the root words next to them and ask the child how the addition changes the meaning:

child*ren*	child
look*ed*	look
animal*s*	animal

New Words Introduced in Unit 3

Lesson #1: car, go, good, oh, ride, stay, zoo
Lesson #2: laughed, may
Lesson #3: got, rode
Lesson #4: *No new words*
Lesson #5: child, pond, swim, water
Lesson #6: pony
Lesson #7: home, looked, time
Lesson #8: *No new words*

LESSON 1

A Ride to the Zoo

Father came home. He said, "We will go to the zoo."

Mother said, "I cannot go. You and the children go. I will stay at home. I will stay with the pets."

Father said to the children, "We will ride to the zoo. We will ride to the zoo in the car."

Pam said, "Oh! Oh!"

Tom said, "Good, good!"

Jim said, "Oh, good! We will ride to the zoo in the car."

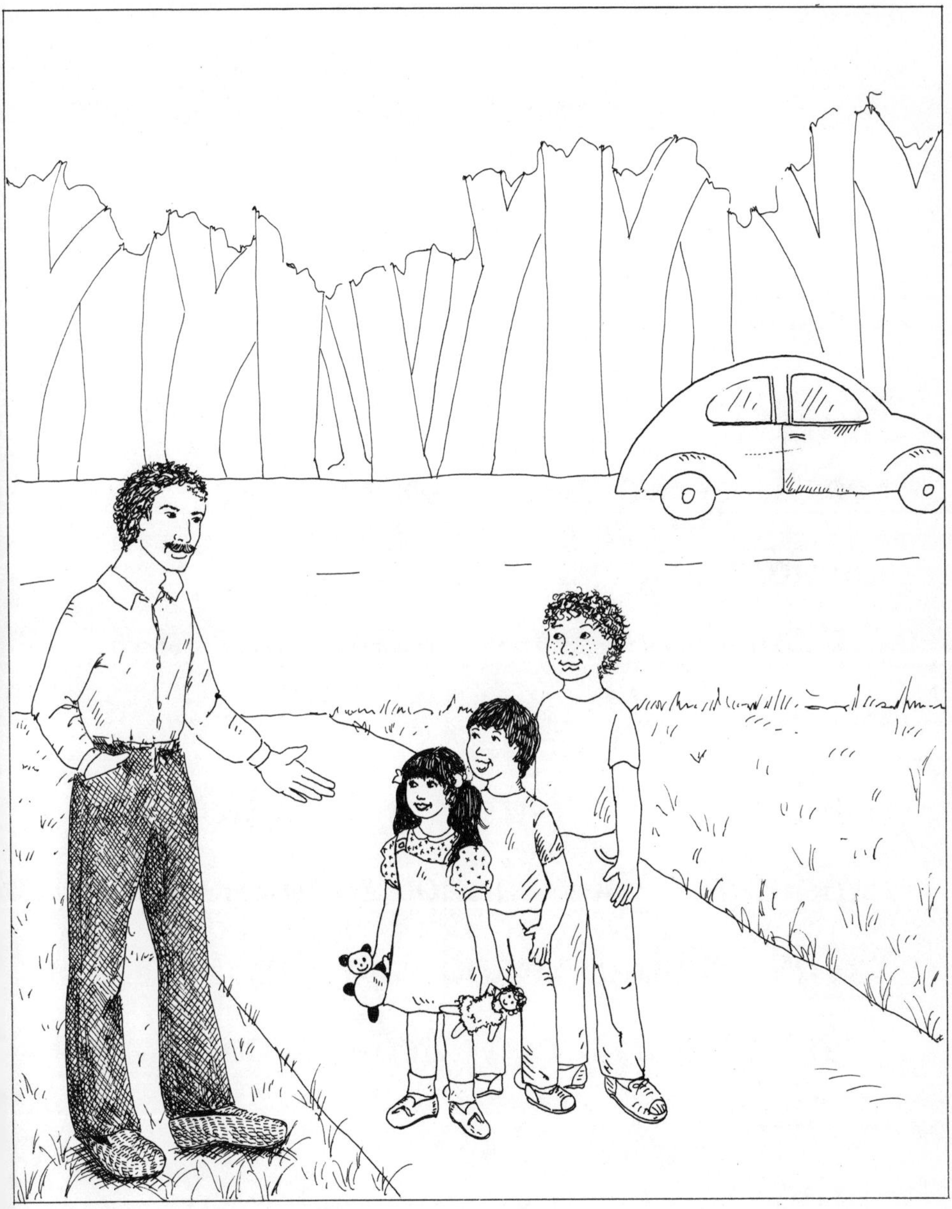

May the Pets Go?

Jip ran to Father. Meow-Meow ran to Father. They wanted to go to the zoo. They wanted to go with the children.

Pam asked, "May the pets go? May they go to the zoo?"

Father said, "No, Pam. The pets cannot go. They cannot go to the zoo."

Father laughed and said, "Jip is not a zoo animal. Meow-Meow is not a zoo animal."

Pam laughed too. She said, "No, they are not zoo animals. They are pets."

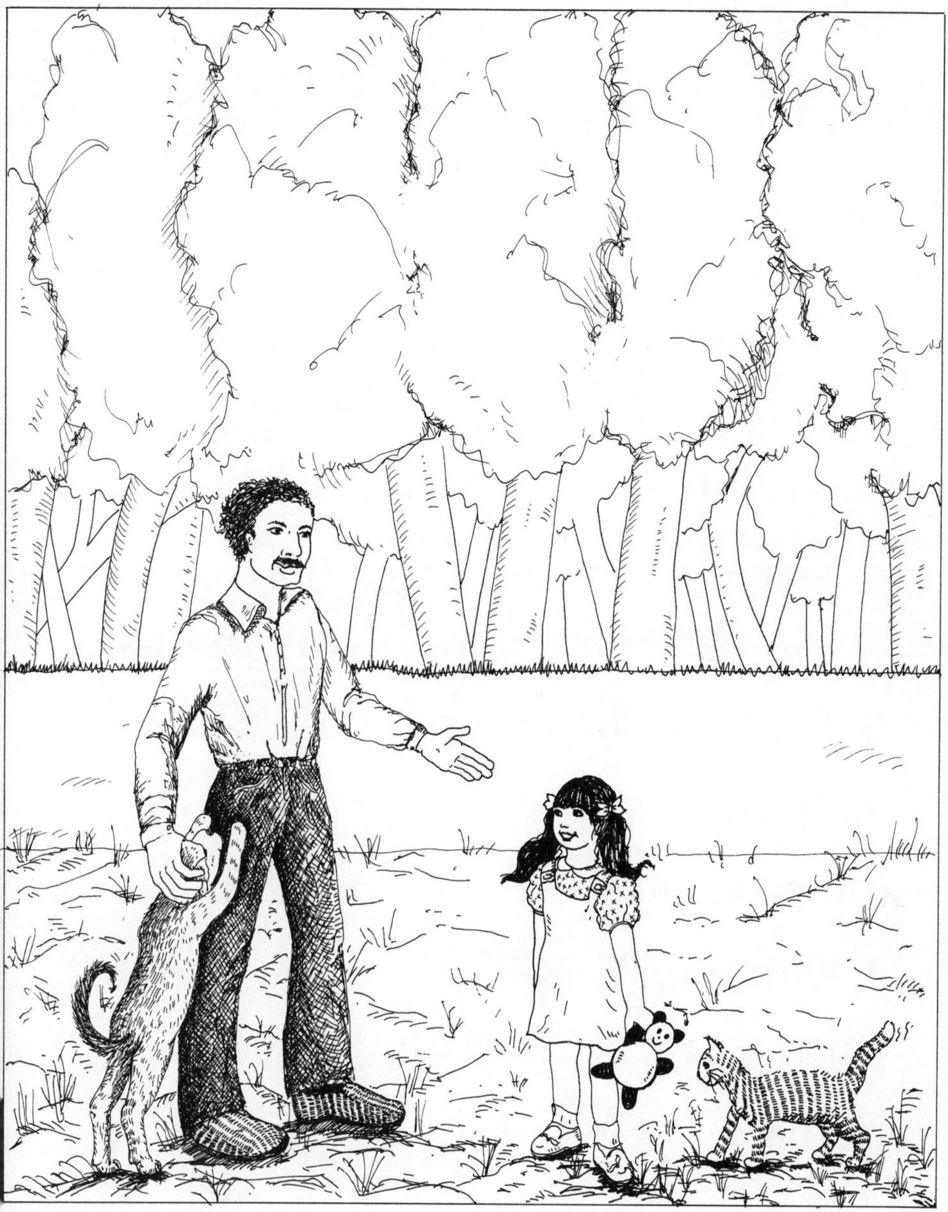

LESSON 3

The Ride to the Zoo

Father got in the car. He said, "Come on children. Get in the car. Get in and we will ride to the zoo."

The children got in the car and rode to the zoo. The children said, "We will see the animals at the zoo. We will see the zoo animals. We will see big animals at the zoo. We will see little animals. We will see all the zoo animals. Come and we will go fast."

And they did.

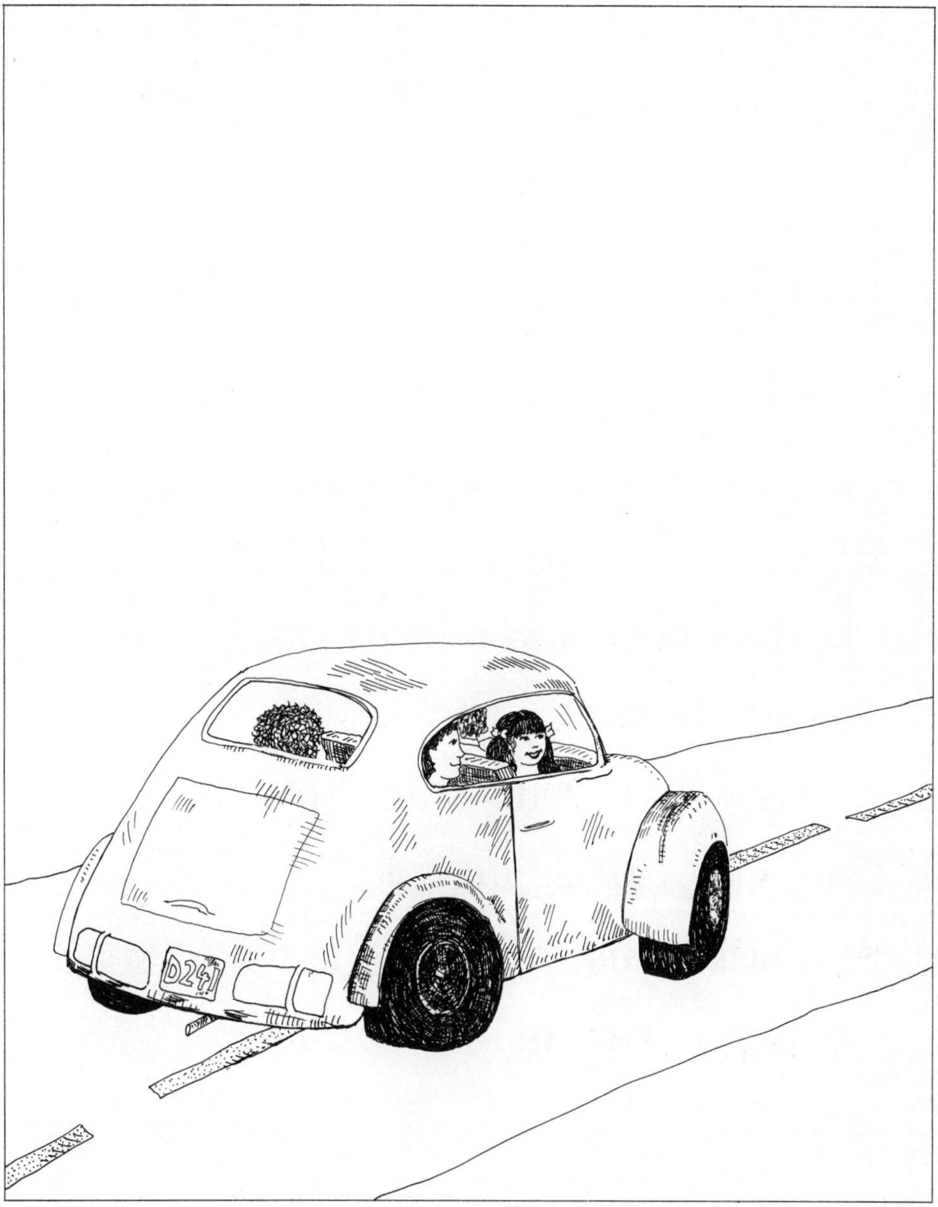
D241

Ducks at the Zoo

Here is the zoo. Look at the ducks. Here are big ducks and little ducks. They saw white ducks. They saw father ducks and mother ducks. They saw baby ducks, too.

Pam said, "Ducks are not zoo animals. Ducks are pets."

Father said, "This zoo is for children. The animals are for children."

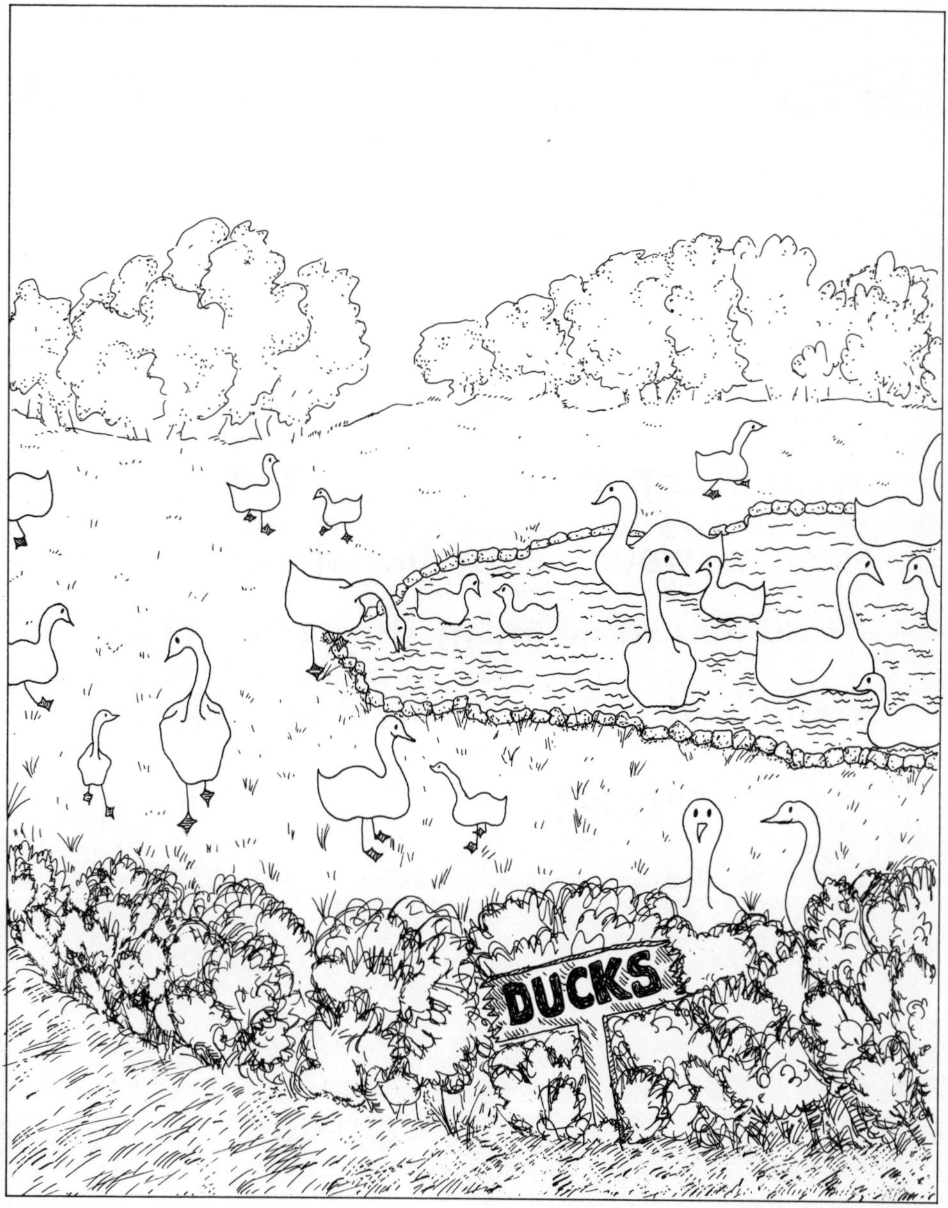
DUCKS

LESSON 5

In the Pond

The ducks were in a pond. They were in a pond of water. The ducks like the water. They like the pond. They like to swim in the pond. They swim and swim. The children like to see the ducks swim.

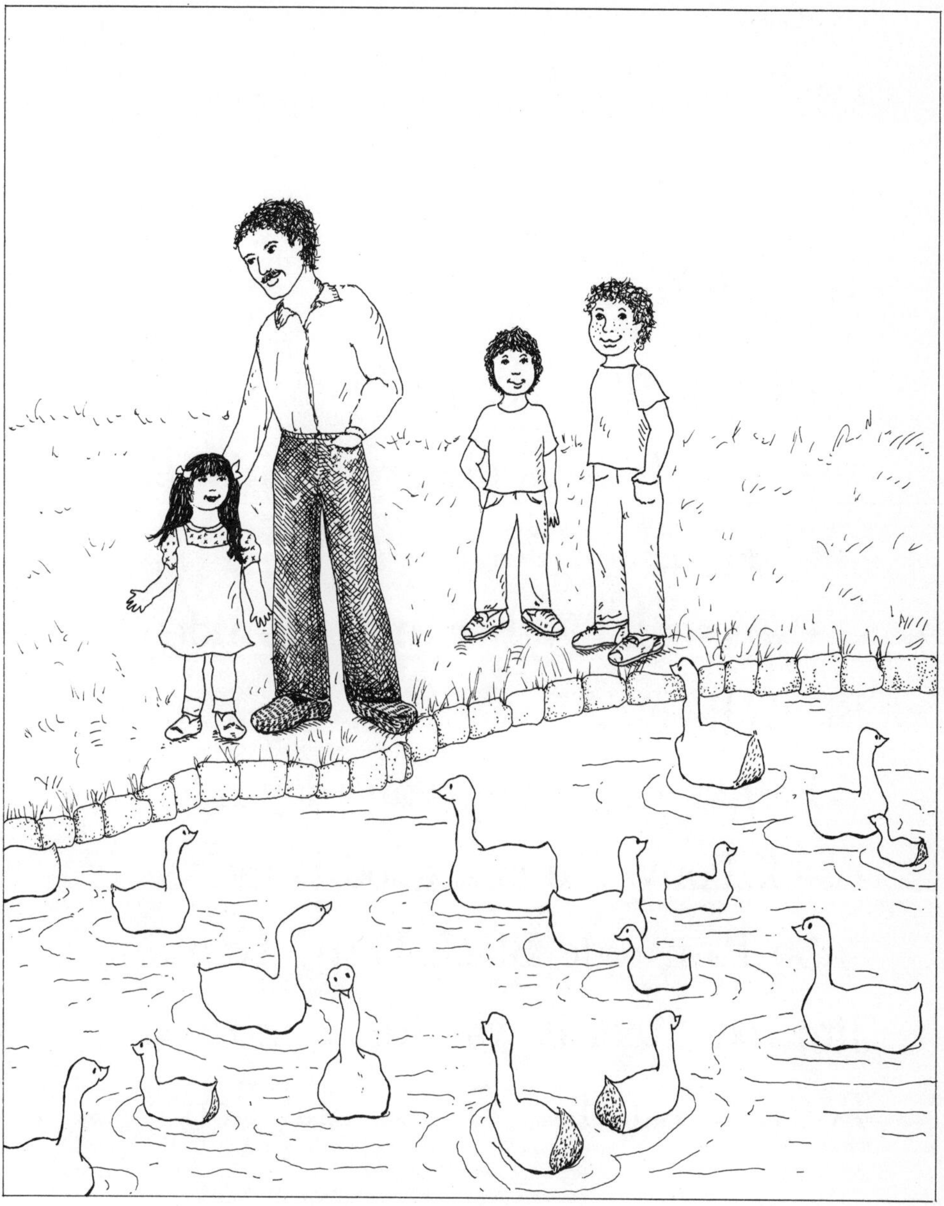

LESSSON 6

The Pony

Here is Black Pony. Black Pony is in the zoo. He likes children. Children can ride Black Pony.

Pam said, "Father, may we ride Black Pony?"

Father said, "Yes, you may ride Black Pony. He is a good pony."

So Pam rode Black Pony. Tom and Jim rode, too. It was fun to ride Black Pony. It was fun to ride and ride.

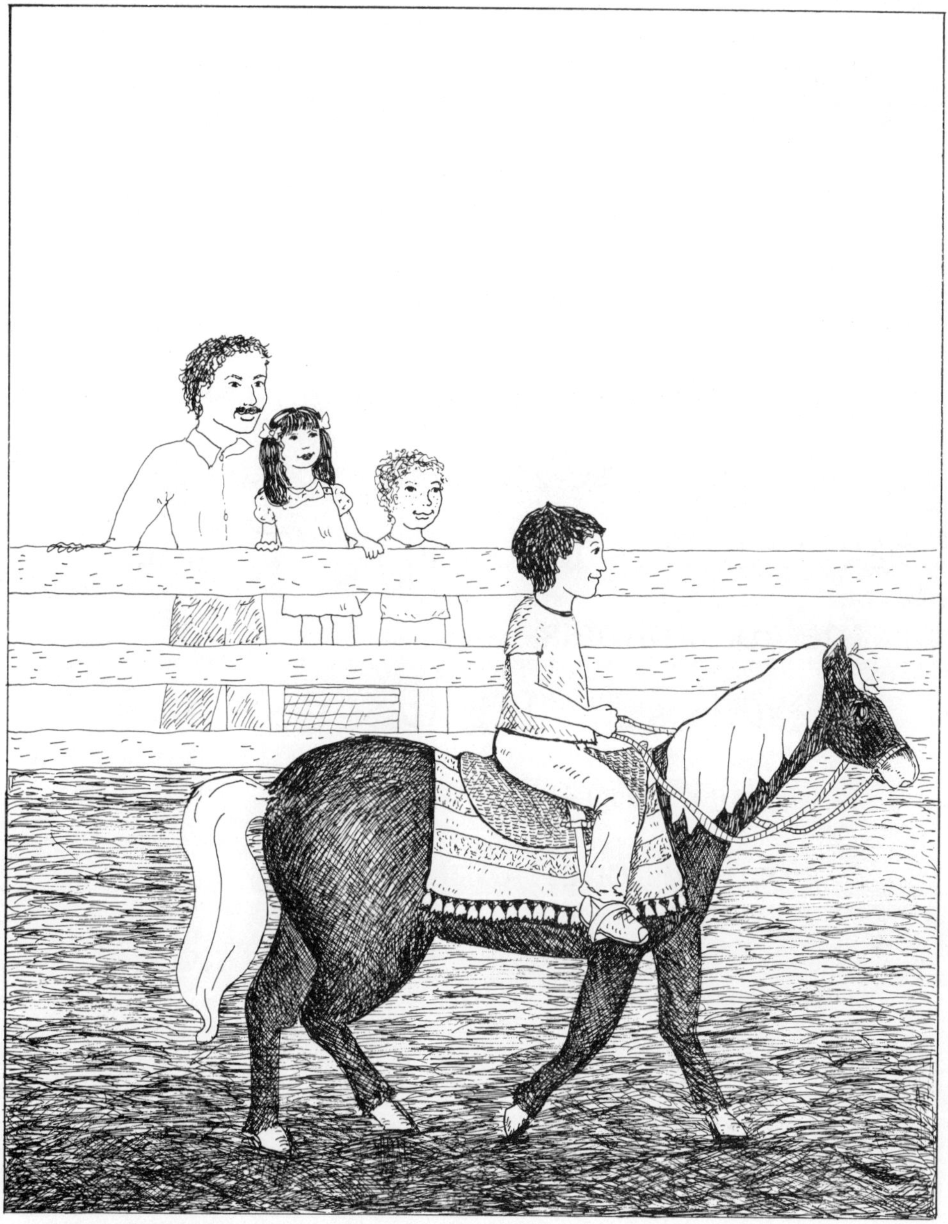

LESSON 7

Time to Go Home

The children looked at all the animals in the zoo. They looked and looked. They liked the zoo. They liked the zoo animals.

Father said, "It is time to go. It is time to go home."

So they rode home.

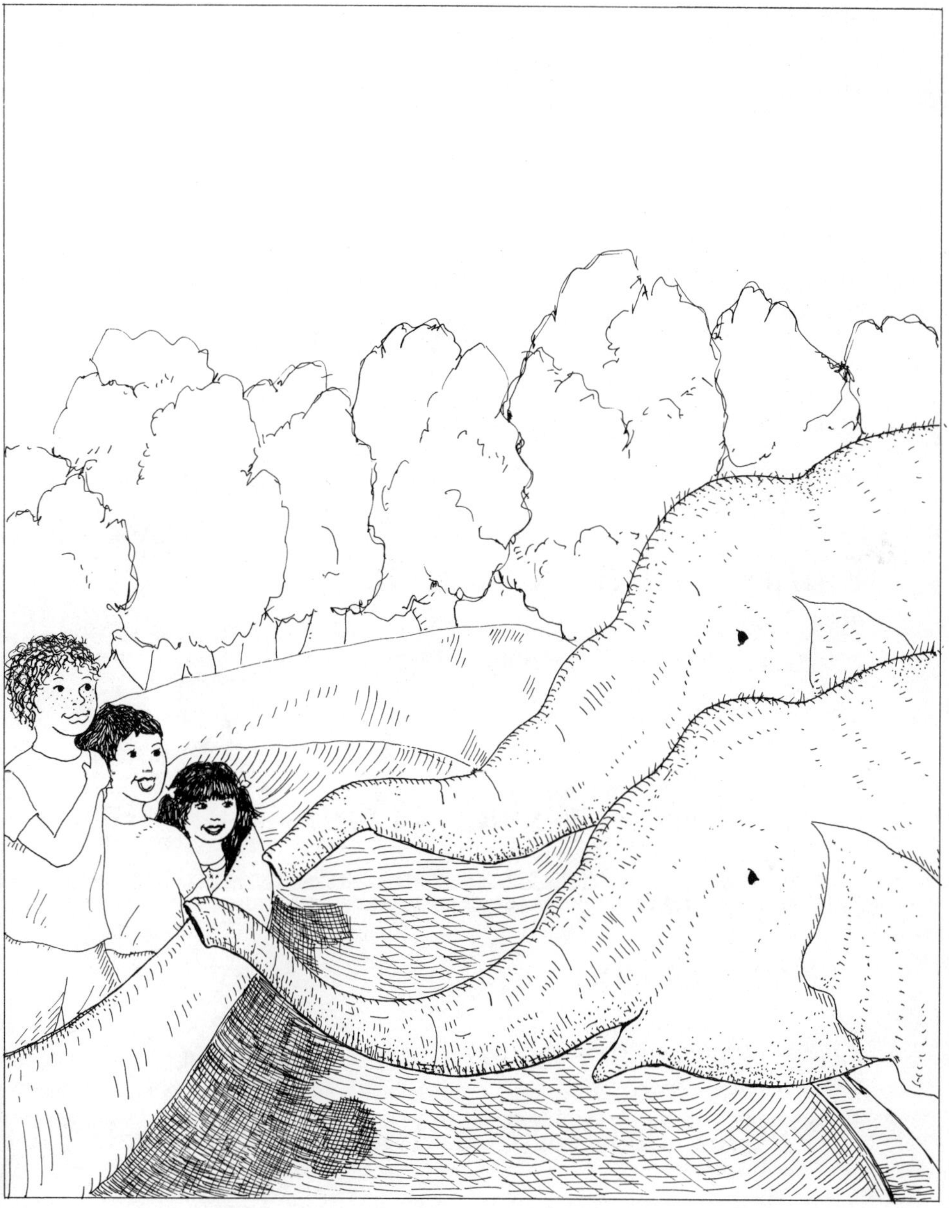

LESSON 8

At Home

Here are the children. Here is Father. They are home.

Jip and Meow-Meow ran to see Father and the children.

Pam said, "Good, Jip! Good, Meow-Meow! You are good pets."

Meow-Meow said, "Thank you." Jip said, "Thank you, too."

Pam laughed and said, "They are pets. Pets can be zoo animals, too."

Father laughed and said, "Yes, pets can be zoo animals at a zoo for children."

249

REVIEW

1. Take the nineteen word cards representing words introduced in Unit 3 from the Word Box and present them to the child one at a time. Place all the words with which he has trouble in a separate stack.

2. As you did previously, compute the percentage of success and record the figure with your other performance records.

3. Reproduce the list below and mark the words which gave your child trouble.

___car	___pony
___child	___ride
___go	___rode
___good	___stay
___got	___swim
___home	___time
___laughed	___water
___looked	___zoo
___may	___oh
___pond	

4. Make sentences containing the words your child missed, or as a variation of that theme you might construct some "silly" sentences using words he has already learned. Examples are:

    The car laughed and laughed.
    Can a pond swim?
    The zoo rode in the car.
    The pond got into the car.

Or, examples of proper sentences:

    The children got into the car.
    May we go?
    I rode to the zoo.
    Stay in the car.
    It is a good zoo.
    The ducks swim in the water.

5. After working on the words your child missed, test him again on only those words. If he misses any again, make a special note of them so that you can work on them in the future, or put them in the "Jail" envelope.

6. Other optional review activities might include work with rhyming words such as having the child read the following pairs.

ride—side
got—not
zoo—too
go—no
car—far
may—stay

7. Another, more advanced, activity could involve working with word endings. You could say to the child, for example, *Look at these words and see how the s, ing, and ed change the words.* (Discuss the change in meaning with him and have him use each word in a sentence.)

look	looks	looking	looked
play	plays	playing	played
stay	stays	staying	stayed
help	helps	helping	helped

8. If time permits, review the function of adding an s to a noun. *The s changes the word from meaning one to meaning more than one.* Have the child read them.

boy—boys
girl—girls
ball—balls
day—days
rabbit—rabbits
kite—kites
balloon—balloons
bird—birds
egg—eggs
cat—cats

WORD RECOGNITION COMPETENCY TEST FOR PREPRIMER #2

Listed below are the seventy-one words introduced in the second preprimer. The test is given the same way as that following Preprimer #1 (Chapter Six, page 179). Refer to it for procedures, materials, and directions for evaluating the results.

Word Recognition Competency Test for Preprimer #2

cannot	thank you	plays
child	Yellow Duck	rode
did	can	swim
feed	chickens	water
good	comes	black
home	fast	chicken
laughed	go	come
looked	high	family
me	jump	girl
pen	look	helps
pond	may	Jip
run	Pam	lives

man	Jim	fun
oh	live	got
played	loves	house
ride	no	Little Chick
stay	play	love
Tom	Mother Hen	Meow-Meow
boys	said	pets
cat	time	pony
cluck	boy	runs
eat	car	this
get	children	zoo
help	dog	

Word Recognition Competency Test
Preprimer #2—Worksheet

Date _____ _____ # correct (+)

_____ % correct = $\dfrac{\text{\# pluses}}{50}$

Word	Unit	Lesson #	Word	Unit	Lesson #
cannot _____	2	5	man _____	1	3
child _____	1	5	oh _____	3	1
did _____	2	4	played _____	2	4
feed _____	2	6	ride _____	3	1
good _____	3	1	stay _____	3	1
home _____	3	7	Tom _____	1	2
laughed _____	3	2	boys _____	1	6
looked _____	3	7	cat _____	2	1
me _____	2	4	cluck _____	2	6
pen _____	2	6	eat _____	2	6
pond _____	3	5	get _____	2	6
run _____	2	2	help _____	1	4
thank you _____	2	6	Jim _____	1	2
Yellow Duck _____	2	1	live _____	1	2
can _____	2	3	loves _____	1	3
chickens _____	2	6	no _____	2	5
comes _____	2	6	play _____	1	7
fast _____	2	3	Mother Hen _____	2	1
go _____	3	1	said _____	2	4
high _____	2	3	time _____	3	7
jump _____	2	2	boy _____	1	6
look _____	2	6	car _____	3	1
may _____	3	2	children _____	1	1
Pam _____	1	2	dog _____	2	1
plays _____	1	7	fun _____	2	2
rode _____	3	3	got _____	3	3
swim _____	2	5	house _____	1	1
water _____	3	5	Little Chick _____	2	1
black _____	2	3	love _____	1	3
chicken _____	2	1	Meow-Meow _____	1	2
come _____	2	4	pets _____	2	1
family _____	1	1	pony _____	3	6
girl _____	1	7	runs _____	2	3
helps _____	1	4	this _____	1	6
Jip _____	1	2	zoo _____	3	1
lives _____	1	2			

HOW TO USE THE RESULTS FOR PLACEMENT IN THE BOOK

If you are not using this book from cover to cover, but want to know *where* in the book to start working with your child, follow these guidelines:

1. If the child knows 63–71 words (90–100%) he does not need to study Preprimer #2 (Chapter Seven). Give him the Word Recognition Competency Test at the end of Preprimer #3 (Chapter Eight). Keep a record of the few words he missed so you can teach them later.

2. If the child knows 56–63 words (80–90%) go back only to those lessons in Preprimer #2 that present the missed words and pay particular attention to the word study activities. Then administer the Word Recognition Competency Test at the end of Preprimer #3 and follow the accompanying placement directions.

3. If the child knows fewer than fifty-six words (less than 80%) begin teaching him with Preprimer #2 proceeding from the beginning to the end. Then go on to teach Preprimer #3.

8

Reading the Third "Book": Preprimer #3

Preprimer #3 introduces thirty new words in ten stories which carry the family to a fast food restaurant, a playground, and the post office. Since your child undoubtedly has had considerable experience with these settings, generating discussion and interest should not be difficult.

The lessons themselves will be taught in exactly the same way as were the ones in Preprimer #2. We suggest that you follow the suggestions presented both there and in Preprimer #1. You should by no means skimp on word study activities, however, and we will offer a few ideas for each lesson to supplement those already presented.

LESSON #1
Fast food

    a. To help the child recognize "what," have him locate "white" in the "w" envelope. Place the two cards ("what" and "white") together and discuss how they are alike.

    b. "So" can probably be best recognized by the fact that it rhymes with "go." If trouble is encountered, place the two word cards together and remind the child that the word in question begins like "see" and "sun."

    c. Other words in the story can be reinforced by constructing sentences in which they fit but leaving the word out in a blank large enough into which to fit a word card. Show the child the sentences and allow him to place the appropriate word card in the proper blank. (Note that sentences 1 and 2 are interchangeable.)

1. I ———— a pet. (have)
2. I ———— to go. (want)
3. ———— is my dog. (There)
4. ———— is it? (What)
5. I play ————. (there)

LESSON #2
The food

a. Have the child look at "hamburger" and say it slowly, listening to the word's parts. After the word has been pronounced slowly, write it as follows: "ham   burg   er."

When you said "hamburger" slowly I heard these parts. How many did I hear? (3)

Now let's look at this word's parts and read them.

Read "ham   burg   er" together.
b. Repeat the process for "milk shake" and "milk shakes."
c. "Wanted" gives a good opportunity to work on verb endings, if needed. Feel free to use additional verbs as well, such as "play," "look," "jump."

LESSON #3
Ice cream

a. Teach "who" in relation to "what" and "white" (note the **wh** sound is slightly different for "who"). The word "wants" should be easily recognized if the final s sound is known. If it isn't, work on it.

b. "Paid" can be introduced as the past of "pay." Pay can be sounded out if the child is shown "day" and "may" word cards and told that the final sounds are identical. Once "pay" is known the child can be told that the "y" turns to "i" when it becomes past and the final "d" sound is added.

c. When teaching "again" point out the fact that "a" placed on the front of some words makes them completely different. (Example: away)

d. "Ice cream" can be introduced through context clues. Ask the child what else might be eaten at the fast-food place, or what could be eaten for dessert. Context clues, in fact, can be very helpful in identifying many nouns and verbs.

LESSON #4
The playground

Compound words can be discussed in this lesson by showing the child the two parts of "play—ground" and "to—day." Other words that might be used are:

    into upon cannot maybe

LESSON #5
The walk to the playground

a. "Away" should not be a problem if it is shown in relationship to "day" and "may" to arrive at the final sound. You may need to review the w sound again.

b. Endings could be reviewed with:

    walk walk*s* walk*ing* walk*ed*
    talk talk*s* talk*ing* talk*ed*

Here are some exercises you might have the child complete to assess his understanding of verb endings:

    I like to _____ to school.
            walk walking

    Jim is _____ to Father.
          talking talk

    Father _____ to Mother.
          talk talks

    Do you _____ fast?
          walk walked

LESSON #6

a. After the child has read the word "funny," cover the ending and ask him to read the root word (fun). Next ask him to read the entire word slowly and listen to the two parts (syllables).

b. Write "cat" and ask the child to cover the "c" and read the part left (at).

Now let's see how many words we can make from "at."

b__, c__, f__, h__, m__, r__, p__, v__, s__

LESSON #7

a. *Look at "slide" and tell me the first two letters.* (sl)

That's right, the first sound in "slide" is sl. Listen to these words as I say them.

Write and pronounce: slow   slang   slid   slim

Did they all sound alike at the beginning? (yes) *That's right, they all began with the sl sound.*

b. Do the same thing for "play."

Note that these exercises are the beginning steps in recognizing consonant blends, which will be taught in more detail in Chapter Ten.

LESSON #8

a. Point out that the **ow** in "slow" is pronounced the same as the **o** in "go." Other words to illustrate this sound are **crow, show, grow**.

b. Once "round" is taught, "merry-go-round" should be recognized at once if the child is taught to read the known words first: (_____-go-round). This is an example of using context clues in word recognition.

LESSON #9

a. Write "good" and "by" separately and have the child read them (both have already been introduced). Write them together on the word card and have "good-by" read orally.

b. Have the child read the first two sentences silently in order to find a new word which tells *when* the family will go home. (Answer: now) Do the same type of exercise for "soon."

LESSON #10

a. Write "send" and "sent" together and ask the child how they are similar and how they differ. Explain the difference in tenses, perhaps illustrating with "bend"—"bent."

b. You might wish to review by having the child point out and read all words beginning with "w" in the story (will, wants, went, with, walked), "th" (the, they, then), and other letters.

(Note that if "who" is given as an example of a word beginning with "w" you should point out that **wh** represents a different sound than **w** in the other words.)

New Words Introduced in the Preprimer #3

Lesson #1: have, place, so, want, what
Lesson #2: hamburger, milk shake, wanted
Lesson #3: again, ice cream, paid, wants, who
Lesson #4: playground, today
Lesson #5: away, walk, walked
Lesson #6: at, funny
Lesson #7: slide
Lesson #8: merry-go-round, round, slow
Lesson #9: now, good-by, soon
Lesson #10: post office, send, sent

LESSON 1

Fast Food

Father said, "Come on. We will go to eat. We will all have a ride. We will ride to a fast food place. We will eat there."

"What will we eat?" asked Tom.

"We will see," said Father. "We will eat what we want."

So away they went. Away they went to the fast food place.

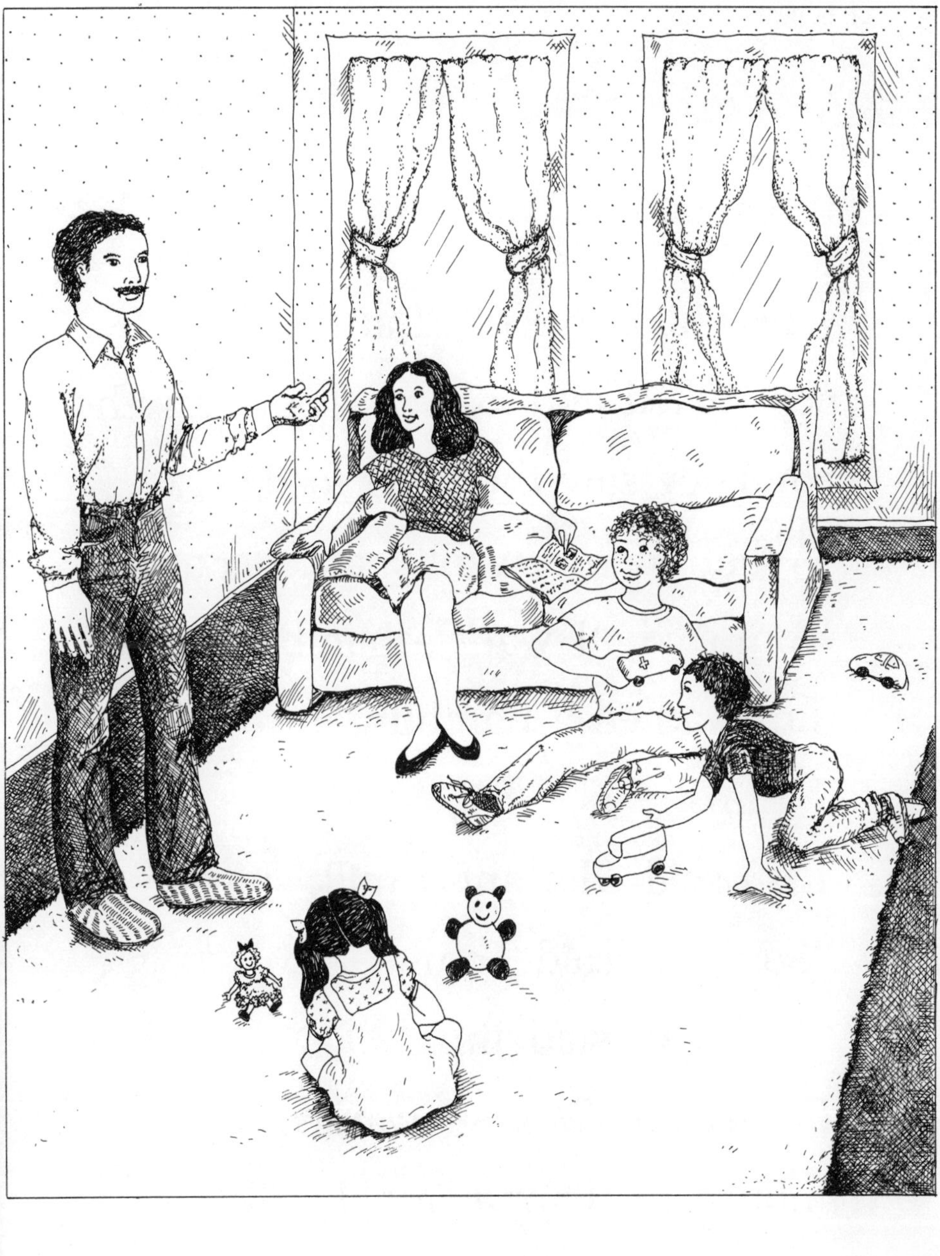

The Food

The children looked at the food. They looked and looked. They saw the food. They saw the good food.

"What do you want?" asked Father.

Tom said, "I want a hamburger!"

Jim wanted a hamburger, too. So did Pam.

Pam said, "I want a milk shake."

"So do I," said Tom.

"Me, too!" said Jim.

Father and Mother wanted hamburgers. They wanted milk shakes, too. So they all ate at the fast food place.

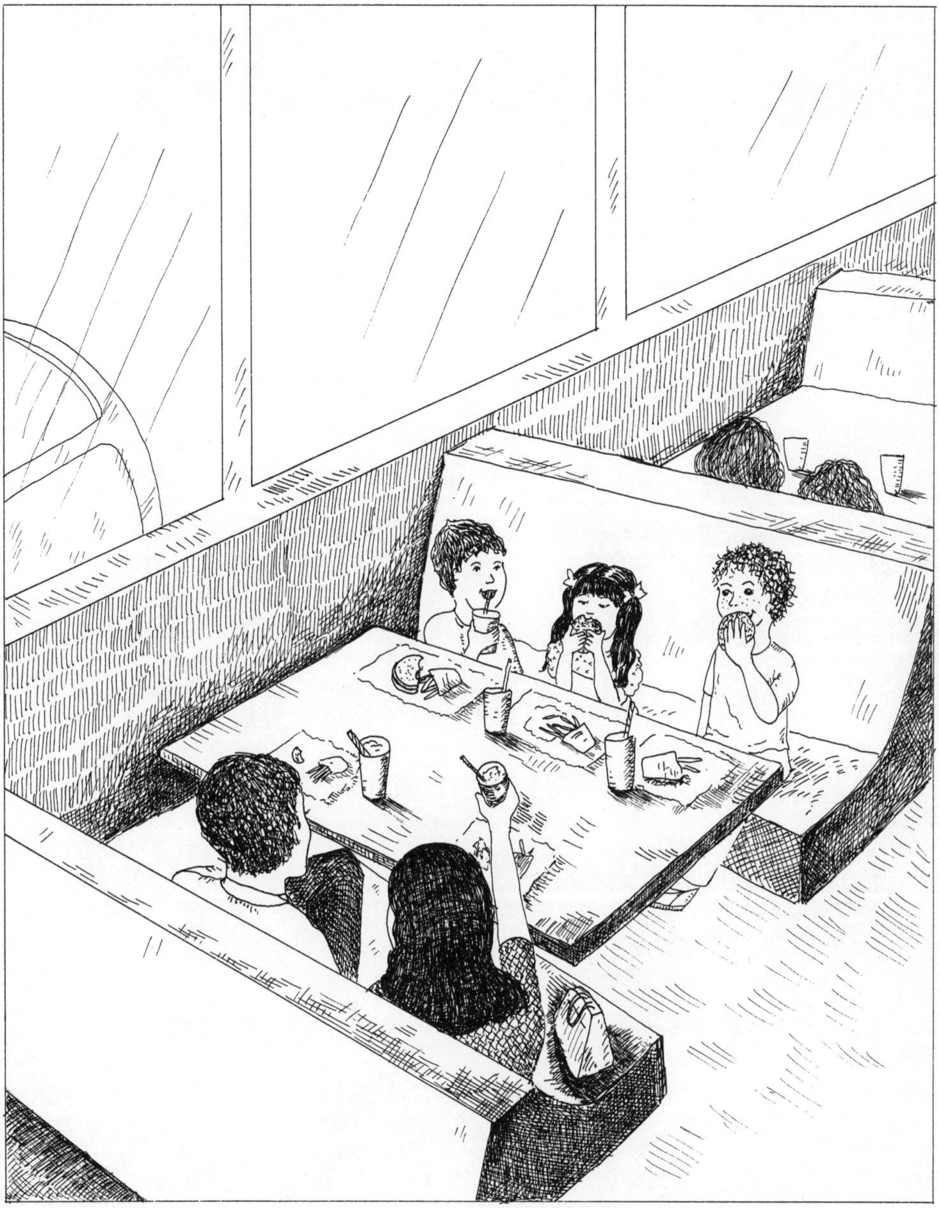

LESSON 3

Ice Cream

Mother said, "Who wants ice cream?"

"I do," said Pam.

"So do I," said Tom and Jim.

Father had ice cream. So did Mother. They all had ice cream.

Father paid for the food, and they all went home.

"That was a good ride," said Jim.

"And good food," said Tom.

"Good, good food," said little Pam.

"We will go again," said Mother.

And they did.

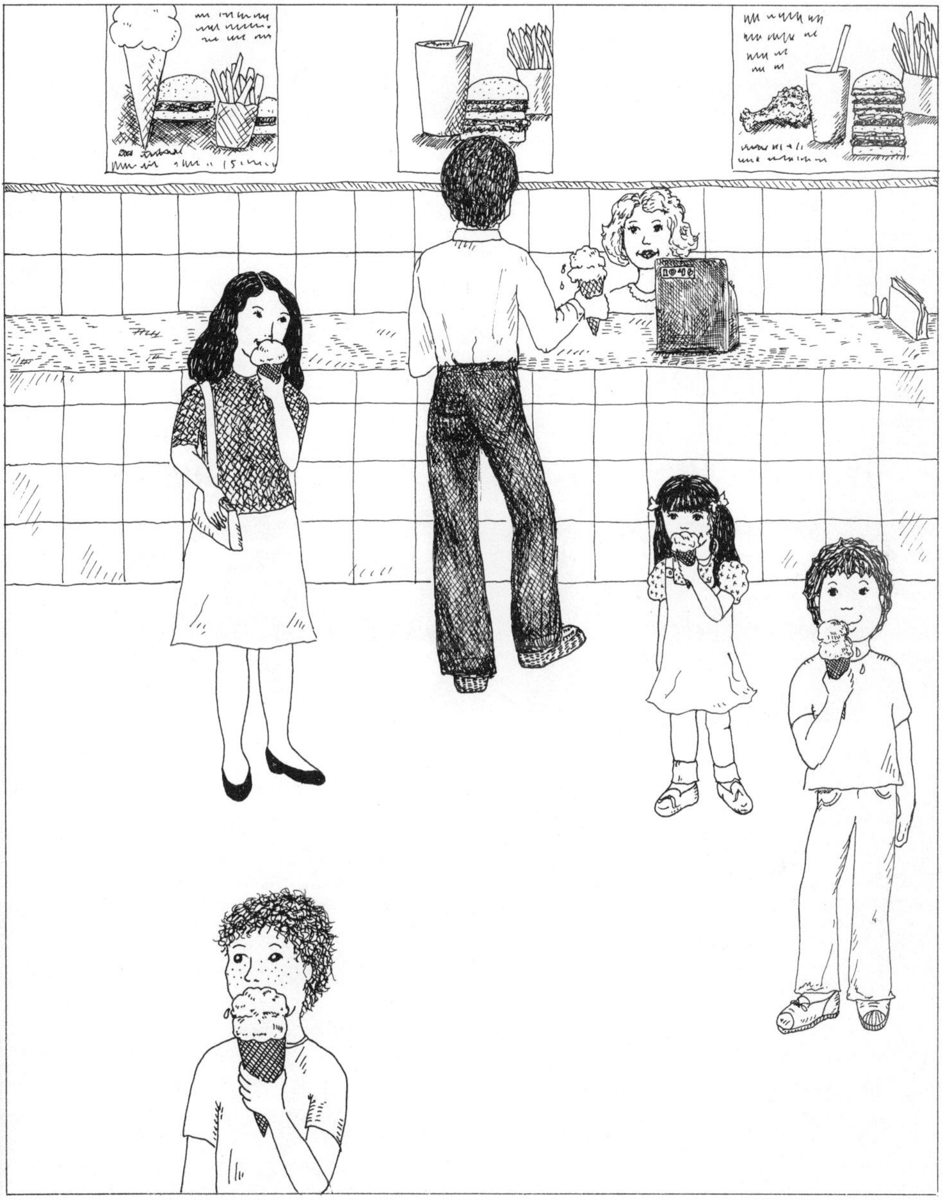

LESSON 4

The Playground

"We will go to the playground today. Do you want to go?" asked Mother.

"Yes, yes," said the children. "We want to go. We will have fun at the playground today."

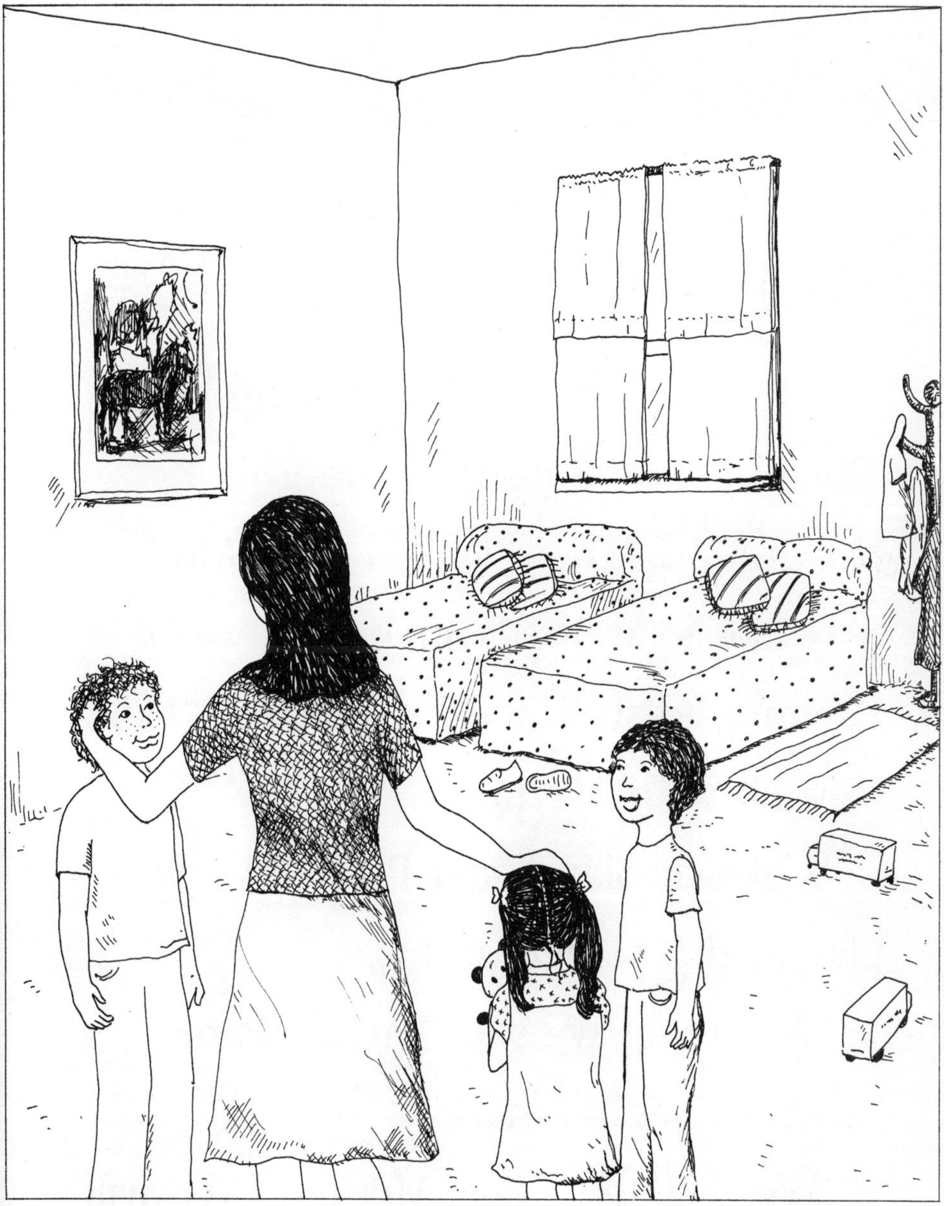

LESSON 5

The Walk to the Playground

Away they went to the playground. The children walked to the playground. They walked with Mother.

"I like to walk," said Jim.

"I like to walk too," said Tom. "I like to walk with Mother."

"I like to play," said Pam. "We will play at the playground."

"What will we see?" asked Pam. "Will we see animals?"

"We will see," said Mother. "We will see."

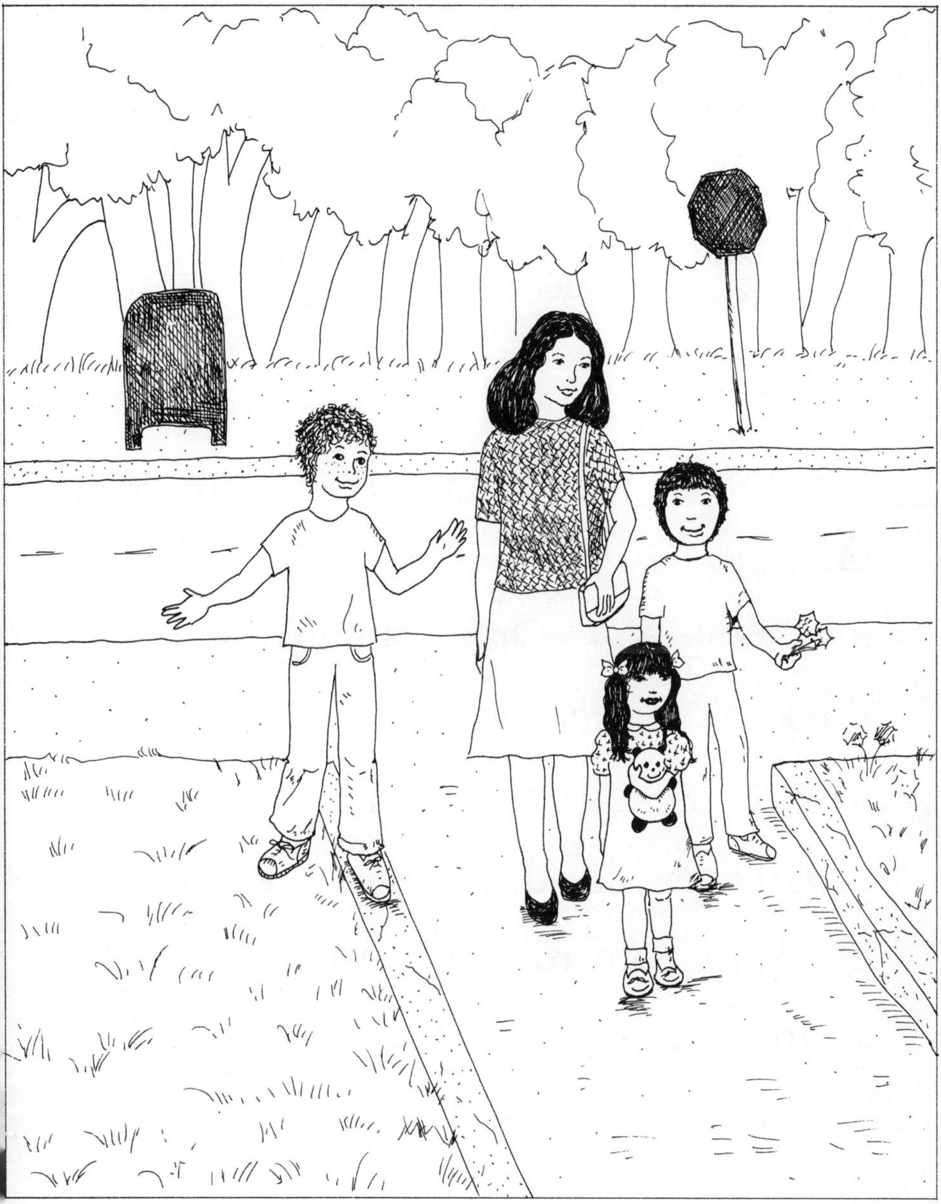

LESSON 6

Animals at the Playground

The children did see animals at the playground. They were funny animals. One animal was a dog. A funny black and white dog. One animal was a duck. The duck was funny, too. They saw a chicken, a cat, and a rabbit.

Jim rode the duck. Ram rode a chicken. Tom rode a funny rabbit. The animals went up and down.

273

The Slide

The children saw the slide.

Mother said, "You may play at the slide."

The children did slide and slide. It was fun to slide down. Up they went and down they came. Up and down. Down and up.

Oh, what fun! What fun for children. They went up. They went down. What fun! What fun!

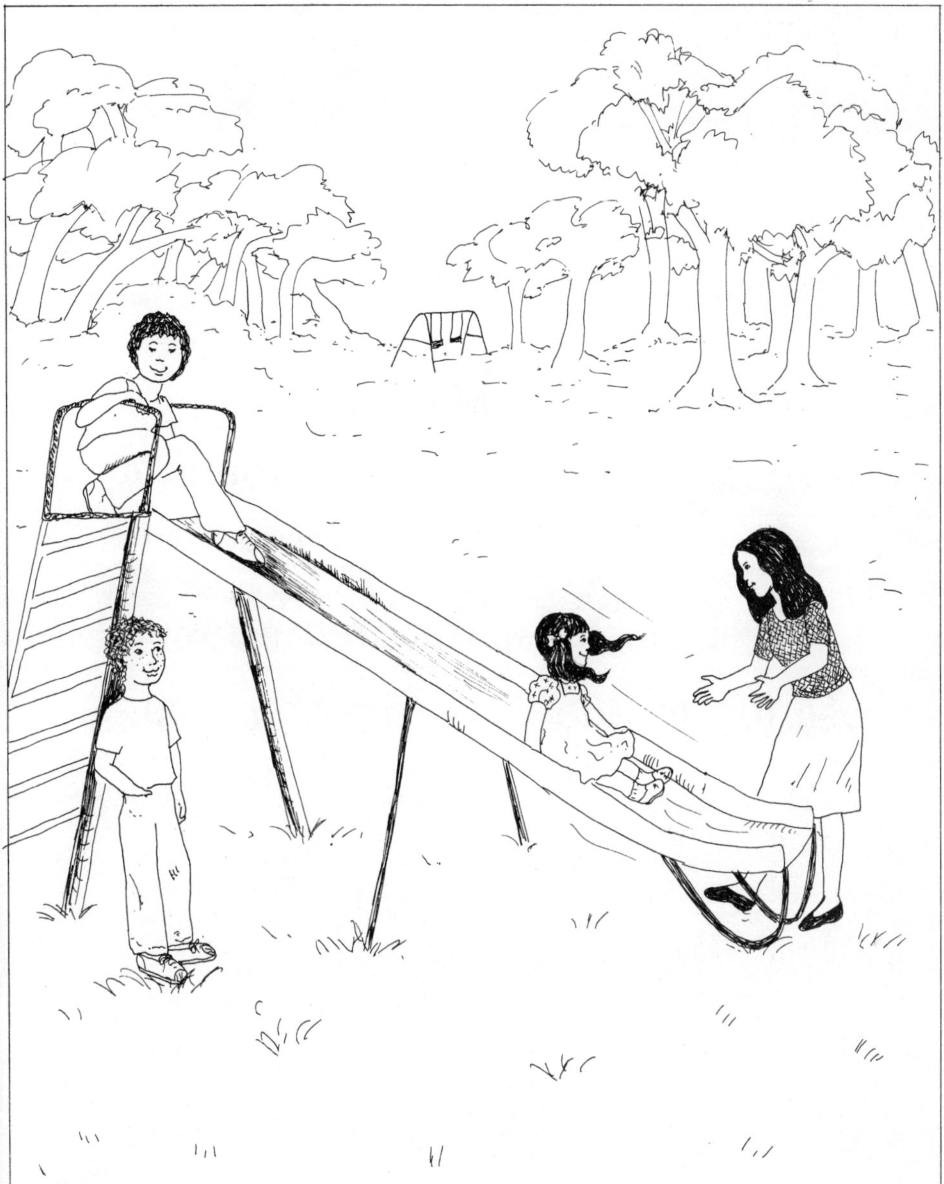

LESSON 8

The Merry-go-round

The children looked at the merry-go-round. Round and round it went.

It went fast. Then it went slow. It was fun to ride the merry-go-round.

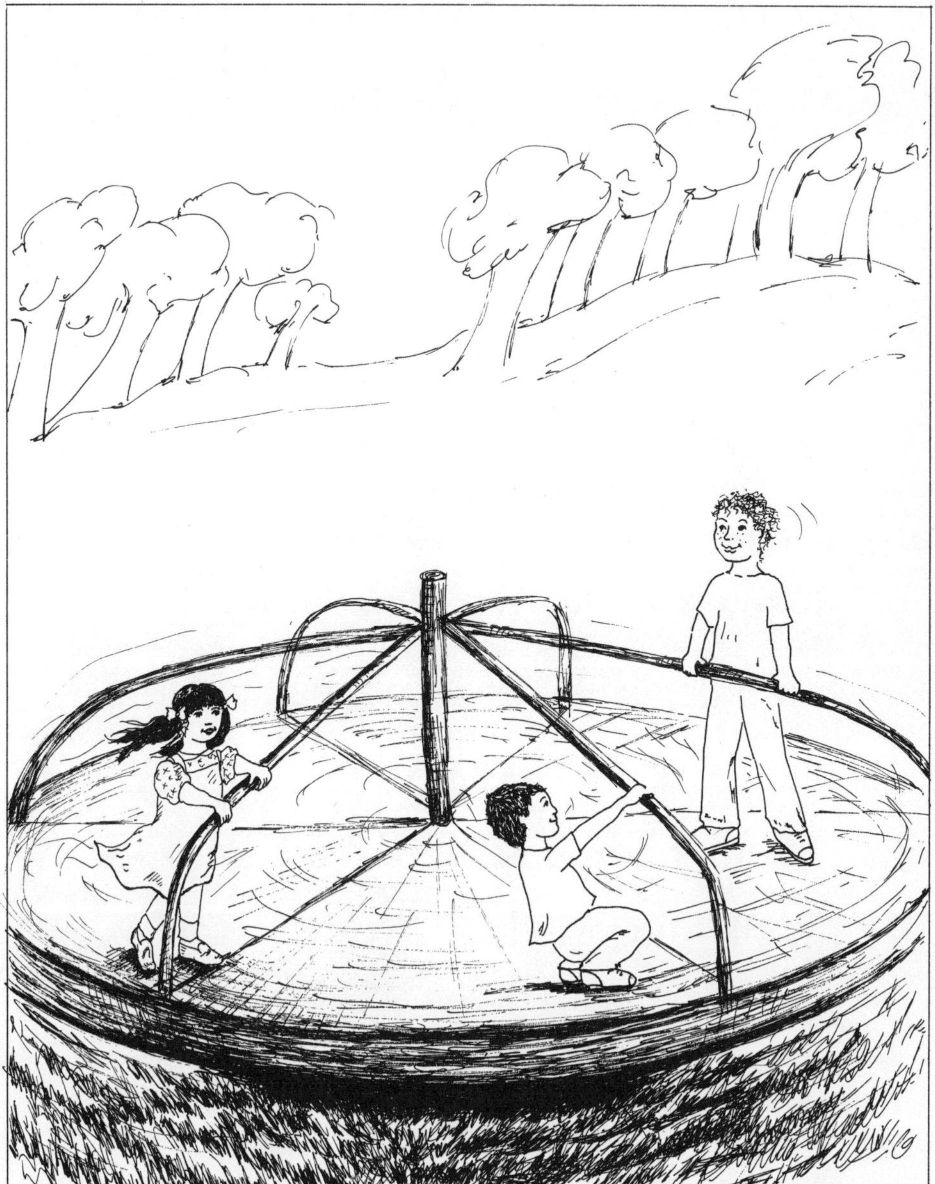

Good-by to the Playground

Mother said, "We will go home. We will go home now."

The children said, "May we come again? May we come again soon?"

Mother said, "Yes, we will come again soon."

The children said, "Thank you! Thank you, Mother. We will come again soon."

Pam said, "Good-by! Good-by! The playground is fun."

The boys said, "Yes, the playground is fun."

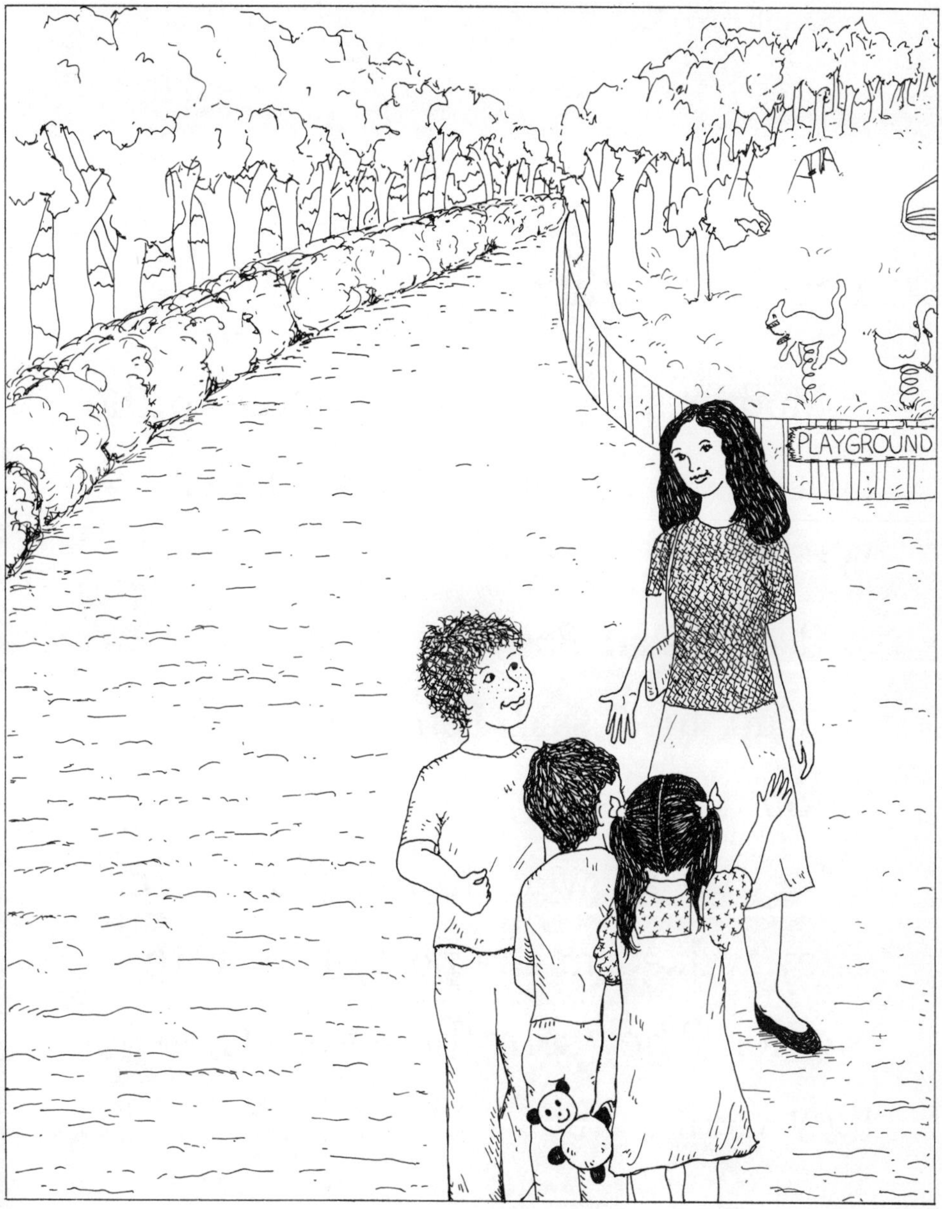
PLAYGROUND

LESSON 10

The Post Office

Mother said, "Today I will go to the post office. I need to send a letter. Who wants to go?"

"I do," said Pam.

"I do, too," said Tom.

"So do I," said Jim.

So they all went to the post office. They walked to the post office with Mother. They sent the letter. Then they went home.

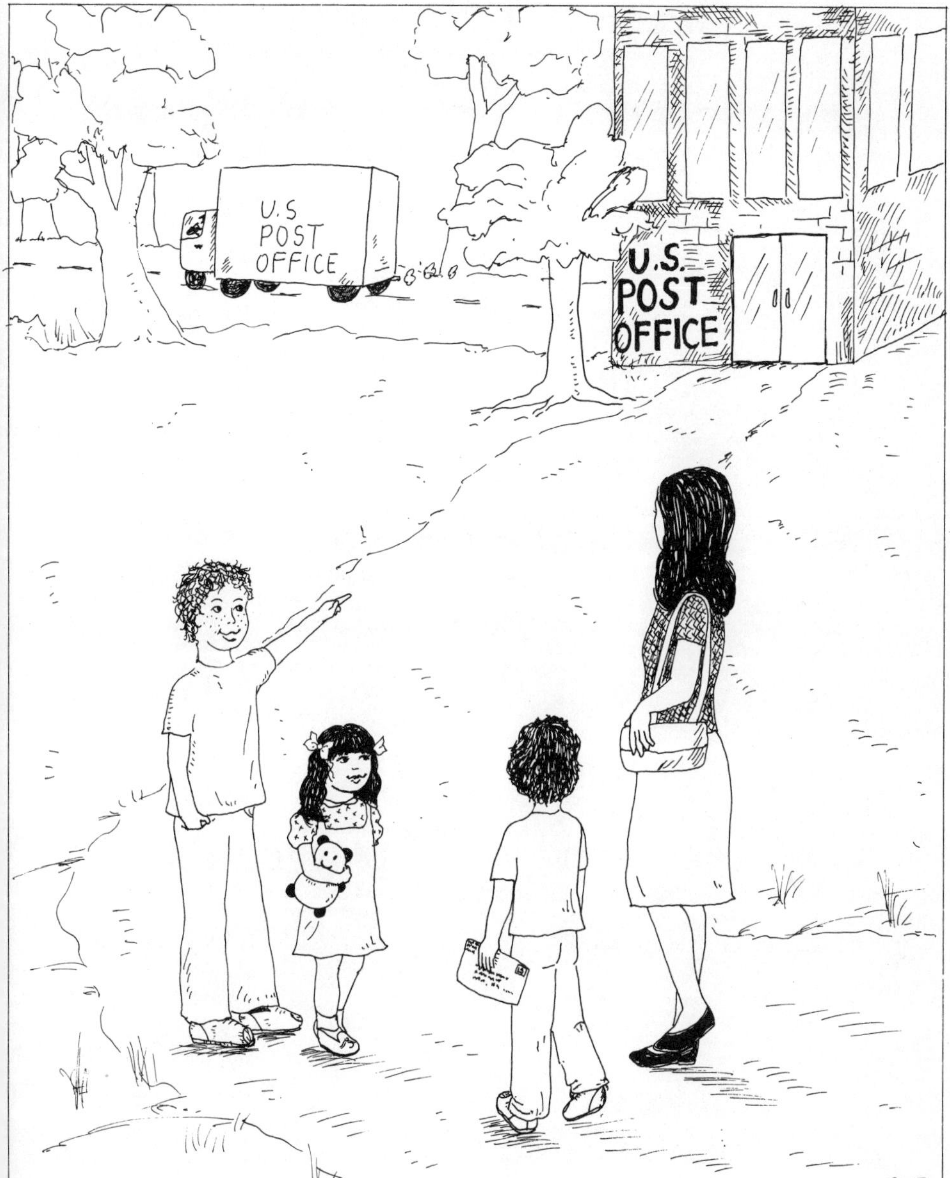
U.S
POST
OFFICE
U.S.
POST
OFFICE

WORD RECOGNITION COMPETENCY TEST FOR PREPRIMER #3

Listed below are the thirty words introduced in Preprimer #3. Refer to the test at the end of Preprimer #1 (Chapter Six, page 118) for procedures, materials, and evaluating the results.

Word Recognition Competency Test For Preprimer #3

so	round	away
wants	have	at
walked	hamburger	slow
funny	ice cream	place
good-by	walk	milk shake
what	slide	paid
post office	send	playground
wanted	now	merry-go-round
again	want	soon
today	who	sent

HOW TO USE THE RESULTS FOR PLACEMENT IN THE BOOK

If you are not using this book from cover to cover, but want to know where in the book to start working with your child, follow these guidelines:

1. If the child knows 27–30 words (90–100%), he does not need to study Preprimer #3. Begin work with Chapters Nine and Ten (to be used together), administering the Competency Tests in Chapter Ten for proper placement. Keep a record of the words missed here so you will be sure to teach them later.

Word Recognition Competency Test
Preprimer #3—Worksheet

Date _____ ____ # correct ÷ 30 = ____ % correct

Word	Lesson #	Word	Lesson #
so _____	1	slide _____	7
wants _____	3	send _____	10
walked _____	5	now _____	9
funny _____	6	want _____	1
good-by _____	9	who _____	3
what _____	1	away _____	5
post office _____	10	at _____	6
wanted _____	2	slow _____	8
again _____	3	place _____	1
today _____	4	milk shake _____	2
round _____	8	paid _____	3
have _____	1	playground _____	4
hamburger _____	2	merry-go-round _____	8
ice cream _____	3	soon _____	9
walk _____	5	sent _____	10

2. If the child knows 24 to 27 words (80–90%), go back only to those lessons in Preprimer #3 that present the missed words, paying particular attention to the word study activities. Then proceed to Chapters Nine and Ten.

3. If the child knows fewer than twenty-four words (less than 80%), begin teaching him with Preprimer #3 proceeding from the beginning to the end. Then readminister this test to check on words learned and proceed to Chapters Nine and Ten.

9
Reading the Child's Own Experience Stories

Your child has now begun to read. A basic group of words can be recognized on sight, beginning phonics skills have begun to be acquired, and simple stories can be read with understanding.

Obviously this momentum must be maintained. The best way to do this is to continue the process by extending reading instruction to more complex stories and phonics instruction to other basic sounds. In this chapter the first task is accomplished through a teaching strategy in which the child dictates his own stories.* The extension of phonics to include other basic sounds is accomplished by combining the lessons contained in Chapter Ten with the process of reading those stories which your child dictates.

Phonics Instruction

As you are well aware of by now, teaching reading includes more than having the child learn whole words in stories. We believe strongly in making a commitment to phonics instruction in order to give your child the capability of discovering new words when no one is around to help him.

---

* The language experience techniques used in this chapter have been adapted from the work of Dr. Russell G. Stauffer, both from his book, *Teaching Reading as a Thinking Process* (Harper and Row, 1969), and from his graduate reading courses conducted at the University of Delaware.

Since the best way to teach phonics is by combining it with actual reading activities, we suggest that you teach the lessons given in Chapter Ten *at the same time you teach your child to read his own stories.* To simplify this process the final portion of each lesson in this chapter will be devoted to a phonics lesson from Chapter Ten.

Advantages of Using the Child's Own Stories in Reading

Learning to read would be a great deal more fun if children could choose books and stories which specifically interested them to serve as texts. The problem is that it is difficult to locate interesting stories that can be read with a sight vocabulary of 150 to 200 words. We could have continued and expanded the stories begun in Chapter Six until a sufficiently large sight vocabulary was built in order to permit reading of more varied materials, but that goal can be reached by a faster, more interesting way. It is called the *language experience approach* and it is based on the theory that (1) children have less difficulty learning those words that are in their spoken vocabulary and (2) they will most enjoy reading about things with which they have personal experience.

Language experience incorporates both these factors by having the child dictate and then read a story about any topic that interests him, using any words he pleases. In doing so he usually learns more words per story than in other methods simply because he is not so easily overwhelmed by words of his own choosing. Equally important, the process sharpens oral communication skills and lays the foundation for future writing success. From an instructional point of view, the language experience approach has the added benefit of being an open-ended process not dependent upon the availability of texts and therefore can be continued as long as the child continues to profit from it.

Materials

The basic materials you will need for teaching this chapter include:

1. 3" by 5" word cards,

2. a felt tip pen,
3. crayons,
4. pencils, and a red pencil
5. a loose-leaf notebook,
6. wide-lined paper, and
7. a word window, which consists of an index card with a small rectangle cut out of its center.

Format of the Lessons

The process of dictating a story, reading it, learning the new words introduced, and interspersing phonics lessons from Chapter Ten will be spread over three sessions.

SESSION #1

This session is primarily given over to the dictation and illustration of a story.

1. Selecting a Topic

The child should feel free to choose any topic that interests him. You may stimulate interest in a topic discussion of an experience you share. You might, for example, point out a toad in the backyard or talk about something the two of you saw while shopping. With a little help the child will have no difficulty coming up with topics, whether from a story you have just read to him, a television show, something he and a friend did together, or something he would like to do. Anything, in short, is a reasonable topic for a story as long as it interests the child.

2. Discussion

Once a topic is selected it is usually a good idea to spend a few minutes discussing it. This will help supply ideas for things to include in the story and makes for clear thought processes.

3. Dictation

Following the discussion, take out a lined sheet of paper and a felt tip pen. Print exactly what the child dictates in clear block letters, supplying appropriate punctuation and capitalization. Don't worry about grammar at this point; the closer it is to actual speech patterns the better. When finished, ask for a title for the story and print it at the top of the page.

Be sure to make a big deal out of the fact that your child is actually writing his own stories. Children really enjoy keeping all of them in a loose-leaf notebook entitled something like:

>MY STORIES
>by
>Jan

4. Parent-Assisted Reading

Once the story is written, read it back to the child slowly but with enough rhythm to convey its meaning and tone. Next suggest that the two of you read it together by pointing to each word and saying them in unison. Reread the story in the same way.

5. Illustrating the Story

After the story has been read and reread, suggest that the child illustrate it with pencil and crayon. Be sure to discuss the picture and show your approval. (It is enough if the artist recognizes its relevance to the story!) Place the picture facing the story in the language experience notebook, numbering both in the upper right-hand corners for future reference.

6. Phonics

If time permits, finish the session with one of the phonics lessons in Chapter Ten.

SESSION #2

This session will be primarily devoted to reading the story again, identifying known words, reviewing previous stories, and phonics activities from the next chapter.

1. Identifying Known Words

The first thing you will do when you sit down is have the story read by the child, supplying words as needed. Reread, if necessary, then have the child identify those words in the story which he has previously learned. Give him a pencil and ask him to draw two lines under each word in the Word Box. If he forgets to underline one, simply say:

I think you forgot this one. What is it?

When he reads it correctly, have him draw two lines under it as before. If he incorrectly identifies a word as having been previously learned that was not, express your doubt and have him see if he can locate it in the Word Box. If you are correct, erase the lines.

After sight words have been identified, have the child go through the story and draw *one* line under each word he *thinks* he knows. At this point some words may be underlined that are not really known since the story itself has been read several times. Don't worry about that now; you will discover which words are really known during the third session.

2. Review

Have the word cards constructed from the previous language experience story (they will be filed in the "New Words" section of the Word Box) read by the child. If any trouble is encountered, have him read the entire story.

3. Phonics

Teach the next phonics lesson from Chapter Ten. If the sounds taught in that lesson happen to be included in some of the words used in the new story (and chances are they will be), be sure to point that out. The more that phonics instruction can be integrated into actual reading instruction, the more meaningful it will be.

SESSION #3

This session will be devoted primarily to identifying words in the story which have been added to the child's sight vocabulary.

1. Identifying Learned Words

After having the story read again, take out the word window and tell the child you are going to point out some words for him to read. Move the frame around the story randomly, bracketing each word that has been underlined *once* (which indicates that the child thinks he knows it).

For each word that he recognizes, compliment the child, have him underline it with a red pencil, and make up a word card for it as he watches, placing the number of the story in the upper right-hand corner. When finished, place the word cards in a row on the table and have the child read each word again. When you are through, place them in the "New Words" section of the Word Box and have the story read one last time. (Both it and the word cards will, of course, be reviewed during the next three lesson sequences.)

2. Phonics

Go on to the next phonics lesson in Chapter Ten. As always, make a special effort to apply that instruction to the new words just learned in the story.

A CASE STUDY

An illustration of how an actual language experience lesson might progress will help solidify the process in your mind.

Jan Montand is a bright five-year-old who is being taught to read by her parents prior to going to school. She has already attained a quite impressive sight vocabulary and has dictated and read several of her own stories.

SESSION #1

After a brief discussion of possible topics, Jan decided that she would like to write about her friend Scott. Her mother was receptive to the idea, asking her questions about things the two of them did together, what good friends they were, and so forth, to stimulate ideas for the actual story.

Jan dictated the following story, with her mother printing it clearly on a lined sheet of paper.

Scott is my friend.
I like Scott and he likes me too.
Scott and me play baseball together.
I can hit the ball longer than Scott.

Jan decided to name the story "Scott" after her friend. Her mother wrote that at the top of the page, along with "Story #7" in the upper right-hand corner for future reference. (Jan had written six previous stories and all were placed in a notebook entitled "Jan's Stories.")

Mrs. Montand next read the story back slowly as Jan watched. (Note that she did not correct the grammar in line 3 nor suggest that "farther" might be more appropriate than "longer" in line 4. She reasoned that plenty of opportunities existed every day to correct Jan's grammar. Her focus at this point was teaching Jan to read.)

Jan's mother next suggested that the two of them read the story together. They did so with the mother pointing to each word as they read. Since Jan stumbled several times they read the story a second time.

Jan needed little encouragement to draw a picture of her and Scott playing ball. She seemed quite content with the work which was placed in the storybook along with her story after she discussed it with her mother.

Jan's mother had planned to also begin Lesson #3, Part II, of Chapter Ten but Jan took longer than expected in drawing her picture so the lesson was ended at that point.

SESSION #2

Jan read the story herself this time with her mother supplying words as needed. Jan indicated that she would like to read the story once again before she underlined her "Word Box words" as she called them. (Jan already knew the entire language experience routine by heart.)

After placing two pencil marks under each previously studied word, Jan went on to underline once each new word she thought she knew. (When picking out words in the Word Box, Jan sometimes liked to go through its entire contents one word at a time. Although time consuming, her mother did not discourage the practice since it afforded an excellent chance to review the entire sight vocabulary.)

As indicated by the fact that only two words were not underlined, Jan felt she knew most of the words she had dictated:

Scott
Scott is my friend.
I like Scott and he likes me too.
Scott and me play baseball sometimes.
I can hit the ball longer than Scott.

Since the entire process took only a very few minutes, Jan and her mother decided to see how many new words were remembered from Story #6. The word cards with a "6" in their upper right-hand corners were pulled from the "new words" envelope and placed in a row on the table. Jan read three of the four with absolutely no problems so those three were filed in the Word Box with the troublesome fourth placed back in the "New Words" envelope for future review.

After reading Story #6 again, Jan and her mother went on to the above-mentioned lesson in Chapter Ten dealing with the **short i** sound. Mrs. Montand made a special effort to point out the fact that two of the words in the story contained the **short i** sound (**is** and **hit**). This proved especially beneficial since Jan no longer failed to recognize "hit."

SESSION #3

Jan again read the story, without her mother having to help her at all this time. Her mother knew from experience, however, that this didn't necessarily indicate that Jan knew all the words since she tended to memorize very easily.

Mrs. Montand then moved the word window around the story randomly and Jan tried to read all the words which were underlined once. When she recognized words, she underlined them again in red. Jan knew "baseball," "Scott," "friend," "hit," and "too." She failed only to recognize "sometimes."

Mrs. Montand made word cards for each of the five words Jan had recognized and placed them on the table in a row. After Jan read each word again, they were placed in the "New Words" envelope for future review.

Because Jan was a perfectionist, and because "sometimes," and the two words which were not underlined ("longer" and "than"), would not be considered further, Mrs. Montand assured her that these words would probably come up in the future and she would get to put them in her Word Box then. In the meantime, Jan's mother reminded her that she would be able to write a new story the next day, so she could begin thinking about a topic. The pair next went on to work on the **short o** lesson in Chapter Ten. Mrs. Montand pointed out the fact that the "o" in "Scott" conformed to Rule I for short vowels and thus represented the **short o** sound.

General Guidelines

1. Language experience is a fun activity. Keep it so. *Never* criticize a child's story. If he consistently makes them too short, spend more time on discussion prior to dictation and suggest other things he could say about his topic; if they seem uninteresting or of poor quality, don't worry about it as long as he is learning to read.
2. As always, don't drag a lesson out beyond your child's interest threshold. Remember that there's no rule that says you have to finish, or even start, a phonics lesson if the language experience portion takes longer than expected or if your child seems tired.

3. Continue to keep careful records. The Word Box continues to be an extremely valuable tool. Keep it updated.
4. It is not necessary nor expected that your child learn every word in each story. It is not necessary that your child learn a great many words quickly, either. Let him proceed at his own pace without pressure.
5. If your child enjoys language experience, continue it as long as he is learning new words. Just because you exhaust the phonics lessons in Chapter Ten does not mean that you have to stop the language experience portion of your instruction. All the word attack strategies discussed in Chapter Eleven are as applicable to your child's own stories as they are to the materials suggested in that chapter. Keep in mind, however, that one of your chief objectives is an increased sight vocabulary. Children often reach a point at which fewer and fewer new words are introduced in each story. When this happens, it is time to go on to Chapter Eleven.

10

Teaching More Advanced Phonics Skills

The importance of teaching phonics has already been discussed. So far only beginning and ending consonant sounds have been taught, however, and since the ultimate goal of teaching phonics is to make possible the recognition of new words, the beginning reader is obviously going to have to become familiar with some additional sounds.

Vowels, for example, play such a major role in English that without knowledge of them, few words can be sounded out successfully. By the same token many consonants (and some vowels) appear together to form blended or new sounds. Knowledge of these elements, taken for granted by adults, plus some conception of syllabication will go a long way toward assisting the recognition of *most* new words. This will become even more apparent once the word attack strategies presented in the next chapter are learned.

As explained in Chapter Nine, the phonics lessons contained in the present chapter are to be taught together with the dictated language experience stories. Each story is taught in a three-session framework with the final portion of each set aside for one phonics lesson.

These phonics lessons are therefore designed to be of rather short duration. The basic steps involved are:

1. Introducing the letter sound, in which the child is taught to recognize a sound by listening to words containing it.

2. Distinguishing the sound, in which words which contain a particular sound are distinguished from those that do not.

3. Miscellaneous activities, designed to teach rules and to review particular sounds.

If for some reason all these steps cannot be completed in a single lesson, however, each contains several natural and obvious breaking points which will permit continuation the following day.

If you are dealing with a preschool child you will, as always, go through the chapter in order. School-age children's placement will be determined by the competency tests, but the lessons themselves will still be taught at the end of a language experience session.

The final section dealing with syllabication may be taught in any way you please, whenever you please. The division of words into syllables is a relatively complex skill which requires a continuing effort to teach properly.

Materials

The materials necessary to teach the lessons in this chapter will be identical to those in Chapter Nine with the addition of those necessary to construct a sound book or sound cards (see Chapter Five). These include:

1. Heavy construction paper and/or 6″ by 8″ cards,
2. Envelopes large enough to contain these cards and/or
3. A loose-leaf notebook (if you choose to make a sound book).

General Guidelines

The same general teaching principles apply here as in previous chapters. Four that are specific to this kind of phonics instruction are:

1. The concepts taught in these lessons are hard to learn thoroughly and even harder to retain. Therefore do not be surprised if your child has forgotten several lessons by the time he takes the competency tests. Simply decide to teach each sound as many times as necessary.

2. Phonics should not be taught in a vacuum. Wherever possible try to relate the concept being taught directly to the words being studied in the language experience story for that session. If such a tie cannot be made, find a previous story in which it can.

3. Should language experience not work out as an appropriate method for your child, or should you wish to go on to the materials suggested in Chapter Eleven before completing this chapter, continue teaching the remaining phonics lessons at the end of these formal reading sessions instead.

4. Phonics rules can be found throughout this chapter. It is helpful to some children to learn these rules by heart; to others it is cumbersome. Discuss the rules with the child until he understands them. Use your judgment as to whether or not to require learning them.

PART ONE
Learning the Long Vowels

Since the child already knows many of the initial and final consonant sounds, learning the sounds made by the five main vowels will greatly increase his word attack capabilities. Although each vowel can represent several different sounds, depending upon the word in which it appears, the long- and short-vowel forms which will be taught in this chapter cover the majority of these sounds. The vowel lessons have been organized so that the easiest ones come first and the phonics rules build on one another. Long vowel sounds will be taught first because they are identical to the letter names with which the child is already familiar. Prior to that, however, it is of course necessary to explain what vowels are.

PRELIMINARY LESSON
Teaching the vowel names

Today we're going to learn what vowels are. Some of the letters in the alphabet are called vowels, the rest are called consonants.

Write the vowels clearly on a card while saying the letter names out loud: A E I O U. (Leave room under each letter to write the lower-case version later.)

A E I O U

Now let's say the names of the vowels together (read them in order). *O.K. How many vowels do we have?* (five) *Good! Now say the names of the vowels while I write them again in small letters.*

A E I O U
a e i o u

Have the child say the five vowel names until he can repeat them without looking at the card.

ACTIVITY #1
Using the letter cards

Take out all the letter name cards you constructed for Chapter Four. (It doesn't matter whether you have upper- and lower-case versions on the same cards or on separate ones.)

	A	a	B	etc.
or	Aa	Bb	Cc	etc.

Ask the child to sort through the letter cards and pull out only those that are vowels. If he has trouble, allow him to use as a reference the vowel card you prepared.

ACTIVITY #2
Distinguishing vowels from consonants

I'm going to say the names of letters in the alphabet and I want you to clap your hands when you hear me say the name of a vowel.

Again you may allow the child to have the vowel card in front of him as a reference until he seems to know the vowels, but you should gradually wean him away from its use. Say some of the letters in a series like this, or just make them up as you go along.

```
R  C  J  O  L  B  A  T  D  U  N  X  E  F
I  G  M  A  K  P  I  O  Z  S  U  R  Q  E
```

ACTIVITY #3
Circling the vowels

Write a series or several short series of letters, mixing capital and lower-case forms. Have the child circle the vowels. After he has finished, give him the vowel card to check his answers and correct any mistakes. Examples of the letter series you might make up are:

```
E  j  O  t  Z  d
I  N  s  X  C  h
M  r  X  b  G  u
L  q  V  a  D  k
l  A  s  F  o  B
c  H  e  T  p  J
g  U  v  Q  f  R
a  K  i  P  m  N
```

ACTIVITY #4
Introducing the long vowel concept

By now the child should be able to recognize the names of the five vowels. Learning the long vowel sounds should not be difficult since they are identical to the letter names.

Now that you know the names of the vowels, you are going to learn that every vowel makes a long sound and a short sound. The long sounds are fun to learn because you'll hear the vowel say its name!

LESSON #1
Long E

ACTIVITY #1
Recognizing the **long E** sound

*The **long E** sound says its name. I'm going to say some words that have a **long E** at the end. Listen and tell me if you can hear **long E** say its name.*

Read the following words slowly, dragging out the **E** sound to make the point.

    me   he   she   we   be

What did you hear at the end of "me"? (E)
At the end of he? (E)
At the end of she?
At the end of we?
At the end of be?

*Do you see why we say that **long E** says its name?*

ACTIVITY #2
Distinguishing the **long E** sound

Now that you can hear long E say its name, I want you to listen to some more words and tell me every time you hear a long E. When you hear a word with a long E in it, say "Long E!"

Read the following word list to the child, giving him sufficient time to indicate whether or not he hears the sound in question. When he makes an error, reread the word, emphasizing the sound that gave him trouble and ask him if he is sure of his answer.

green	(yes)	tree	(yes)
eat	(yes)	need	(yes)
lie	(no)	today	(no)
pony	(no)	play	(no)
be	(yes)	feed	(yes)

ACTIVITY #3
Rule I for long vowels

We heard the long E at the end of words like "he," "she," and "me." Let's look at those words now.

(These words should be in the child's sight vocabulary.)

Write the words on a sheet of paper labeled **Long E** in a column. (See Supplementary Activity #1 for illustrations of how this page may be laid out if you are making a sound book).

$$\bar{E}$$

he
she
me

Now read each word and tell me where the e is.

(Answer: at the end of each word.)

How many vowels are in each word?

(Answer: one)

That's right! You've just learned the first rule for long vowels!

RULE I

When there's only one vowel in a word and it comes at the end it is usually a long vowel.

---

*Let's mark these **E** vowels to show that they're long. Watch me mark the first two so you can mark the last one.*

$$\text{hē}$$
$$\text{shē}$$
$$\text{mē}$$

*Here are some new words that end in **long E**. Let's see if we can figure them out together.*

You can help your child read these words himself without your reading them first by reminding him of the initial consonant sound as well as the long "E" sound, and suggesting that he put the two together. Since they rhyme with the words above all he really needs to do is to substitute the first sound (which he probably already knows).

Write "be" and "we" on the same sheet of paper.

After the child has read the words, with or without your assistance, ask him to *mark the **long E**'s to show that they say their names.*

ACTIVITY #4
Rule II for long vowels

Write the following words on a sheet of paper or in the child's sound book if you have made one, arranged as below:

      tree   need   green
      see   feed   eat
                             cream

Look at "tree" and tell me how many vowels you see.

(Answer: two, since there are two **e**'s.)

How many are in "need"?
How many in "green"?
How many in "eat"?

(Answer: two again, **e** and **a**.)

How many in "cream"?

*That's right. These words all have two vowels and they all make a long **E** sound. You've just learned another rule!*

RULE II

When two vowels are together, the first one is usually long and the second one is not heard.

Go back to the last set of words you wrote on the child's sound sheet and demonstrate the rule with all seven words.

*Here are some new words and some old words that have the long **E** sound. See if you can figure out what the new word is by looking at the word you already know.*

Point to the first word in each column and ask the child if he remembers what that word is. If he does, ask him if he can guess what the second word is. For example, he should know "feed." If he sees, or is helped to see, that "seed" differs from "feed" only in its initial consonant, and if he remembers the **S** sound, then he should be able to sound out "seed." If he cannot (or if he does not remember "feed"), help him.

feed	green	be	eat
seed	seen	beet*	meat
	queen		

SUPPLEMENTARY ACTIVITY #1
Adding to the sound book

By following the instructions for this lesson you should have constructed a page labeled **"Long E"** which looks something like this:

Long E

Ē
he
she
me

be*
we*

tree	need	green	eat	cream
see	feed			
feed	green	be	eat	
seed*	seen*	beet*	meat*	

* New words.

---

* Note these two words begin alike rather than end alike as do the others.

The first group of words illustrate Rule I, the second (beginning with "tree") Rule II. You may even divide the page into two halves and write out the two rules if you prefer:

Ē

RULE I
Word has one vowel and it is at the end

Old Words
he
she
me

New Words
be
we

RULE II
Word has two vowels together, and the first is usually long

Old Words

tree	need	green	eat	cream
see	feed			
feed	green	be	eat	
seed*	seen*	beet*	meat*	

* New words.

This sound sheet can now be filed in a sound book as suggested in Chapter Five and used periodically to review both the vowel and other sounds taught in this chapter.

SUPPLEMENTARY ACTIVITY #2
Sound cards

Instead of, or in addition to, the sound book illustrated in Supplementary Activity #1, each of the words used to illustrate the **long E** sound may be written separately on a 6" by 8" index card and placed in an envelope marked **Long E** or simply $\bar{\text{E}}$'s. Like the sound book, this envelope can then be pulled out periodically to review the **long E** sound as well as the words containing it. On the back of one or more of the cards a picture can be drawn or pasted which illustrates the word with that particular sound.

LESSON #2
Long O

This lesson should be taught basically in the same way as the previous lesson dealing with the **long E** sound.

ACTIVITY #1
Recognizing the **long O** sound

Remind the child of the identity of the five most common vowels, that each one has both a long and a short sound, and that the long vowel "says" its name. Tell him that the two of you are now going to study **long O**.

What do you think long O will sound like?

(He should give you the letter name; if not, supply the sound for him.)

That's right. The long O says its name. I'm going to say some words that have a long O. See if you can hear it.

As in the previous lesson, read the following words dragging out the **O** sound.

no　　so　　go　　pony　　slow　　rope　　home

Now listen to these long O words and tell me if the O is at the beginning, end, or inside of the word.

(Do not show the child these words; there are so many vowel generalizations involved that he may become confused.)

oats	(beginning)
coat	(inside)
toe	(end)
road	(inside)
note	(inside)
old	(beginning)
hold	(inside)
snow	(end)

ACTIVITY #2
Distinguishing the **long O** sound

As in the previous lesson have the child say "**Long O**" when he hears that sound in a word:

no	(yes)	ride	(no)
stay	(no)	blue	(no)
so	(yes)	slow	(yes)
shake	(no)	tree	(no)
pony	(yes)	go	(yes)

ACTIVITY #3
Rule I applied to **O**

Ask the child if he remembers the first rule for when vowels are long (that is, when there is only one vowel in a word and it comes at the end). If he doesn't, remind him. Write the words "no," "so," and "go" on a sound sheet as in the previous lesson (labeled **Long O** or **Ō**) and allow the child to mark the vowel with a long sign (n**o**).

Note that these rules are not infallible, as with "do," which does not contain a long "O" sound.

ACTIVITY #4
Rule II applied to **O**

Repeat the process for Rule II: When two vowels are together, the first one is usually long and the second one is not heard. Unfortunately, the child may not know any words containing a **long O** to illustrate Rule II, but this gives you an excellent excuse to teach a few:

coat   road   boat   goat

Have the child mark the **long O** in each word.

ACTIVITY #5
Rule III for long vowels

There is a definite danger of overloading the child with complex phonics rules, especially if you are dealing with a very young child. The best advice we can give you at this point is for you to *use your judgment*. If the child had no trouble learning the previous two rules, teach him this one. If he did have trouble, simply present him with the following "family" of words to learn; he will eventually make up his own rules, even if it is only on a very intuitive level.

RULE III

If a word has only two vowels and one is an "e" at the end, the "e" is usually silent and the other vowel is long.

Words you can teach to illustrate this rule:

note   hope   rope   broke   rose

Have the child mark the vowel.

SUPPLEMENTARY ACTIVITY #1
The sound book

The **O** page in the sound book could look something like this:

Long O   **ō**
RULE I   **Word has one vowel and it is at end**   no   so   go
RULE II   **Word has two vowels together; first is usually long**   boat   coat   goat   road
RULE III   **Word has two vowels one of which is an "e" at end; "e" is silent and other vowel is long**   (If you don't formally teach the rule, just list these words separately for the child.)   note   hope   rope   broke   rose

SUPPLEMENTARY ACTIVITY #2
O followed by **ld**

If you are dealing with an older child, or feel especially adventuresome, you can point out the following family of words which contain the **long O** sound:

    bold   fold   hold   sold
    cold   gold   mold   told

LESSON #3
Long A

ACTIVITY #1
Recognizing the **long A** sound

Words to read orally following discussion as in previous lesson:

    baby   day   may   play   stay
    place   shake   paid   away   today

ACTIVITY #2
Distinguishing the **long A** sound

baby	(yes)	slow	(no)
need	(no)	stay	(yes)
shake	(yes)	today	(yes)
paid	(yes)	ice	(no)
eat	(no)	play	(yes)

ACTIVITY #3
Rule II applied to **A**

Words which illustrate this rule:

paid   rain   train   sail

Have the child mark the **long A**.

ACTIVITY #4
Rule III applied to **A**

Words illustrating this rule:

made	wade	fake	make
jade	bake	Jake	rake
fade	cake	lake	take
			wake

Don't forget to help the child guess the identity of each of these words by consonant substitution.

ACTIVITY #5
Rule IV for long vowels

Usually when a vowel is followed directly by "y," the y is silent and the vowel is long. Unless your child is very adept at rules, the best way to teach this principle is by simply teaching him the following list of words and entering them on his sound sheet.

Words he knows: day   may   play   stay   away   today
New words: bay   gay   hay   Jay   Kay   lay   Ray   say   way
(Allow the child to mark the **long A**.)

Although this may seem like an inordinate number of words to teach the child, you will find that he will have very little trouble with them, as long as they are in lists such as these which allow him to substitute consonants. Teaching him words in this manner is excellent practice in actually applying his phonics skills, and with a little review these words can become a permanent part of his sight vocabulary.

SUPPLEMENTARY ACTIVITIES (AS DESIRED)

LESSON #4
Long I

ACTIVITY #1
Recognizing the **long I** sound

Words to read orally:

kite   white   I   child   high   ride   ice   time

Ask the child to tell you the location of the **long I** in the following list (that is, beginning, inside, or end):

ice   my   pie   light   child   kind   find   lie

ACTIVITY #2
Distinguishing the **Long I** sound

I'm going to read you a list of words that have vowels that say their names. I want you to tell me the name of the vowel in each word.

kite	(i)	child	(i)
white	(i)	ripe	(i)
day	(a)	he	(e)
pony	(o)	place	(a)
slide	(i)	I	(i)

ACTIVITY #3
Rule III applied to **I**

As always, prompt the child to see if he can verbalize the rule. If not, help him.

Words he knows	New Words
like	hike
kite	bite
white	mine
time	dime
ride	hide
slide	fine

SUPPLEMENTARY ACTIVITY #1
Y

If the child had no trouble with any aspect of **I**, you might explain to him that "Y" at the end of a one-syllable word (since he doesn't yet know what a syllable is, you might say "a very short word") is pronounced the same way as a **long I** if no other vowel is present. Examples are: my, by, try, fly.

SUPPLEMENTARY ACTIVITY #2
I followed by **nd** and **gh**

Again, teach the following families of words only if you think your child is ready for them.

gh	*nd*
fight	find
light	kind
might	mind

gh
night
right
sight
tight

OTHER SUPPLEMENTARY ACTIVITIES (AS DESIRED)

LESSON #5
Long U

The **long U** sound is not encountered as commonly as the other vowel sounds, and the child probably has not yet learned a word actually containing it. (Words like "blue" which at first glance may appear to have a **U** sound actually have an **oo** sound like **boot**.) At this point, therefore, it is probably enough to familiarize the child with the **long U** sound and make sure that he can differentiate it from the other long vowel sounds.

ACTIVITY #1
Recognizing the **long U** sound

Words to read orally:

use   cube   cute   fuse   mule

ACTIVITY #2
Distinguishing the **long U** sound

Have the child tell you the long vowel contained in each of the following words:

use	(u)	cube	(u)
pray	(a)	slow	(o)
white	(i)	fuse	(u)
cute	(u)	mule	(u)

ACTIVITY #3
Rule III applied to **U**

Show the child the following list and ask him if he can think of a rule that will indicate why the **U** sound should be long. If he cannot verbalize the rule (III), help him.

use   cube   cute   fuse   mule

Allow the child to draw the long sign over the vowels when you are through.

SUPPLEMENTARY ACTIVITIES (AS DESIRED)

COMPETENCY TEST
Long vowel sounds

Listed below in random order are ten nonsense words by means of which you will evaluate your child's competence in recognizing the long vowel sounds.

Approach this test as you would any activity in order not to intimidate your child. After giving the test, use the section "How to evaluate the results" to decide which sounds still need to be taught.

HOW TO ADMINISTER THE TEST

The materials you will need are: 1. a copy of the Long Vowel Sounds Competency Test, 2. a copy of the corresponding worksheet, and 3. a pencil or crayon for the child to use.

Starting at the top of the list on the worksheet, read each nonsense word *twice* slowly. In parenthesis is a real word indicating how it should be pronounced. Do not hold the list in the child's line of vision. Allow him sufficient time to examine the options on the test and then circle the letter corresponding to the long vowel sound he heard.

When the entire test has been given, score it by writing in the blanks on the worksheet in the following manner:

correct response : +
no response : −
wrong sound : Write the letter representing the actual sound that was given.

To use the test you should say something like:

I am going to read you some silly words that don't mean anything. All of them have long vowel sounds. Listen carefully while I say each word. Then look at your paper and circle the long vowel sound you heard. Let's practice together so you will know what to do.

Direct the child to where it says "sample" on the test paper.

Listen to the word I say. Then circle one of these letters to show which vowel sound you heard.

bafe (safe)
bafe

After you have said the word twice the child should circle the letter "a" on his paper. Practice with the sample until you are sure he knows what to do.

Long Vowel Sounds Competency Test

Sample	a	e	i	o
1.	u	a	e	i
2.	o	u	a	e
3.	u	a	i	o
4.	o	u	e	i
5.	a	e	i	o
6.	o	a	e	i
7.	i	u	a	e
8.	u	a	e	o
9.	o	u	a	i
10.	u	e	i	o

Long Vowel Sounds Competency Test Worksheet

				Part I Lesson #
1.	bute	(cute)	(u)	5
2.	mo	(no)	(o)	2
3.	pide	(ride)	(i)	4
4.	dee	(bee)	(e)	1
5.	sate	(late)	(a)	3
6.	tay	(bay)	(a)	3
7.	kuse	(fuse)	(u)	5
8.	lope	(hope)	(o)	2
9.	fi	(hi)	(i)	4
10.	beek	(seek)	(e)	1

HOW TO EVALUATE THE RESULTS

Count up the number of correct responses (the number of plus marks) and record it at the top of your worksheet. You now have a record of how many and which sounds are in your child's *functional phonics repertoire*. These are the sounds you can expect him to use in unlocking unknown words. The letters marked with a minus will need to be retaught. In cases where the wrong answer was given, both sounds should be retaught.

Praise your child for those sounds that he knew (never make him feel badly for those he didn't know). Use the test results constructively. You now know which lessons to go back to. Included next to every test item on your worksheet is the lesson in which it was introduced. For every sound there are two test items. If either one has been missed, the particular lesson should be reviewed. This can be done directly or, preferably, when the problem sound comes up in the child's reading. In a perfectly staged scenario you would see the sound *before* your child started reading his language experience story or his book. You would then go back to teach the phonics lesson *prior* to his reading. Afterwards, when he went to read the story he would have the opportunity to apply the lesson contents to the new word. You would have the chance to see whether he could *use* his new skills.

You do not need to postpone teaching the rest of this chapter until a certain percentage of the test items are answered correctly, as long as you continually review those lessons which are not within your child's functional phonics repertoire. He may have less difficulty learning the material in other sections. As always, you must use your judgment.

HOW TO USE THE RESULTS FOR PLACEMENT IN THE BOOK

If you are not using this book from cover to cover, but want to know where in the book to start working with your child, follow these guidelines. If a perfect score was attained, proceed to administer the Competency Test in Part Two; otherwise:

1. Teach only the lessons in Part One for those sounds missed on the test, preferably in conjunction with actual reading experience as described in Chapters Nine and Eleven. Refer to rules that may be taught in other lessons and teach them when they apply.

2. Readminister the test and file the worksheet in your records so you will know which lessons to reteach in the future.

3. Give the other competency tests in this chapter and incorporate the lessons for those sounds your child does not know in your regular reading instruction.

PART TWO
Learning the Short Vowels

The short vowels are a little more difficult to learn than the long ones since the actual sounds they represent are different from the letter names. As there are only five of them, however, the task shouldn't take too long.

Before teaching them you should first familiarize yourself thoroughly with the sounds represented by each since they will be pronounced in isolation. The following chart may be of help in this regard if you memorize the word associated with each short vowel. (If you still have trouble isolating the vowel sound, go to the other examples in Activity #1 of each of the five lessons contained in this section.) A chart made up of words chosen by you and the child may be used as well.

	A	E	I	O	U
long	ate	me	kite	no	use
short	at	met	it	not	up

LESSON #1
Short a

We've learned the long sounds which each of the five vowels stand for. Now we're going to learn their short sounds.

Can you make the sounds of the five long vowels?

As always, help the child if necessary.

ACTIVITY #1
Recognizing the **short a** sound

Today we're going to learn a different sound for a. The long a sound is a (pronounce it). The short sound which a sometimes stands for sounds like this: ă (pronounce it).

You already know many words which have this sound. Listen to these carefully and see if you can hear it:

        and   rabbit   has   can   Thank

Do you hear the ă (pronounce it) sound?

Let's hear you say it.

Help the child arrive at a reasonable approximation of the sound, then read the rest of the list to him.

black   fast   man   cat   hamburger   at   ham

ACTIVITY #2
Distinguishing the **long** and **short a** sounds

---

*O.K. Now that you know the sound that **short a** stands for, I want you to see if you can tell which words have **short a** and which have **long a**.*

*First say the sound **long a** stands for again.*

*Now the sound for **short a**.*

*Good. Now after each word I read I want you to say "**short a**" if the sound is short and "**long a**" if the sound is long.*

track	(short)	had	(short)
baby	(long)	stay	(long)
bag	(short)	grass	(short)
at	(short)	place	(long)
play	(long)	tap	(short)

ACTIVITY #3
Rule I for short vowels

Write the following words on the child's sound sheet, having him read each as you write it. If he doesn't know a particular word, remind him of a similar one he does know.

at   an   am   and

How are these words alike?

Elicit the fact that they all begin with **short** a.

Good, you've just learned the first rule for short vowels.

If a word only has one vowel and it is at the beginning of a word, then that vowel is usually short.

Show the child the "short sign" (˘) and have him place it over the four words you just wrote.

*We can make many new words out of these words by adding one letter. They all have the **short a** sound. See if you can read these families.*

Administer help with the initial sound as needed.

an	at	am	and
ban	bat	dam	land
can	cat	ham	sand
Dan	fat	jam	band
fan	hat	Pam	hand
Jan	mat	Sam	
man	rat		
Nan	sat		
pan	vat		
ran			
tan			
van			

How are these words alike?

Elicit the fact that all contain a **short a** and it is inside the word.

That's right, so let's add something to our rule.

RULE I

If a word only has one vowel and it is at the beginning or inside (emphasize "inside") of the word, then that vowel is usually short.

SUPPLEMENTARY ACTIVITY #1
Sound book or cards

As in previous lessons, the words learned illustrating the **short a** sound can be written on (1.) a piece of paper and filed in the sound book or (2.) on word cards and filed in an envelope labelled ă.

SUPPLEMENTARY ACTIVITY #2
Sentences containing **short a** words

It is a good idea to have actual sentences read containing words with the **short a** sound. Children often enjoy this activity if the sentences are purposefully contrived such as:

> A fat cat ran back.
> Nan can fan Jan.
> Dan and Jan had jam and ham.
> Pam has a black mat.
> Sam has a hat.

SUPPLEMENTARY ACTIVITY #3
Changing short vowels to long

For the older child, demonstrate how a one-letter addition to certain words changes them from fitting Rule I for short vowels to Rules II or III for long ones (see Part One):

Rule I for short vowels	*Rule III for long vowels*
can	cane
cap	cape
rat	rate
tap	tape
hop	hope
at	ate
hat	hate
ran	rain
man	main
pan	pain

LESSON #2
Short e

Follow the same format as for Lesson #1.

ACTIVITY #1
Recognizing the ĕ sound

    red   helps
    nest   get
    eggs   help
    pen   Red Hen
    yellow   pets

ACTIVITY #2
Distinguishing the ĕ sound

Long versus short e.

1. After reading these words, write them and have the child mark the vowels ("ē" or "ĕ").

    yes   me
    be   eggs
    well   nest

2. ĕ versus ă. Read these words to the child, letting him decide which ones have **short e** and which ones **short a**.

    Red   ham
    at   pets
    fast   help

ACTIVITY #3
Families of words containing ĕ

Have the child read the following lists. Add the words to the sound book/cards, whichever strategy is being used.

red	hen	get
bed	pen	bet
fed	Ben	let
Jed	den	met
led	men	net
Ted	ten	set
wed		vet
		wet
		yet

ACTIVITY #4
Review

Ask the child the following questions, plus any you wish to add:

Name the vowels.
What are the two short vowels we've studied so far?
Can you say the rule which tells us when a vowel is short?

(See Rule I.)

What sound is this?

Write ă and have the child pronounce it.

What sound does ĕ stand for?

SUPPLEMENTARY ACTIVITIES (AS DESIRED)

LESSON #3
Short ĭ

ACTIVITY #1
Recognizing the ĭ sound

After reading the list, point out how the words conform to Rule I for short vowels.

in	sits	swim	Jip
is	Chick	sick	Dick
big	this	rib	lip

ACTIVITY #2
Distinguishing the ĭ sound

Write the following words on a page in the sound book (or sheet of paper if this activity is not being used). Have the child tell you whether each word contains a long or short i. Allow him to draw the appropriate symbol over the ones correctly distinguished.

Chick	(short)	bike	(long)
like	(long)	Dick	(short)
this	(short)	bite	(long)
time	(long)	swim	(short)
gives	(short)	Jim	(short)

ACTIVITY #3
Word families containing ĭ

Add these words to the sound book/cards.

in	is	it	did	sing	ill	big
fin	his	bit	bid	ring	Bill	pig
kin		fit	hid	king	will	wig
win		hit	lid		hill	dig
sin		kit	rid		mill	fig
pin		lit				
		pit				
		sit				

SUPPLEMENTARY ACTIVITY #1
Sentences containing ĭ

Have the following sentences read by the child, pointing out words containing the ĭ sound (all the words with i are short).

This pig can dig.

He is king of the big hill.

Will did sing on the hill.

Bill hid the lid.

SUPPLEMENTARY ACTIVITY #2
Child-constructed sentences

The more advanced student might enjoy making up his own sentences. These can be dictated to you, then read after you have printed them clearly on a sheet of paper. Have the "ˇ" symbol drawn over the short vowels.

OTHER SUPPLEMENTARY ACTIVITIES (AS DESIRED)

LESSON #4
Short o

ACTIVITY #1
Recognizing the ŏ sound

on	soft
got	John
dog	knock
Tom	rock
pond	boss

ACTIVITY #2
Distinguishing the ŏ sound

pond	sat
this	not
boss	got
pets	has
jog	Don

ACTIVITY #3
Word families containing ŏ

not	*stop*	*Bob*
got	cop	rob
lot	hop	sob
hot	pop	cob
tot	mop	mob
rot	top	job
cot		
dot		

SUPPLEMENTARY ACTIVITIES (AS DESIRED)

LESSON #5
Short u

ACTIVITY #1
Recognizing the ŭ sound

up	cluck
Run	fun
Duck	run
jump	funny

ACTIVITY #2
Distinguishing the ŭ sound

Have the child tell when he hears a word with **short u**. If he is successful, repeat the list, this time asking him to name the short vowel in each word:

jump	(ŭ)	is	(ĭ)
black	(ă)	bug	(ŭ)
run	(ŭ)	dog	(ŏ)
pen	(ĕ)	but	(ŭ)

ACTIVITY #3
Word families containing ŭ

Add these words to the sound book/cards.

jump	run	*Duck*
bump	bun	buck
dump	fun	cluck
hump	sun	muck
lump		puck
pump		suck

ACTIVITY #4
Review

Have the following lists read. If one word per list is known, the child should be able to pronounce the rest by supplying the appropriate short vowel sound. If a word is missed, review the appropriate short vowel. (This activity is hard for beginners.)

bat	sit	run	tin	big
bet	set	ran	tan	beg
bit	sat		ten	bag
but				bug
				bog

Expand the lists to include nonsense words:

fun	sit	tell	spell	dress
fan	sat	tall	spall	drass
fin	set	tull	spill	druss
fon	sot	till	spull	driss
fen	sut	toll	spoll	dross

SUPPLEMENTARY ACTIVITIES (AS DESIRED)

COMPETENCY TEST
Short vowel sounds

Listed below are ten nonsense words by means of which you will evaluate your child's ability to recognize the short vowel sounds. Refer to the test on long vowels (page 314) for procedures, materials, and how to evaluate the results.

To use the test you should say something like this:

I am going to read you some silly words that don't mean anything. All of them have short vowel sounds. Listen carefully while I say each word. Then look at your paper and circle the short vowel sound you heard. Let's practice together so you will know what to do.

Direct the child to where it says "sample" on the test paper.

Listen to the word I say. Then circle one of these letters to show which vowel sound you heard.

  bab (cab)
  bab

After you have said the word twice the child should circle the letter "a" on his paper. Practice with the sample until you are sure he knows what to do.

Short Vowel Sounds Competency Test

Sample	a	e	i	o
1.	u	a	e	o
2.	o	u	a	i
3.	u	e	i	o
4.	o	a	e	i
5.	i	u	a	e
6.	u	a	e	i
7.	o	u	a	e
8.	u	a	i	o
9.	o	u	e	i
10.	a	e	i	o

Short Vowel Sounds Competency Test Worksheet

				Lesson #
1. um	(gum)	(u)		5
2. ig	(pig)	(i)		3
3. mun	(sun)	(u)		5
4. ob	(mob)	(o)		4
5. en	(pen)	(e)		2
6. med	(bed)	(e)		2
7. mot	(cot)	(o)		4
8. lat	(sat)	(a)		1
9. fid	(did)	(i)		3
10. ab	(cab)	(a)		1

PART THREE
Consonant Blends

When two or more consonants are used in such a way that both sounds are heard together, this mixed sound is called a *consonant blend*. Usually they are learned easily by children who have mastered the initial and final consonant sounds, and their knowledge can be a great help in attacking unfamiliar words.

Although there are a great many consonant blends, the two consonants which blend most readily are **l** and **r**, such as **bl, cl, fl, gl, pl, sl, br, cr, dr, fr, gr, pr**, and **tr**, all of which will be studied in this chapter, along with two other commonly occurring combinations: **sw** and **st**.

MODEL LESSON

ACTIVITY #1
Recognizing the **bl** sound

Watch as I write these words and tell me how they are all alike.

The child will most likely notice that they all begin with **b**. Tell him that he is correct but they all have something else in common. They also have an **l**.

blue	blame	block
black	blaze	blood
blend	bloom	blind
blank	blow	blown

Now listen as I read them so you can tell me how else they're alike.

(Answer: they begin with the same sound.)

That's right! They all begin with a bl (pronounce it) *sound.*

ACTIVITY #2
Distinguishing the **bl** sound

Now I'm going to read you some words which begin with the **bl** *(pronounce it) sound and some which do not. I want you to clap your hands when you hear it.*

black	boom
boy	fly
toy	glare
blue	blare
sue	blossom
bloom	block

ACTIVITY #3
Learning a **bl** word

Let's read our list of words containing the **bl** *sound together. Watch carefully because I want you to pick out one that you want to learn.*

Place the sheet of paper upon which you wrote the words used in Activity #1. Read the words slowly so that your child can follow the words with you. Emphasize the initial consonant blend.

Now let's read them together.

Read the list again allowing the child to join in.

Which word would you like to learn?

Allow the child to choose one of the words, preferably not one he already knows (such as "blue" or "black").

Write the word on a sound card and place it in an envelope marked BLENDS. In later lessons you will ask the child to supply a word beginning with the **bl** sound. If he cannot come up with one you will show him this sound card and ask him to read it (see Activity #4 in Lesson #2).

SUPPLEMENTARY ACTIVITY #1
Sound book and/or word cards

As in previous lessons. Label the page/envelope **bl**.

SUPPLEMENTARY ACTIVITY #2
Nonsense words

One good way to make sure that the child has mastered a consonant blend is to make up nonsense words and see if he can pronounce them. If he can, he has mastered the blend and is probably ready to incorporate it in his word attack repertoire.

*I'm going to write some words beginning with **b**, then I'm going to add an **l** after the **b**. I want you to read both the **b** and the **bl** words and show me how they are different.*

(The child may need help initially but he will soon catch on.)

big	blig
boy	bloy
bird	blird
ball	blall

This exercise may be done with any of the blends taught in this chapter if your child seems to profit from it.

LESSON #1
bl

See Model Lesson.

LESSON #2
cl

ACTIVITY #1
Recognizing the **cl** sound

cluck	clam	clan
clown	cloud	clear
clean	clap	click
clay	climb	club

ACTIVITY #2
Distinguishing the **cl** sound

curtain	cluck
clan	kangaroo
click	keep
color	climb
keep	cold
clay	clown

ACTIVITY #3
Learning a **cl** word

See Model Lesson.

ACTIVITY #4
Review

Can you think of a word that begins like this?

Show him **bl** on a piece of paper. If he can, compliment him. If he does not name the specific word he chose to learn in Activity

#3 of the previous lesson, take the **bl** word card from the BLENDS envelope and ask him to read it. If he has trouble, help him sound the word out.

SUPPLEMENTARY ACTIVITIES

Pick the sound book, word cards, and/or nonsense word activities from the Model Lesson, as desired.

LESSON #3
fl

ACTIVITY #1
Recognizing the **fl** sound

fly	flat	flood
flop	flag	flap
flip	flash	flake
float	flavor	floor

ACTIVITY #2
Distinguishing the **fl** sound

flood	flag
Father	flake
fun	fair
floor	fish
float	flop
fire	fly

ACTIVITY #3
Learning a **fl** word

See Model Lesson.

SUPPLEMENTARY ACTIVITIES (AS DESIRED)

LESSON #4
gl

ACTIVITY #1
Recognizing the **gl** sound

glad	glint	glee
glass	glum	glide
glow	glimpse	glitter
glare	gleam	glue

ACTIVITY #2
Distinguishing the **gl** sound

glad	get
guy	glue
garden	glitter
glare	game
glimpse	gave
gas	glutton

ACTIVITY #3
Learning a **gl** word

See Model Lesson.

SUPPLEMENTARY ACTIVITIES (AS DESIRED)

LESSON #5
pl

ACTIVITY #1
Recognizing the **pl** sound

play	playground	plot
place	plop	plum
plant	plump	plus
plow	plan	please

ACTIVITY #2
Distinguishing the **pl** sound

play	pig
puddle	pillow
plop	playground
pond	Peter
plus	paid
please	place

ACTIVITY #3
Learning a **pl** word

See Model Lesson.

SUPPLEMENTARY ACTIVITIES (AS DESIRED)

LESSON #6
sl

ACTIVITY #1
Recognizing the **sl** sound

slide	slant	slam
slow	sled	slick
slap	sleep	slipper
slip	sly	slope

ACTIVITY #2
Distinguishing the **sl** sound

simple	sly
Sunday	shy
slide	said
super	sled
slope	slipper
super	slap

ACTIVITY #3
Learning a **sl** word

See Model Lesson.

ACTIVITY #4
Review

Make an answer sheet for the child as follows:

1.	bl	cl	fl
2.	bl	cl	fl
3.	bl	cl	fl
4.	gl	pl	sl
5.	gl	pl	sl
6.	bl	pl	sl
7.	bl	pl	sl
8.	bl	pl	sl
9.	cl	fl	gl
10.	cl	fl	gl

I'm going to read you some words and I'd like you to circle the letters that you think each one begins with.

Read the following list of words, emphasizing the consonant blend, and indicating to the child which row he should circle:

1. black
2. clean
3. fly
4. glass
5. slow
6. play
7. plate
8. slip
9. flap
10. clap

If he has trouble with a blend, remind him of the word in his BLENDS envelope he chose to learn for that particular blend. If he still doesn't recognize the letters, show him "his" word.

SUPPLEMENTARY ACTIVITY #1
Nonsense words

Make an answer sheet identical to the one in Activity #4 above and read the child the following nonsense words:

1. blat
2. clut
3. floam
4. glang
5. slun
6. flim
7. plike
8. slig
9. flid
10. cloat

Have the child circle the appropriate blend as before.

OTHER SUPPLEMENTARY ACTIVITIES (AS DESIRED)

LESSON #7
br

ACTIVITY #1
Recognizing the **br** sound

brown	brick	breakfast
bring	brag	break
brother	brain	branch
bright	brave	brush

ACTIVITY #2
Distinguishing the **br** sound

brown	brick
black	brag
break	bland
blame	blond
bake	brave
brush	brown

ACTIVITY #3
Learning a **br** word

See Model Lesson.

ACTIVITY #4
Review

Can you think of a word which begins like this?

Show **fl** in written form. Accept either a word or the sound itself. Review the appropriate word in the BLENDS envelope, if necessary.

Repeat for **gl**, **pl**, **sl**, and **br**.

LESSON #8
cr

ACTIVITY #1
Recognizing the **cr** sound

cream	crop	crime
cry	crash	creep
crab	cross	crown
crib	crooked	crumb

ACTIVITY #2
Distinguishing the **cr** sound

clown	crime
cream	climb
crab	club
cluck	crown
cold	cloud
crooked	creep

ACTIVITY #3
Learning a **cr** word

See Model Lesson.

SUPPLEMENTARY ACTIVITIES (AS DESIRED)

LESSON #9
dr

ACTIVITY #1
Recognizing the **dr** sound

drop	drip	dream
drag	draw	dragon
dress	drum	drive
drink	drill	drug

ACTIVITY #2
Distinguishing the **dr** sound

dark	drill
drop	drug
dish	dug
drink	does
do	dress
dull	dragon

ACTIVITY #3
Learning a **dr** word

See Model Lesson.

SUPPLEMENTARY ACTIVITIES (AS DESIRED)

LESSON #10
fr

ACTIVITY #1
Recognizing the **fr** sound

free	frog	friend
fry	fruit	frown
from	freeze	front
fret	frost	fright

ACTIVITY #2
Distinguishing the **fr** sound

from	fry
float	fly
front	flop
flake	freeze
floor	for
fright	friend

ACTIVITY #3
Learning a **fr** word

See Model Lesson.

SUPPLEMENTARY ACTIVITIES (AS DESIRED)

LESSON #11
gr

ACTIVITY #1
Recognizing the **gr** sound

green	grass	great
grow	grape	gray
grip	grease	grind
grab	growl	ground

ACTIVITY #2
Distinguishing the **gr** sound

grape	great
glare	go
gray	glint
glitter	ground
grab	grip
glad	green

ACTIVITY #3
Learning a **gr** word

See Model Lesson.

ACTIVITY #4
Review

Can you think of a word which begins like this?

Show **cr** written down. Accept either a word or the sound itself. Review the appropriate word in the BLENDS envelope, if necessary.

Repeat for **dr**, **fr**, and **gr**.

SUPPLEMENTARY ACTIVITIES (AS DESIRED)

LESSON #12
pr

ACTIVITY #1
Recognizing the **pr** sound

print	prince	press
pride	pretty	praise
price	prey	princess
prank	pro	prize

ACTIVITY #2
Distinguishing the **pr** sound

pride	plum
plant	plow
pretty	price
pro	print
plot	plump
prince	prize

ACTIVITY #3
Learning a **pr** word

See Model Lesson.

SUPPLEMENTARY ACTIVITIES (AS DESIRED)

LESSON #13
tr

ACTIVITY #1
Recognizing the **tr** sound

tree	tray	track
try	trash	trail
trip	trade	trace
trap	truck	true

ACTIVITY #2
Distinguishing the **tr** sound

trash	touch
tell	turn
tug	truck
true	to
tongue	touch
trap	tree

ACTIVITY #3
Learning a **tr** word

See Model Lesson.

ACTIVITY #4
Review

Make an answer sheet for the child as follows:

1.	br	cr	dr
2.	br	cr	dr
3.	br	cr	dr
4.	fr	gr	pr
5.	fr	gr	pr
6.	gr	pr	tr
7.	tr	cr	fr
8.	tr	br	dr
9.	cr	fr	gr
10.	br	tr	cr

I'm going to read you some words and I'd like you to circle the letters that you think each one begins with.

Read the following list of words, emphasizing the consonant blend, and indicating the number if necessary.

1. break
2. cry
3. drive
4. green
5. pride
6. trash
7. frog
8. try
9. cream
10. true

Use the words in the BLENDS envelope for any troublesome sounds.

SUPPLEMENTARY ACTIVITIES
Nonsense words

Conduct the above exercise with the following list of nonsense words:

1. bloy
2. crub
3. druke
4. grake
5. preak
6. trog
7. frack
8. tream
9. cride
10. treen

OTHER SUPPLEMENTARY ACTIVITIES (AS DESIRED)

LESSON #14
sw

ACTIVITY #1
Recognizing the **sw** sound

swim	swoop	sway
swell	sweat	sweet
sweep	swat	swamp
swap	swan	swing

ACTIVITY #2
Distinguishing the **sw** sound

swim	swamp
slide	slope
slip	sly
swan	sweat
swoop	swell
slap	swing

ACTIVITY #3
Learning a **sw** word

See Model Lesson.

ACTIVITY #4
Review

Can you think of a word which begins like this?

Show **cr**. If he cannot, and cannot pronounce the sound as well, refer to the appropriate word in the BLENDS envelope.

Repeat for **dr, fr, gr, pr, tr,** and **sw**.

LESSON #15
st

ACTIVITY #1
Recognizing the **st** sound

---

stay	stop	state
sting	stamp	stand
stink	step	stone
Steve	stomp	stick

ACTIVITY #2
Distinguishing the **st** sound

---

stamp	swim
swoop	sweat
sly	stomp
Steve	sling
stone	stone
stick	stop

ACTIVITY #3
Learning a **st** word

See Model Lesson.

SUPPLEMENTARY ACTIVITIES (AS DESIRED)

Competency Test

Competency test follows Part Four.

PART FOUR
Consonant Digraphs

Sometimes two or more consonants used together produce a single sound rather than a blend of sounds. These consonant combinations are called **digraphs** and four of the more common ones (all involving the letter "h") will be taught in the following four lessons.

LESSON #1
ch

Actually this digraph represents three separate sounds: 1. a **k** sound such as in "chorus"; 2. a **sh** sound such as in "chef"; and 3. the **ch** sound as in "child." Since the first two usages are much less common in beginning reading materials, we will treat only the third **ch** sound in this chapter. You may deal with the others on an individual basis if the need arises later.

ACTIVITY #1
Recognizing the **ch** sound

(See the Model Lesson for Part Three.)

child	chicken	chin
chick	children	chocolate
chest	chuck	chill
chop	chip	chase

ACTIVITY #2
Distinguishing the **ch** sound

(See the Model Lesson for Part Three.)

>   checker   chuck
>   cream   crowd
>   chest   clear
>   chill   cab
>   clown   chicken
>   click   child

ACTIVITY #3
Adding the **ch** sound

I'm going to write some words that you already know. Watch carefully because I want you to read each one.

> in
> at
> ill (The child may not know this word, so you can help him sound it out if needed.)

Now, I want you to add the ch (pronounce it) *sound to each word and tell me what word it makes.*

Print the "ch" in front of each word as your child attempts to sound out the new word. If he needs help with the first word, for example, ask him:

What does i n spell? Point to the word.
What sound does ch make?
O.K. What word sounds like ch (pronounce it) *"in"?*
Good! Now let's do the same thing for "at."

ACTIVITY #4
Sound substitution

I'm going to write some more words you know. See if you can read them as I write each one.

>   Jip   stop
>   nest   will
>   duck   hat

Now, I'm going to cover the first sound of each word and I want you to add the **ch** *(pronounce it) sound and tell me what word it makes.*

>   Jip   (ip-chip)   stop   (op-chop)
>   nest   (est-chest)   will   (ill-chill)
>   duck   (uck-chuck)   hat   (at-chat)

SUPPLEMENTARY ACTIVITY #1
Learning a **ch** word

As in Activity #3 of the previous section, you may find it helpful for the child to learn one word of his choosing beginning with **ch**. We personally recommend this technique, and if you found it helpful with the consonant blends you should include it in the four digraph lessons. See the Model Lesson for Part Three for details.

OTHER SUPPLEMENTARY ACTIVITIES (AS DESIRED [SEE PART THREE])

LESSON #2
sh

This is an easy sound for children to remember because they often hear parents and/or teachers use it when they want children to be quiet: "shhhh."

ACTIVITY #1
Recognizing the **sh** sound

(See the Model Lesson in Part Three.)

she	shall	ship
show	shell	sharp
shot	shoe	shirt
shut	sheep	shame

ACTIVITY #2
Distinguishing the **sh** sound

shake	ship
share	shame
chest	child
shore	chase
chill	shoe
shirt	shot

ACTIVITY #3
Adding the **sh** sound

Have the child substitute the **sh** sound for the first sound in the following list of words as you did in Activity #4 of the previous lesson.

but	(ut-shut)
not	(ot-shot)
stop	(op-shop)
he	(e-she)
bell	(ell-shell)
red	(ed-shed)
Jip	(ip-ship)

ACTIVITY #4
The final **sh** sound

*The **sh** (pronounce it) sound also comes at the end of some words. Listen carefully while I read you these words. If you hear the **sh** sound at the end, clap your hands.*

shop	dash	short	wash	push
dish	ship	Jip	mash	hush

SUPPLEMENTARY ACTIVITIES (AS DESIRED [SEE PART THREE])

LESSON #3
wh

The **wh** sound is in some frequently used words: "why," "what," "when," and "where" being the most obvious examples. It is a peculiar sound in that it is pronounced as if it were spelled "hw," although if your child gives it more of an initial "w" sound you probably shouldn't confuse him at this stage by continually correcting him. (Note that some "wh" words have an initial **h** sound instead of **hw**, such as "who." As with the different **ch** sounds, we suggest that you teach these on an individual basis as they come up in reading.)

ACTIVITY #1
Recognizing the **wh** sound

(See the Model Lesson in Part Three.)

white	what	wheat
when	whale	whether
why	wheel	whip
where	whisper	whisper

ACTIVITY #2
Distinguishing the **wh** sound

    why   three   whip   whistle
    where   wheel   had   whale
    the   chair   whisper   white

ACTIVITY #3
Adding a "w" to make the **wh** sound

I'm going to show you some words beginning with the h sound. Listen carefully as I read them because I want you to tell me what you think each will sound like when we add a "w" to the beginning.

Write the following words, one at a time, reading each as you are writing it. Then place a "w" at the beginning of the word and ask the child:

Now, what word do you think this makes?

    heel (wheel)   heat (wheat)
    hip (whip)   hen (when)

SUPPLEMENTARY ACTIVITIES (AS DESIRED [SEE MODEL LESSON IN PART THREE])

LESSON #4
th

The **th** sound is also commonly used in beginning reading. It might help the child to form the sound if you call attention to the position of the tongue when pronouncing it (right behind the front upper teeth*).

ACTIVITY #1
Recognizing the **th** sound

(See the Model Lesson in Part Three.)

the	there	thumb
they	three	third
this	thing	think
that	thank	thunder

ACTIVITY #2
Distinguishing the **th** sound

---

the	thank	third	hang
tree	tan	herd	thing
thing	whistle	thumb	that
tin		hum	

ACTIVITY #3
Sound substitution

I'm going to write some words you may know. See if you can read them as I write each one.

If the child does not know a particular word, either tell him or help him sound it out.

hen	drink
win	bird
man	bring

* Although the **th** sound in "they" and "this" is slightly different from that in "three" and "think," they are so similar that we find it less confusing to teach them as one sound.

Now I'm going to cover the first sound of each word and I want you to add the th sound and tell me what word it makes.

hen	(en-then)	drink	(ink-think)
win	(in-thin)	bird	(ird-third)
man	(an-than)	bring	(ing-thing)

SUPPLEMENTARY ACTIVITIES (AS DESIRED [SEE PART THREE])

COMPETENCY TESTS
Initial consonant blends and digraphs

Listed below are nineteen short "words," some real and some nonsense. Refer to the first test on initial consonant sounds in Chapter Five for procedures and materials.

To use the test you should say something like this:

I am going to show you a list of words one at a time through a little window. Some of the words will be real and some will be silly words that don't mean anything. Tell me the sound or sounds made by the first two letters of the word, or say the word. Let's practice together so you will know what to do.

Frame the word "blin" at the top of the test with the word window.

Can you think of the sounds made by the first two letters in this word or can you say the word? (Give the child a chance to respond.) *You could say blll for the sound, or you could say "blin."*

Practice using the sample until the task is understood, then go ahead to administer the test. For each item say:

Tell me the sounds or tell me the word.

HOW TO EVALUATE THE RESULTS

If you have gone through all the lessons in the consonant blends and digraphs sections you now know which lessons you need to go back to. (Included next to every test item on your worksheet is the lesson in which it was introduced). You may go directly to those lessons and reteach or review the material. The procedure we prefer, however, is that you wait until one of those troublesome blends or digraphs is encountered in the child's reading (either in a language experience story he has dictated or in a book he is reading with you). At that time go back to teach the particular lesson and then have your student read the story in which the sound will be encountered. Phonics is always

Initial Consonant Blends and Digraphs Competency Test

Sample	blin	10.	prin
1.	plin	11.	clin
2.	frin	12.	crin
3.	stin	13.	whin
4.	slin	14.	trin
5.	chin	15.	flin
6.	grin	16.	drin
7.	blin	17.	swin
8.	brin	18.	glin
9.	shin	19.	thin

Initial Consonant Blends and Digraphs Competency Test Worksheet

Date _____ ___# correct ÷ 19 = _____% correct

		Part	Lesson #
1.	pl_____	3	5
2.	fr_____	3	10
3.	st_____	3	15
4.	sl_____	3	6
5.	ch_____	4	1
6.	gr_____	3	11
7.	bl_____	3	1
8.	br_____	3	7
9.	sh_____	4	2
10.	pr_____	3	12
11.	cl_____	3	2
12.	cr_____	3	8
13.	wh_____	4	3
14.	tr_____	3	13
15.	fl_____	3	3
16.	dr_____	3	9
17.	sw_____	3	14
18.	gl_____	3	4
19.	th_____	4	4

more meaningful if taught in the context of an actual reading experience.

You do not need to postpone teaching the rest of this chapter until a certain percentage of the test items are answered correctly as long as you continually review the contents of the blends and digraphs sections that have not been mastered. He may have less difficulty learning the material in other sections. As always, you must use your judgment.

HOW TO USE THE RESULTS FOR PLACEMENT IN THE BOOK

If you are not using this book from cover to cover, but want to know where in the book to start working with your child, follow these guidelines:

1. Study the Model Lesson for Part Three (Consonant Blends).
2. Teach the lessons in Parts Three and Four for those sounds missed on the test, preferably in conjunction with actual reading experience as described in Chapter Nine.
3. Readminister the test and file the worksheet in your records so you will know which lessons to reteach in the future.
4. Administer the other competency tests in this chapter and incorporate the lessons for those sounds which your child does not know in your regular reading instruction.

PART FIVE
Endings and Special Problems

The five lessons in this section treat structural characteristics of the language with which the child will eventually need to become familiar. The first lesson discusses compound words which children attack fairly easily once they learn to break them apart. This topic also blends naturally into the study of syllabication which, although it cannot be taught in detail within the scope of this book, is crucial to the development of advanced reading skills. The other topics have been introduced in previous lessons (with the exception of the use of contractions) and thus should not create any special problems.

LESSON #1
Compound words

Compound words consist of two or more words joined to make one.* They obviously tend to be longer than most individual words

* The formal definition of compound words involves unequal stress and no pauses between syllables. We feel that this is too complicated for most children, hence have opted for this simpler one. (This means, of course, that in some cases words which are designated as compound by our definition do not meet Webster's criteria.)

and can intimidate a beginning reader until he learns to break them apart.

ACTIVITY #1
Introduction

Print the following words for your child:

> thank you   milk shake   ice cream

Look at these three words you learned earlier. Do you see anything different about them?

(Answer: they are each composed of two separate words.)

Some words are made up of two separate words like this except they are not separated by a space like "thank you," "milk shake," and "ice cream."

(Point out the space between the two words in each.)

These words are called compound words. I'm going to show you some words you already know which can be made into compound words.

Write the following individual words followed by the compound word made from them:

> in + to = into

Ask the child to read both "in" and "to" by pointing to each individually. If he has trouble, help him. Next ask him if he can read the compound word (pointing to "into"). Then have him use "into" in a sentence to be sure he knows the meaning.

Repeat the process for:

> can + not = cannot
> up + on = upon (note the slight variation in pronunciation)

```
with   + out    = without
bird   + house  = birdhouse
dog    + house  = doghouse
with   + in     = within
pig    + pen    = pigpen
chicken + house = chickenhouse
```

ACTIVITY #2
Separating compound words

I'm going to write some more compound words for you and I want you to draw a line between the two words in them.

Give the child a pencil and show him how to draw the line using one of the words above (such as "birdhouse").

        playground   doghouse
        playhouse   into

SUPPLEMENTARY ACTIVITY #1
"Cutting" compound words

Write some of the above compound words on index cards and cut around each word in the shape of a circle, butterfly, or heart as illustrated below:

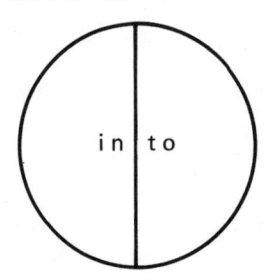

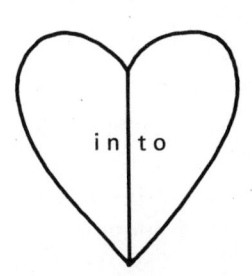

Next cut the word into its two constituents. Do this with several compound words and mix the halves thoroughly. Play a game in which the words are put back together and read.

SUPPLEMENTARY ACTIVITY #2
Distinguishing compound words

Read the following list of words to your child. Ask him to say yes for each that is a compound word, no for those that are not. When he misses a word, point it out to him and ask him to show you the two separate words.

1. mailman (yes)
2. beginning (no)
3. doorbell (yes)
4. anything (yes)
5. sunshine (yes)
6. yellow (no)
7. driveway (yes)
8. women (no)
9. bedroom (yes)
10. inside (yes)

SUPPLEMENTARY ACTIVITY #3
Sentences containing compound words

If you are dealing with an older child, or one who has a large sight vocabulary, you might write the following sentences out for him and ask him to underline or separate the compound words:

1. The airplane is on the runway.
2. The boy rang the doorbell.
3. The sunshine came into the bedroom.
4. Did somebody leave the classroom?
5. The flag is at the top of the flagpole.
6. The bluebird lives in the birdhouse.
7. The mailman delivered the postcard.
8. He lives inside the city.

LESSON #2
Selected noun and verb endings

If you taught your child the preprimers he already has a rudimentary knowledge of plural compared to singular endings for both nouns and verbs, tense changes for verbs, as well as possessive endings. We are going to include a few formal activities which you can employ to reinforce these concepts, but the best way to teach them is in context, that is, as your child encounters them in his reading.

ACTIVITY #1
Plural versus singular endings (regular nouns)

I'm going to write some words you know. Then I'm going to change them just a little bit to see if you can still read them.

Write the following words and their plurals and ask the child to read both. If he has trouble with the plural, remind him of the final **s** sounds learned in Chapter Five.

> kite   kites
> ball   balls
> balloon   balloons

Explain that when an **s** is added to words naming a "thing" it means more than one, and that when it doesn't have an **s** it usually means just one. (You may actually use the singular-plural terminology at this stage if you like.)

Here are some plural words that mean more than one. Tell me how to say each word when you only mean one.

Write and say the plural of each word. When your child supplies the singular, write it alongside the original.

eggs   (egg)
rabbits   (rabbit)
birds   (bird)
boys   (boy)
pets   (pet)
animals   (animal)

Now I want you to read the following words and tell me if they mean one or more than one.

Father
ducks
ponds
animals
chickens

ACTIVITY #2
Plural versus singular endings (irregular nouns)

Unfortunately, all nouns do not simply add "s" to form their plurals. Those ending in "y" normally replace the "y" ending with **ies**, such as "baby"–"babies"; others add **es**, such as "dish"–"dishes," while still others are even odder ("leaf"–"leaves," "child"–"children").

At this point it is enough that the child simply recognize these irregular plurals as plurals of familiar words. Toward this end have the child read the list below and tell you which word in each pair is singular and which plural.

leaf—leaves
baby—babies
families—family
children—child
dish—dishes

ACTIVITY #3
Adding **s** to verbs

Write these sentences for the child to read, underlining the verb, as shown below:

>Jim walks to school.
>The children walk to school.
>Tom plays with Jip.
>Tom and Pam play with Jip.

After each sentence is read, point out that the word that tells what the people do sometimes has an **s**. Make up other sentences and have the child decide whether the verb should have an "s." A more formal explanation of verb conjugation is not necessary at this time.

If the child's oral usage is incorrect, you should always supply the correct form in a friendly but matter-of-fact manner.

ACTIVITY #4
Other verb endings

It is important for a beginning reader to recognize the root word in verbs with **ed** and **ing** endings. (Having to learn each verb form as a new word is senseless.) To help the "spotting" of root words, provide lists like the one below for practice reading. Planting the words in sentences can then afford a more meaningful exercise.

play	plays	played	playing
jump	jumps	jumped	jumping
talk	talks	talked	talking

>Tom and Jim play with Jip.
>Tom plays with Jip.
>Tom played with Jip yesterday.
>Tom is playing with Jip.

LESSON #3
Contractions

Examples of some of the more common contractions follow. Call the child's attention to the fact that contractions always involve the deletion of one or more letters signaled by the presence of an *apostrophe* ('). Read the contractions together in the sentences below. Then write each contraction on a card and let the child practice reading it alone. If he doesn't remember one, refer him back to the sentence in which it is found.

Contractions involving **is** *or* **us**:
    let us—let's
    it is—it's
    that is—that's
    who is—who's

Contractions involving **not**:
    cannot—can't
    do not—don't
    did not—didn't
    is not—isn't

Contractions involving:

will
I will—I'll
He will—he'll

will not
I will not—I won't
He will not—He won't

have
I have—I've
They have—They've

am
I am—I'm

Sentences:
    Let us play ball.—Let's play ball.
    I do not want to go.—I don't want to go.
    I will not go.—I won't go.
    I am not going.—I'm not going.
    I have got to go.—I've got to go.

LESSON #4
Possessives

The apostrophe used in contractions to indicate that certain letters have been left out can also be used to denote possession or ownership. As with the contractions taught in Lesson #3, we assume that the use of possessives is already in the child's spoken and listening vocabulary. All that needs to be taught at this point is his recognition of possessives in print. (He should already know the final s sound from Chapter Five.)

As with the other items in this section, the best way to teach recognition of possessives is to point them out as they are naturally encountered in stories, or to use specially constructed sentences such as the ones below.

> The boy's cap is red.
> Tom's rabbit is big.
> The bird's eggs are in the nest.
> The man's hat is black.

As these words are probably in the child's sight vocabulary you should be able to concentrate entirely upon the use of the possessives. Make up as many sentences as are needed. To help you teach the concept, you can ask after each sentence is read, "Whose cap?" "Whose rabbit?" "Whose eggs?" and so on. The child should be able to answer based on the sentence.

One exercise which might help clear up any confusion between the use of possessives and contractions (after both are taught) follows.

Read the following phrases and fill in the box next to the one which shows possession.

The child should get at least eight correct. If he does not, he needs some more work on both possessives and contractions.

1. ☐ Jim's hat
   ☐ he's here

2. ☐ it's new
   ☐ Jan's book
3. ☐ Let's play
   ☐ Tom's pony
4. ☐ she'll play
   ☐ Kate's doll
5. ☐ I'll go
   ☐ bird's nest
6. ☐ children's mother
   ☐ playful boys
7. ☐ Jim's ball
   ☐ it's here
8. ☐ he'll sing
   ☐ boy's friend
9. ☐ cat's kitten
   ☐ runs fast
10. ☐ Jim's dog
    ☐ dogs run

COMPETENCY TEST
Endings and special problems

The four lessons in Part Five of this chapter have been divided into two competency tests. The first covers all the compound words taught in Lesson #1; the second samples items from the rest of the lessons. The topics treated in Lessons #2, #3, and #4 are potentially complex. Since we have provided an *introduction* to those topics in our text, we have also dealt with them in a more casual fashion in our test. The purpose of these tests is to make you aware of skills that still need teaching or review. Using the test results as a guide will enable you to tailor instruction to your child's needs.

Compound Words Competency Test

HOW TO ADMINISTER THE TEST

You will need a copy of the Compound Words Competency Test and corresponding worksheet. Read aloud each word from the list on the worksheet, keeping it out of the child's line of vision. The child is to decide whether or not each word is a compound word and circle "yes" or "no" on his paper. Read each word twice pausing long enough for him to respond.

After the entire test has been administered, score it by writing in the blanks on the worksheet in the following manner:

> correct response : +
> incorrect response : −

To use the test you should say something like this:

I am going to read you some words. Some of them are compound words and others are not. Remember that compound words are two or more words joined together. I will read each word twice. If it is a compound word, circle "yes" on your paper; if it isn't, circle "no."

HOW TO EVALUATE THE RESULTS

Count up the number of correct responses (the number of plus marks) and record it at the top of your worksheet. Discuss each incorrect response and refer back to Lesson #1 on compound words to review as needed.

Compound Words Competency Test

1.	yes	no
2.	yes	no
3.	yes	no
4.	yes	no
5.	yes	no
6.	yes	no
7.	yes	no
8.	yes	no
9.	yes	no
10.	yes	no

Compound Words Competency Test Worksheet

Date _____ ___# correct ÷ 10 = _____% correct

LESSON 1

1.	mailman	**yes**	no	_____
2.	beginning	yes	**no**	_____
3.	doorbell	**yes**	no	_____
4.	anything	**yes**	no	_____
5.	sunshine	**yes**	no	_____
6.	yellow	yes	**no**	_____
7.	driveway	**yes**	no	_____
8.	women	yes	**no**	_____
9.	bedroom	**yes**	no	_____
10.	inside	**yes**	no	_____

Selected Noun and Verb Endings, Contractions, and Possessives

HOW TO ADMINISTER THE TEST

Have the child read each sentence silently, underline (or point to) the correct word, and then read the entire sentence out loud. Mark the worksheet on the basis of his *both* choosing the right word and reading it correctly. (He does not have to read the whole sentence accurately if this word is given.)

You may find it convenient to use the following symbols to mark the worksheet:

> correct response : +
> incorrect response : −

To use the test you should say something like this:

I am going to show you a few sentences in which a word is missing. Read each sentence silently to yourself. Choose the right word to finish the sentence, and draw a line under it. Then read the sentence out loud with the word you chose.

Selected Noun and Verb Endings, Contractions, and Possessives Competency Test

Sample: Tom is a boy / boys .

1. Tom saw two egg / eggs .
2. The rabbits / rabbit was big.
3. Mother has a babies / baby .
4. The two family / families live here.
5. The cat and dog plays / play .
6. Pam walks / walk to school.
7. Tom playing / played with his dog.
8. The children are playing / played .
9. I isn't / can't play ball.
10. I'm / Let's not going to play.
11. Here is Tom's / Tom pony.
12. Can / Jim's dog jumps.

Selected Noun and Verb Endings, Contractions, and Possessives Competency Test Worksheet

Date _____   ___# correct ÷ 12 = ___% correct

		Lesson #2 Activity #
1. Tom saw two egg/eggs . _____		1
2. The rabbits/rabbit was big. _____		1
3. Mother has a babies/baby . _____		2
4. The two family/families live here. _____		2
5. The cat and dog plays/play . _____		3
6. Pam walks/walk to school. _____		3
7. Tom playing/played with his dog. _____		4
8. The children are playing/played . _____		4
9. I isn't/can't play ball. _____		Lesson #3
10. I'm/Let's not going to play. _____		Lesson #3
11. Here is Tom's/Tom pony. _____		Lesson #4
12. Can Jim's dog jumps. _____		Lesson #4

Let's practice with the sample at the top of the page so you will know what to do. Read the sentence silently and underline the word that makes sense. (Let the child respond.) *Now read the sentence out loud with the word you chose.*

(If he chose "boy" and read "boy" correctly, compliment him. If not, help him arrive at the correct answer.)

Now that you know what to do, go ahead to number one. Be sure to read the whole sentence silently before you choose the word that makes sense.

HOW TO EVALUATE THE RESULTS

Count up the number of correct responses and record it at the top of your worksheet. Included next to every test item on your worksheet is the lesson in which it was introduced. You now have a record of which lessons were successfully learned and which you need to reteach or review. This test covers a variety of skills: noun endings, verb endings, contractions, and possessives. It is unlikely that a child would master them all the first time around. Compliment him on those he knew. Refer back to those lessons he did not master as the problem word forms appear in his reading.

HOW TO USE THE RESULTS FOR PLACEMENT IN THE BOOK

If you are not using this book from cover to cover, but want to know where in the book to start working with your child, follow these guidelines. If a perfect score was attained proceed to read Part Six on syllabication and Chapter Eleven, otherwise:

1. Study and teach the lessons in Part Five for which one or more test items were missed.
2. Readminister the test and file the worksheet in your records so you will know which lessons to reteach in the future.

PART SIX
Syllabication

Most of the phonics elements discussed so far have been introduced through one-syllable words in controlled situations. As more advanced vocabulary is encountered, however, the child will have to learn how and when to break words into syllables. Once this is achieved most of the phonics concepts already learned will be directly applicable to each syllable within any given word. The purpose of this section, therefore, is to present a *few* of the more useful rules concerning the breaking of words into individual syllables which can be taught as the need arises.

DEFINITION: Arthur W. Heilman defines a syllable as a vowel or group of letters containing a vowel sound which taken together form a pronounceable unit.*

Note that the definition implies that a *vowel* (or a vowel sound such as "y") *must be present for a unit to be a syllable.* Furthermore, although two or more vowels may appear in a single syllable, only one vowel sound is pronounced.

Example: The first syllable in "beautiful," "beau," has three vowels but only one vowel sound: ū.

RULE I

Words can be divided into syllables between two like consonants.

Example: Using known words:
funny   fun-ny
balloon   bal-loon
rabbit   rab-bit
little   lit-tle
puzzle   puz-zle

* *Phonics in Perspective* (Columbus, Ohio: Charles E. Merrill Publishing Co., 1968), p. 77.

Note that both consonants aren't pronounced. Usually only the first member of the pair is pronounced, but there are many exceptions to this generalization (ba·lōōn', for example).

You could give some practice in applying this rule and increase the child's sight vocabulary at the same time by adding endings to known words which result in double consonants:

fun	funny	fun-ny
bun	bunny	bun-ny
sun	sunny	sun-ny
big	bigger	big-ger

RULE II

Words can be divided into syllables between unlike consonants unless those consonants represent a digraph or other single speech sound.

Example: Divide between unlike consonants:
    con-test
    car-pet
    mon-key
Single speech sounds stay together:
    fa-ther ("th" is pronounced as a single sound)
    ta-ble ("bl" is pronounced as a single sound)
    tur-tle ("tl" is pronounced as a single sound)

RULE III

A single consonant between vowels usually goes with the second syllable.

Example: ba-by
    a-round
    wa-ter
    a-lone

RULE IV

Words are divided into syllables between two vowel sounds unless the two represent a single sound.

Example: eat (only the **e** is sounded)
great (only the **a** is sounded)
green (only one **e** is sounded)

cre-ate
the-a-ter
i-de-a

ENDINGS

A few helpful miscellaneous facts:

1. The **ed** ending forms a final syllable when the root word ends with "d" or "t". (For example, need-ed; want-ed.)

2. **ble, cle, dle, gle, kle, ple, tle**, and **vle** usually serve as the final syllable in words containing them.

3. **es, er**, and **ing** normally add an extra syllable to a word.

Please note that in this chapter we have attempted to mention only the most common (and therefore most helpful) rules and relationships. There is a great deal more to syllabication than we have included in these few pages. But this content, if thoroughly mastered, will provide the beginning reader with an excellent start in analyzing more complex words.

11

Continuing Reading Instruction

As useful as language experience stories are in beginning reading, they can be used only for a limited time before fewer and fewer new words are introduced in each story (or before the child tires of the process). The purpose of this chapter is therefore to show you how to extend your reading teaching to more advanced materials than those contained in this book and than those likely to be dictated by a child. We will do this by showing you where to obtain and how to select materials appropriate to your child's reading level, how to use these materials, and how to continue teaching those crucial word attack skills which, coupled with meaningful discussion of content, will set your child on his way toward successful, independent reading.

SELECTING INSTRUCTIONAL MATERIALS FOR YOUR CHILD

How

The two most important considerations in selecting reading material for a child are the interest they offer and their level of difficulty.

Interest. You already have a good idea of which topics most interest your child through reading and talking to him. You can use this knowledge either in choosing books for him or helping him choose those he is most likely to enjoy. You can also, of course, stimulate curiosity to some degree. Remember that your main purpose at this stage is to teach your child both *how* to read and how to *enjoy* reading.

Difficulty. The interest a book holds for a beginning reader is not independent of its difficulty level. Reading material that has too many unknown words will not be enjoyed regardless of how interesting a subject may be (unless there are many appealing pictures to look at). The selection of an appropriate level of difficulty also can vary depending on how the materials are to be used; for example:

1. *When you are going to read something to the child,* you need only be concerned with his oral comprehension level; if what is being read can be understood, then the material is not too difficult. Therefore, if a chosen book is too difficult for the child to read by himself, consider reading it to him.

2. *When the child is going to read something primarily for his own entertainment with a minimum of help,* he should not have to struggle with its vocabulary. If such a book has one unknown word for every two pages of text, something easier should be chosen. This may be done in one of two ways: (a) If the child is present, have him read aloud two pages near the middle of the book, counting the number of words missed (don't count names). (b) If the child is not present, you might make an alphabetized list of his sight words from the Word Box (see illustration 11-1) and check the frequency of unknown words for a page or two near the middle of the book. If you end up selecting a book that does have some unknown words, make sure that you or another adult is present to explain them when the book is being read. The best practice is to have your own reading time coincide with your child's, thus being available to answer questions *and* at the same time setting a positive example.

3. *When you select a book which will be used for instruc-*

tional purposes, you should follow the same general procedure indicated above for identifying unknown words. However, unlike books to be read independently, those selected for actual teaching purposes are to be read with your help and *should* contain some unknown words. *One* or *two* new words per page is optimal; as many as three is too difficult.

These guidelines are not absolute. If your child is truly interested in a topic, then a higher number of unknown words can be allowed. If a book is chosen which turns out to be too difficult, or proves uninteresting, don't hesitate to replace it with a more appropriate substitute.

Where

There are basically two sources for obtaining instructional material at the appropriate level of difficulty for your child: reading texts such as the ones used in public schools, and books especially written for children which are to be found in libraries and bookstores.

Reading texts. The reading books used in the elementary schools have several distinct advantages for home teaching purposes:

1. They are written so that words are introduced at a controlled rate and repeated often to aid their retention.
2. They are designed as a series of volumes carefully graded for difficulty, from the preprimer level to what is close to adult prose.
3. They are available together with teachers' manuals and workbooks which can be quite helpful if used with discretion.

In many ways the use of a professional reading series may be your most satisfactory choice. If you choose this course we suggest that you contact your local elementary school and ask if it is possible for you to borrow a book at the appropriate difficulty level. If you are dealing with a preschooler, then a primer or first reader (depending upon how many words were learned in the activities in Chapters Nine and Ten) will probably be appropriate. We suggest that you check a couple of pages in the first quarter of the reading text to determine its level of difficulty.

If your child is of school age, his teacher is in the best position to select an appropriate text for you. Many schools will be glad to lend you the books you need, some will not have enough available, and a few might even try to discourage you from working with your child. In the latter two cases, be understanding, diplomatic, and buy what you need from a textbook company.

Whether you decide to buy or borrow a textbook, we strongly suggest that you *learn what series your local school is using and be sure to obtain a book from a different series.* This is imperative whether your child is a preschooler or already enrolled in school. Using the same books at home and at school would bore your child and mislead his teacher in the diagnosis of his skills. This is not to suggest that you cannot help your child with reading assignments given by his teacher (the word attack and word study activities presented later in this chapter are excellent for that), only that you *not* supplement your child's schooling instruction with materials used at the same school.

Children's books. You should not get the idea from this discussion that you must use a formal reading text for the teaching activities outlined in this chapter. Many children prefer books and stories written by professional writers for strictly entertainment purposes, and, if *carefully* screened with respect to difficulty level, they can be used quite successfully to teach reading. They have the further advantage of being available in great abundance in libraries and well-stocked bookstores, and if you are fortunate enough to live near one specializing in children's books, the variety of titles can be staggering. The chief disadvantage of using such books for formal reading instruction is the fact that their authors are under no constraints to use a controlled vocabulary. This can be a very real problem and may require time on your part in selecting appropriate stories using one of the procedures outlined above. Sometimes a library will have a shelf of "beginning readers," usually written on a late first-grade level. When you visit the library, you might check if they have such books.

LESSON FORMAT

With one exception, the method by which the selected materials will be taught is quite similar to the lesson format used with the preprimers in Chapters Six, Seven, and Eight. You will still generate interest or a reason for reading the story through questions, discuss the story with respect to those questions following reading, and work on the mastery of new words through word study activities and the Word Box. The chief difference now is in the way in which you will deal with new words. Instead of routinely supplying them during reading, you will map out a *word attack strategy* through which you will enable the child to identify words through phonics concepts and context clues. The method we have chosen for this is a synthesis of different schools of thought which can make the most sense for your particular circumstances, given that you (1) probably haven't formally taught reading before; (2) have the luxury of teaching your child individually; and (3) aren't under any externally imposed time constraints.

The basic lesson format we now suggest that you use consists of the following six steps:

STEP I
Word attack preparation

Prior to oral reading you will present a list of words designed to *familiarize* the reader with the sounds contained in the new words being introduced in the story. In order to do this you will obviously have to identify words the child is not likely to know in advance. To ease this process, we suggest that before teaching any of the lessons in this chapter, you prepare the following two aids:

An alphabetized list of sight words. This list will be used as a reference to indicate which words in the upcoming lesson will probably *not* be recognized. Knowledge of which words are new in a story allows the teaching procedures for word attack to be mapped out *before* the actual lesson; thus, for every new word

Illustration 11-1

SIGHT WORD TABLE

a	d	i	p	t
a	day	I	paid	time
again	did	ice cream	Pam	to
all	dog	in	pen	today
and	down	is	pets	Tom
are			pond	
at	**e**	**j**	pony	**th**
away	eat	Jim		thank you
	eggs	Jip	**pl**	the
b		jump	place	they
baby	**f**		play	this
ball	family	**k**	played	
balloon	fast	kite	playground	**tr**
big	Father		plays	tree
bird	feed	**l**		
boy	food	laughed	**r**	**tw**
boys	for	little	rabbit	two
	four	Little Chick	rabbits	
bl	fun	live	red	**u**
black	funny	lives	Red Hen	up
blue		look	ride	
	fl	looked	rode	**w**
br	fly	love	round	walk
brown		loves	run	walked
	g		runs	want
c	get	**m**		wanted
can	girl	man	**s**	wants
cannot	go	may	said	water
car	good	me	see	will
cat	good-by	Meow-Meow	sits	with
come	got	merry-go-round	so	
comes		milk shake	soon	**wh**
	gr	Mother		what
ch	green	My	**sh**	white
chicken			she	who
chickens	**h**	**n**		
child	hamburger	need	**sl**	**y**
children	has	nest	slide	Yellow Duck
	have	no	slow	
cl	he	now		**z**
cluck	help		**sw**	zoo
	helps	**o**	swim	
	here	Oh		
	high	on		
	home	one		
	house			

you will have at your fingertips "old" ones with similar characteristics. Your child's list of sight words might look something like illustration 11-1 (note that blends and digraphs are listed separately).

A word ending list. Next you should copy the alphabetized list of word endings from our table below. Copy only the word endings, then fill in words under each from your child's sight vocabulary. An example of what this list could look like is provided in the illustration. You may find that you have no words to place under certain endings. Don't worry about it since as more and more words are learned, you will have plenty to fill in. (You will eventually need to add new endings as well.)

Illustration 11-2

WORD ENDINGS TABLE

-ace/-ase	-ack	-ad	-ain	-air
place	black	sad	rain	fair
race	tack	bad	train	hair
face	back	glad	brain	chair
base		had		
-alk	-all	-am	-an	-and
walk	ball	Sam	man	band
talk	wall	ham	can	land
stalk	fall	tam	fan	sand
	tall		ran	stand
	call			
-ank	-ar	-as	-ast	-at
sank	car	has	fast	cat
drank	far		last	rat
	star		mast	that
				mat
-ay	-aw	-eck	-ed	-ell
play	saw	deck	red	bell
day	jaw		bed	sell
stay	raw		sled	tell
tray			shed	well
way				
hay				

-en	-er	-est	-et	-ew
men	Father	nest	pet	new
hen	Mother	west	let	blew
then	hamburger	best	met	few
when	water		wet	chew
chicken			set	flew
children				

-ey	-id	-ide	-ig	-ight
they	did	wide	big	fight
	slid	slide	pig	bright
	hid	side	wig	light
		tide		might
		ride		sight
		hide		

-ild	-im	-in	-ink	-ird
child	Jim	tin	sink	bird
wild	swim	thin	drink	third
mild		chin		
		sin		
		win		
		fin		

-irl	-is	-it	-ite	-ly
girl	this	bit	bite	family
		sit	site	silly
		rabbit	kite	Billy
		wit		
		hit		
		lit		

-ode	-og	-om	-ome	-on
rode	dog	Tom	come	son
mode	log		some	ton
	hog			
	bog			
	fog			
	jog			

-one	-onk	-or	-ound	-ove
bone	honk	for	playground	love
			round	

-ow	-own	-oy	-uck	-ump
meow	town	toy	duck	jump
now	brown	boy	buck	
	clown	joy	luck	
			truck	
			stuck	

-un   -unk
fun   sunk
gun   drunk
run
bun

Once these two lists have been prepared, you will be ready to teach the materials you have selected for this chapter. The first thing you should do is to read through the passage to be read in the first lesson and write down all the words that are not in the list of sight words (see illustration 11–1). Examine each new word carefully for sounds and component parts with which the child is familiar, and prepare a list of three or four words, some familiar, some not, to illustrate each sound.

For example, suppose the following sentence occurred in a story selected for study:

"Jip wanted to chase the two rabbits."

By comparing the words in the sentence to the list in Illustration 11–1, you would know that the child was familiar with all the words except "chase."

"Chase" would, therefore, be earmarked for study, so the first step would be to examine the word for familiar sounds. The **ch** digraph and the **ase** ending might come to mind first (although the **a** might be an equally good choice).

From Illustration 11–1, two or three sight words beginning with the **ch** sound could be written down (such as "chick," "children," "chicken") and "place" could be lifted from the list of endings under **-ace/ase.**

These words would be used just before reading the story in the following way.

Write out the three selected words beginning with the **ch** sound:

chick   children   chicken

How are these words alike?

(They begin with the **ch** sound.)

Do you hear the ch (pronounce it) *sound?*

Here are some other words.

Write "place," "face," "race," "base."

See if you can read them.

The child knows "place." If he stumbles on one of the others, help him sound it out by asking him what sound **f**, **r**, and **b** represent at the beginning of a word, and then have him add the ending sound of "place" to each.

You will note that the actual word encountered in the story ("chase") has not been presented, only its constituent sounds. This is to teach work attack skills that can enable the child to figure out unknown words. If the word itself is presented, then no real practice in this skill is given.

To summarize, the Word Attack Preparation portion of the lesson consists of the following five steps, the first four of which are accomplished before actually sitting down with the child:

1. A personal Sight Word Table is prepared listing all the words known by the child (see Illustration 11–1). Obviously, this table need be prepared only once, as long as it is periodically updated with the new words learned through the materials used for this chapter.

2. A Word Endings Table like the one in Illustration 11–2 is prepared, also using all the words known by the child. Like the Sight Word Table this aid need be prepared only once if updated. It will contain many of the same words as the former, the only difference being that the words in the Sight Word Table are listed alphabetically by *beginning* sounds, those in the Word Ending Table being alphabetized by *ending* sounds.

3. The reading passage is screened in order to identify new words. This is done by checking them against the Sight Word Table.

4. For each new word, familiar initial sounds and/or word endings are identified using both the Sight Word and Word Ending tables.

5. A few sight words *and* unknown words that illustrate the familiar initial sounds and word endings identified earlier are presented to the child to read. The actual new words from the story are *not* presented.

STEP II
Laying the groundwork

As always, it is extremely important to generate motivation *before* reading the story. This not only makes reading more fun, but also prepares the child to reflect on what is being read. Below are some suggestions as to how to do this (for more ideas, refer to the sample lessons in Chapter Six):

a. Read the title of the story and ask the child what he knows about the topic and what he would like to find out. Previous personal experiences may be discussed.
b. Look at the picture together and have him describe it.
c. Develop questions which can be answered by reading the passage. Have the child repeat those questions before reading.

You will have the benefit of using all of these strategies only when you start a lesson with the beginning of a story. For a lesson which begins in the middle of a story, you can adapt this by basing the discussion on what has been learned so far and setting up new reasons to read on. Try to develop questions which will be answered in the next few pages of text. Use a picture in the middle of the story for discussion when possible. The point is always to get the reader thinking about what he reads.

STEP III
Reading the story using formal word attack strategies

We are going to present a routine series of steps to use whenever unknown words are encountered in the reading portion of each lesson. These steps are based on strategies that we want the child ultimately to use on his own, and if the routine is used with your guidance often enough, it will eventually become second nature to the child. The strategy will not work for every word right away but keep in mind that you are teaching for the *long haul*: the more experience a child gets and the more words he hears, the more useful this word attack strategy will become.

To begin, have the child read the selected passage orally. When the first sentence with a new word is encountered ("Jip wanted to *chase* the two rabbits."), the child probably will stop abruptly at the point of difficulty:

"Jip wanted to _____."

If you are sure the word is in the child's spoken vocabulary, have him skip it, read the rest of the sentence, and take a guess at the unknown word based on the meaning implied in the sentence. There are many words that could fit in the blank, however, so the choice has to be narrowed. The best way to do that is to point out the beginning sound of the unknown word, in this case **ch**.

To do this, cover everything in the word except "ch" and say:

*What sound does **ch** stand for?*

If the child pronounces it, ask him to read the sentence, substituting the **ch** sound for the word in question. If he doesn't remember the digraph sound, show him a word containing it that you are sure he knows ("children" for example) and have him read that word, then make the **ch** sound.

The child should now read the sentence substituting the **ch** sound for the unknown word:

"Jip wanted to **ch**- the two rabbits."

You are, in other words, having a known sound substituted for an unknown word into the context of the sentence, thereby bringing both phonics and contextual meaning clues to bear on the problem of identifying the word.

Do you know what Jip wanted to do to the two rabbits?

If the word is recognized at this point, be lavish with your praise. If it still isn't known, you have two options. If the child seems bored with the whole process, simply supply the word "chase" emphasizing the initial **ch** sound and have the sentence reread. If he is interested in the "guessing game" (and you can influence that interest greatly by exuding enthusiasm and *never* approaching it as a task made necessary by any failure on his part), cover the **ch** digraph and ask:

Do you know any words which end like this?

If a word does not come to mind, print "place" and "base" and ask the child to read them.

These words end the same way (point to "chase"). *Do you know what it is now?*

If the word isn't recognized, have the sentence read again, this time substituting both known sounds (**ch** and **ace/ase**) for the unknown word. If the word still isn't recognized, supply it, have the sentence reread, and go on with the story.

Obviously all new words are not going to fit this initial sound-word ending model so neatly and some sentences will be richer in context clues than others. When a word does not seem appropriate for this process (such as in cases where the child does not know other words with similar sounds, or you are not sure about a particular sound), simply *tell the child the word* and go on with the reading.

Other word elements that can be used similarly in word attack are: root words, compound words, shorter words embedded in longer ones, syllabication, and more advanced sounds such as **oy, or, ur, ar,** and others.

Summary

The word attack process involves the following two steps:

1. *Advance familiarization* (which was accomplished in Step I). Identify known sounds in the words to be taught and construct a list of two or three words containing each sound. Have the lists read, supplying help in sounding out the unknown words.
2. *The use of phonic and context clues in word attack.* When a new word is encountered in the story, have the child: identify the initial sound; read the entire sentence, substituting the initial sound for the unknown word, and; attempt to name the word. If the word is not forthcoming: identify other familiar elements (such as the ending, root word, syllables, and so on); and again read the sentence substituting these additional sounds for the word in question.

Supply the word at this point if it is not known, have the sentence reread, and continue with the story.

General Guidelines

1. *If at any point you are in doubt, simply supply an unknown word as you did in Chapters Six through Eight.* You know that *works* and, although in general it is not as efficient as the method presented above, there are some words that just are not amenable to any set of phonics rules and are best taught as whole words.
2. *Don't dwell on any given word at any great length.* Once you have mastered the general strategy indicated above, the whole process normally won't take longer than a few seconds. If a word or sound isn't recognized fairly quickly, supply it and go on with the story. Word attack skills must not be used at the expense of interest in what is being read. You can always go back to a word during the word study activities.

STEP IV
Discussing the reading

Following completion of Step III you should make sure that each question asked before the reading (Step II) is followed up to make sure the original purposes were met. You should also think of additional questions of a factual nature to determine how well the material was understood. When the child does not know the answer to a particular question, have him reread appropriate sections silently to find the answer. Being able to find information in a text is a very important skill to develop, a skill that greatly enhances your child's chances of becoming a reflective reader.

After you are satisfied with this phase of the lesson, discuss the passage with the child in a general manner. If a story has been completed, give him the opportunity to say whether or not he liked it and how he felt about whatever took place.

STEP V
Word study activities

At this point in the lesson the focus will be on the learning and internalization of word attack skills. However, you should also continue to teach and review the new words introduced in each lesson. Continue to write them on word cards, file them in the "new words" section of the Word Box following each lesson, and review them subsequently until you are sure that they have been mastered (see the discussion on the use of the Word Box in Chapter One).

Phonics. What you will be striving especially hard to do at this point is to teach your child to *apply* the phonics lessons presented in Chapters Five and Ten to the independent identification of new words. This will ultimately involve the review of each concept taught in those chapters as they are applied in the word attack portion of each lesson. (Also remember, as discussed in the previous chapter, that the phonics lessons in Chapter Ten which were not taught with the language experience should be taught with the lessons in this chapter.)

In the hypothetical situation discussed earlier, for example, in which the new word "chase" was encountered embedded in the sentence, "Jip wanted to *chase* the two rabbits," you would want to plan the word study activities around reviewing the **ch** digraph, the **ase/ace** ending, and the **a** sound. This could be done by (1) reviewing other words with these sounds, and (2) making sure that the child recognized the **ch**, **ase**, or possibly **a** in the new word.

You can also teach *new* word endings and sounds based on your child's reading experience. If a new word is encountered for which there are no familiar words or endings to help figure it out, there is no reason why you cannot expand your child's phonics repertoire during this stage of the lesson. Suppose the word "climb" was encountered in a story, for example. You could explain that when **b** follows **m** it is often silent, illustrating the generalization with other examples such as "lamb," "limb," and "thumb."

Another aspect of word study you should not neglect is to discuss word meanings whenever words are encountered which are not yet in your child's spoken vocabulary. The possibilities for word study are almost endless, so the best advice we can give you is simply to exercise your judgment as to how much to introduce to your child and how soon.

Context. The use of context clues in identifying new words should also be reinforced in the word study activities, by saying something like this:

Let's think of some other sentences in which "chase" might appear. Can you make one?

Write whatever sentence is offered and have it read back. If trouble is encountered, you might construct some sentences using the list of sight words (see Illustration 11–1). Examples could be:

Look at Meow-Meow chase the merry-go-round!
Look at Jip chase the ice cream man.

Another activity that is especially helpful involves the selection of a word from two or more alternatives involving the same sound, such as:

The dog $\genfrac{}{}{0pt}{}{\text{chased}}{\text{chicken}}$ the cat.

The cat $\genfrac{}{}{0pt}{}{\text{placed}}{\text{chased}}$ the rabbit.

These exercises require careful reading on the child's part and *force* him to consider context clues before making a choice. They are also very helpful to use with troublesome words such as "their"/"there," "this"/"that," "hear"/"here," and "was"/"saw."

If time and interest permit, you can continue the lesson by using the new words to teach other concepts you feel need reinforcing such as verb endings:

Let's look at some other ways to write "chase." See if you can read these sentences.

Jip wanted to chase the two rabbits.
Jip chased the two rabbits.
Jip chases the two rabbits.
Jip is chasing the two rabbits.

The possibilities are almost endless, especially when you consider the fact that you will eventually be teaching *new* word endings and sounds as your child's word experiences widen. Like the word attack strategies discussed above, however, and like the framing of questions to ask both before and after the reading of a passage, word study activities require preparation on your part prior to your actual teaching sessions.

Summary

Word study activities for new words contained in materials you select to teach include:

1. **Preparation.** Just as you plan the word attack strategies you wish to teach your child to use for a given word, so you must plan a means of reinforcing both the word *and* the strategy.

2. **Word cards.** Use word cards and the Word Box as in previous chapters.

3. **Teach the word attack process** as well as recognition of the new words themselves.

4. **Review** other phonics concepts as needed and as the opportunity arises.

5. **Teach meanings** of new words where appropriate.

6. **Use your judgment** as to how much time to spend on the word study portion of your lessons, based on your child's interest level and the time available.

STEP VI
Review

The need for review is a fact of life for all teaching and all learning, especially when new vocabulary and new word attack skills are being introduced at each lesson. You will have to use your judgment as to how much review your child needs. Remember, however, that all children require some periodic review. (This also applies to the contents of the Word Box, as discussed in Chapter Six.)

If you have worked your way through Chapters Six through Nine, you probably won't have much trouble following the six-step lesson format presented above. If you are using the book for remedial purposes, however, and did not find it necessary to teach the preprimer stories or use the language experience approach, you will probably not be comfortable with this format until you have *studied* this chapter again thoroughly and actually taught a few lessons.

Conceptually, the lesson format is really quite simple, as the following synopsis should indicate:

Step I. **Word attack preparation.** Prior to oral reading you will present a list of words designed to familiarize the reader with the main sounds contained in the new words being introduced in the story.

Step II. **Laying the groundwork.** Before reading the story, generate interest through the development of questions and ideas which can be answered in the reading process.

Step III. **Reading the story using formal word attack strategies.** The story is read for the first time by the child orally. The identities of new words are discovered by the use of *phonics* concepts in combination with *context* clues.

Step IV. **Discussing the reading.** The story is discussed to make certain that it was understood. Questions posed before reading are answered, with passages being reread silently in order to answer missed and additional questions.

Step V. **Word study activities.** After the story has been read and possibly reread, both the new words and word attack skills are reinforced.

Step VI. **Review.** New words and new word attack skills from the present and previous lessons are reviewed.

12

Where Do We Go From Here?

Your child has now acquired a very impressive array of reading skills thanks to your considerable efforts. He knows the letter names, the sounds they represent, a large number of sight words, and word attack skills by which even more can be learned. Most important, *he knows how to read with understanding* and this will prove an increasingly valuable asset as time goes on.

We would like to discuss four questions which may still concern a parent who has successfully taught all the lessons in this book:

1. *How can this early momentum I have generated be maintained?*
2. *What happens if after all this my child falls (or remains) behind?*
3. *What sort of control do I have over what happens to my child in school?*
4. *How can I be sure of my child's success in life?*

Maintaining Momentum

Regardless of whether you began this book teaching a preschool or a school-age child, it is likely that he will be enrolled in school by the time you complete it. If he was not behind in school when you started teaching, chances are that he is doing well now.

Although you certainly have a right to feel good about this, you shouldn't feel *too* comfortable. Obviously if you have taught your child prior to, or in addition to, school he is going to read better initially than children not so fortunate. (At the very least he will read better than he would have read without your help!) If a child gained a half year's skills with outside help and that help is suddenly taken away, however, there is no reason to believe that he will continue to learn at an accelerated rate even though he will most likely continue at a better than average rate.

We suggest, therefore, that you continue your reading instruction as in the procedures outlined in Chapter Eleven, while encouraging him to read more and more on his own. At first this independent reading can take any form your child wishes; quantity is more important than quality. If he wants to read all the *Hardy Boys* or *Nancy Drew* mysteries, let him. Later, when he becomes a more facile reader and reading has become part of the everyday routine, more discrimination may be encouraged by actually planning a literary program (for example, biographies, books about fascinating phenomena, literature, history, and so on).

You must also not lose sight of the fact that although reading may be the most important subject for young learners, other important subjects also exist. Don't neglect writing and arithmetic skills. They become more and more important in later academic pursuits, and by teaching them early you not only prepare for that time but also give the child another arena in which he can succeed. It is not that unusual, for example, for a child who has difficulty with reading to learn arithmetic quite easily (and certainly the opposite can also be true).

Besides teaching there are many other enriching and expanding opportunities you can provide whenever possible, across the whole range of music, art, drama, science, and any number of other areas offering both direct and indirect experiences.

Finally, no matter how faithfully you teach your child, his primary education (in terms of sheer instructional time) is still going to occur in school. It goes without saying, therefore, that you should encourage your child to take a serious interest in school and the experiences it provides. Show genuine interest in what goes on in the classroom, compliment him on small successes, and provide constructive suggestions when improvement is called for. If schooling is not seen as an important enterprise, then it is doubtful if a great deal of success will be encountered there. For this to happen would be the negation of everything this book was designed to accomplish.

If the Child Does Not Succeed

It is always possible that a child may drop behind in school despite his teachers' and parents' best efforts. Some children never learn as quickly as their parents think they should; others are "late bloomers" who don't achieve anywhere near their potential until high school (or even graduate school).

Your best option is to continue giving help and encouragement. Help may include seeking out diagnostic testing, tutoring, and/or counseling services, which are available either within the school or from private sources. Breaking learning tasks into smaller steps and spending more time on each step increases the chances of success in your tutoring sessions. Praising small efforts and accomplishments helps diminish the child's sense of frustration with difficult assignments. Most of all, believing in your child's ability to become whatever he wants to be will give him the courage to try.

Some children never develop an appetite for learning academic subjects no matter how hard their parents or teachers try to motivate them, just as some never enjoy playing the piano despite the Steinway and expensive lessons their parents purchase. The best advice we can give these parents is to find out what does interest their children and supply reading materials dealing with those interests.

Dealing With the School

The vast majority of teachers share the same goal you do: they want your child to achieve as well as he possibly can. The best way to meet that objective is for teacher and parent to cooperate and be as supportive of one another as possible. Teachers generally are pleased to share information with parents who want to know more about their children's education than what grade they received. Teachers can also provide you with valuable advice on how best to help at home.

What goes on in school, however, is not entirely determined by teachers, who often have little choice in matters such as curriculum, textbook selection, length of teaching periods, and the structure of the school day. You don't have a great deal of control over what goes on within the school either, so if you have doubts about the quality or quantity of instruction, there is very little you can do other than provide it yourself. This situation may be in the process of changing as federal legislation requires more and more parental involvement, but any changes that do occur will probably come too slowly to affect you. You and your child do have certain basic rights of which you should be aware. Among them are:

1. access to public school education at public expense regardless of race, religion, income, or special handicapping conditions,
2. access to compensatory educational programs if you live in a low income area and have an underachieving child,
3. participation in the planning of your child's educational program if he has a handicapping condition (including a learning disability), and
4. access to the contents of your child's permanent school record at any time, along with the right to contest inaccuracies in it.

Your Child's Ultimate Success

The answer to the question of how parents can be sure of their children's ultimate success in life is simple. They cannot. You as a parent can provide encouragement, help, opportunity, and support to the best of your ability and, in the final analysis, that is all you can do. The rest is up to your child.